TENDING THE GARDENS OF CITIZENSHIP:
CHILD SAVING IN TORONTO, 1880s–1920s

Tending the Gardens of Citizenship

Child Saving in Toronto, 1880s–1920s

Xiaobei Chen

UNIVERSITY OF TORONTO PRESS
Toronto Buffalo London

© University of Toronto Press Incorporated 2005
Toronto Buffalo London
Printed in Canada

ISBN 0-8020-3913-8

Printed on acid-free paper

Library and Archives Canada Cataloguing in Publication

Chen, Xiaobei, 1969–
    Tending the gardens of citizenship : child saving in Toronto,
    1880s–1920s / Xiaobei Chen.

    Includes bibliographical references and index.
    ISBN 0-8020-3913-8

    1. Child welfare – Government policy – Ontario – Toronto – History –
    19th century.   2. Child welfare – Moral and ethical aspects – Ontario –
    Toronto – History – 19th century.   3. Child welfare – Government policy –
    Ontario – Toronto – History – 20th century.   4. Child welfare – Moral and
    ethical aspects – Ontario – Toronto – History – 20th century.   I. Title.

    HV887.C32T65 2005   362.7'09713'541'09034   C2004-907040-1

This book has been published with the help of a grant from the
Canadian Federation for the Humanities and Social Sciences, through
the Aid to Scholarly Publications Programme, using funds provided by
the Social Sciences and Humanities Research Council of Canada.

University of Toronto Press acknowledges the financial assistance to
its publishing program of the Canada Council for the Arts and the
Ontario Arts Council.

University of Toronto Press acknowledges the financial support for
its publishing activities of the Government of Canada through the
Book Publishing Industry Development Program (BPIDP).

To my parents, who provided the inspiration,
     and
to Ercel, who made it possible

Contents

viii   Contents

Acknowledgments

This book would not exist without the support of many people and organizations. The research was originally conducted for a doctoral dissertation, which was made possible by fellowships and scholarships from the University of Toronto and the Ontario government. This book has been published with the help of a grant from the Canadian Federation for the Humanities and Social Sciences, through the Aid to Scholarly Publications Programme, using funds provided by the Social Sciences and Humanities Research Council of Canada.

The staff of the Toronto Children's Aid Society, especially Bruce Rivers, Bruce Leslie, and Deborah Goodman, was very helpful to my research. Archivists and staff at the City of Toronto Archives, the Archives of Ontario, and the National Archives of Canada made contributions to this book.

Many academic teachers and colleagues helped me through their encouragement, support, ideas and thoughtful critiques at various times over the years, including Carol Baines, Toba Bryant, Cecilia Chan, Nelson Chow, Kari Dehli, Bryan Hogeveen, Franca Iacovetta, Allan Irving, Kirsten Johnson, Nigel Parton, Ken Moffatt, Dawn Moore, Karen Murray, and Karen Swift. While in Toronto I was fortunate to be part of the Dorothy Livesay Collective and the History of the Present Group, where I benefited from both the moral support and the constructive criticism of friends in both groups. In the later stages I benefited from the interest and encouragement of colleagues in the Department of Political Science at the University of Alberta, where I was awarded a Killam Postdoctoral Fellowship, especially Janine Brodie and Linda Trimble. I also thank Andrew Armitage and Marilyn Callahan, my colleagues in the School of Social Work at the University of Victoria, for their wise counsel.

I would like to offer a special word of thanks to two people. Sheila Neysmith has taught me many things and has generously given me essential and wise guidance and encouragement throughout the years. Mariana Valverde has offered substantial teaching, guidance, and support, which have been indispensable to this book and many of my other publications.

My thanks to the editors at the University of Toronto Press, Virgil Duff, Lauren Freeman, Chris Bucis, Stephen Kotowych, and Anne Laughlin, who have been very supportive. I would like to thank the reviewers for their care and diligence in providing comments on the manuscript. Their suggestions were extremely insightful and a significant contribution to improving the manuscript. I would also like to thank my copy-editor, Harold Otto, for his thorough help.

I am grateful to my mother, Chen Lan, and my father, Chen Lihao, who have always encouraged and supported my studies; they taught me much by their examples. I am also grateful to Ercel Baker, who has read every word I have written in English for almost a decade. He has provided unconditional support to me through his love, patience, inspiration, and practical help.

Material now in Chapter 8 appeared as part of 'Constituting "Dangerous Parents" through the Spectre of Child Death: A Critique of Child Protection Restructuring in Ontario,' in *Making Normal: Social Regulation in Canada*, edited by Deborah Brock (Scarborough: Thomson Nelson, 2003). A portion of Chapter 2 was published in 'The Birth of the Child-Victim Citizen,' in *Re-Inventing Canada: Politics of the 21st Century*, edited by Janine Brodie and Linda Trimble (Scarborough: Pearson Education Canada, 2003). An earlier version of Chapter 3 appeared as '"Cultivating Children as You Would Valuable Plants": The Gardening Governmentality of Child Saving, Toronto, Canada, 1880s–1920s,' *Journal of Historical Sociology* 16, no. 4 (2003): 460–86.

When you think of the ill-treatment, the friendlessness, the homelessness of children, remember that the

CHILDREN'S AID SOCIETY

is organized for their protection and is your willing servant for their relief.

1 Illustration from scrapbook, n.d. National Archives of Canada, MG30-C97, vol. 12, John Joseph Kelso Fonds, p. 69.

2   Illustration from a circular, 'Notice to Parents or Guardians,' issued by the Children's Aid Society of Toronto, c. 1899. National Archives of Canada, MG30-C97, vol. 4, John Joseph Kelso Fonds.

3   Illustration of the emblem of the Toronto Humane Society on the title page of pamphlet 'The Toronto Humane Society for the Prevention of Cruelty,' n.d. National Archives of Canada, MG30-C97, vol. 5, John Joseph Kelso Fonds.

4 'The Flaming Youth Problem,' from the *Chicago Daily Tribune*, c. 1920s. National Archives of Canada, MG30-C97, vol. 13, John Joseph Kelso Fonds, scrapbook, p. 109.

NEGLECTED!

One of the Products of a Selfish Social System.

In the person of this neglected child a true picture of 19th century civilization is presented to you for contemplation

Is he to be left to drift into Ignominy, Ignorance, and Vice, to become a danger and a curse?

Is he to be ignored and lost to all Honor, Virtue and Usefulness for ever, or is he to be rescued?

WHAT WILL HIS FATE BE?

" I looked on my right hand and beheld, but there was no man that would know me: refuge failed me; no man cared for my soul."—*Psalm cxlii, 4.*

The mind of a child is the tenderest and holiest thing on earth, for it is begotten of heaven, not earth. To misrule and misguide this heaven-born mind, is to rob it of its promise and purpose, is to cripple its powers of being and doing, is to extinguish its latent virtues and graces, and is an injury and a sin that may never be forgotten nor forgiven.

"It is wiser and less expensive to save children than to punish Criminals."—*Child and State.*

---

5   A neglected boy who would become 'a danger and curse' to society if he were not rescued, cover of pamphlet 'Neglected', c. early 1890s. National Archives of Canada, MG30-C97, vol. 4, John Joseph Kelso Fonds.

6   Children as crop. National Archives of Canada, MG30-C97, vol. 13, John
Joseph Kelso Fonds, scrapbook, n.d., p. 34.

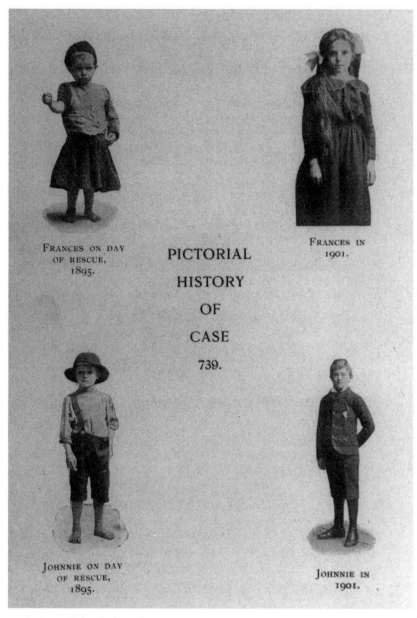

FRANCES ON DAY OF RESCUE, 1895.

PICTORIAL

HISTORY

OF

CASE

739.

FRANCES IN 1901.

JOHNNIE ON DAY OF RESCUE, 1895.

JOHNNIE IN 1901.

7 'Pictorial History of Case 739.' Children's Aid Society of Toronto, Tenth Annual Report, 1901, p. 21. City of Toronto Archives, Children's Aid Society of Metropolitan Toronto Fonds, 1001, Series 532, File 6.

Children's Aid Society

:: OF TORONTO ::

INCORPORATED 1891

NINETEENTH ANNUAL REPORT

NINETEEN HUNDRED AND TEN

MOTTO:

"It is wiser and less expensive to save children than to punish criminals."

OFFICE OF THE SOCIETY

229 SIMCOE STREET

TORONTO

TELEPHONE MAIN 1357

WM. DUNCAN, *Secretary*

8   Title page of Children's Aid Society of Toronto, Nineteenth Annual Report, 1910. City of Toronto Archives, Children's Aid Society of Metropolitan Toronto Fonds, 1001, Series 532, File 13.

9   Case 1594, Children's Aid Society of Toronto, Fifth Annual Report, 1896, p. 49. City of Toronto Archives, Children's Aid Society of Metropolitan Toronto Fonds, 1001, Series 532, File 1. Illustration from cover, Children's Aid Society of Toronto, Eighteenth Annual Report, 1909, File 13. Illustration from cover, Children's Aid Society of Toronto, Nineteenth Annual Report, 1910, File 13.

TENDING THE GARDENS OF CITIZENSHIP:
CHILD SAVING IN TORONTO, 1880s–1920s

Introduction

Experience has taught me that the history of various forms of rationality is sometimes more effective in unsettling our certitudes and dogmatism than is abstract criticism.[1]

In this book I show that the protection of children from violence, abuse, and neglect, especially mistreatment by their parents, is best understood not as part of some essential human morality or a transhistorical ethic, but rather as an interest that has undergone radical historical transformations, depending on the political and social projects within which it was articulated. Child protection, also known as child saving in its early history, emerged in the midst of social and moral reform in urban English-speaking Canada at the turn of the twentieth century. At the time child saving was part of a citizenship project. The problematization of cruelty and neglect arose from citizenship concerns in two aspects. Anti-cruelty activities criticized the immoral use of force, especially by working-class men, on animals and innocent children, who were regarded as harmless, weak, and lowly subjects. The problematization of neglectful parenting emerged from the fear that a lack of discipline and supervision of children would result in a failure to shape children into proper citizens.

When child saving appeared, children were not necessarily considered innocent, as they are today. In fact, neglected children were often regarded as criminals in the making – hence, the felt need to either reform the parents or remove the children. At the turn of the twenty-first century, child protection is embedded in mechanisms that seek to root out and punish bad parents, especially single mothers, not because their children will grow up to be bad citizens, but simply out of a concern to punish evil-doers. In this new paradigm, children are always victims or potential victims whose 'personal safety' is threatened, while parents, especially single and/or young mothers, are always potential perpetrators. Child protection is today linked to a broader tendency to assume the victim perspective and to define citizenship from the victim's point of view, or the point of view of the advocates for victims.

Studying child protection historically is studying changing forms of citizenship, given that protecting children from violence and neglect historically had been an integral part of the citizenship project, and protecting children and ensuring their personal safety has become crucial to citizenship today. The constitution and effects of children's identity as 'citizens in the making' who did not have individual rights stand in contrast to today's identity of children as proper citizens who bear rights to personal safety in the area of child protection. I argue that the crucial position of children in contemporary citizenship politics in Canada as well as in other Western states signifies profound transformation of citizen identities, infantilized distribution of rights and obligations favouring the child (or the infantilized subject), and modes of power for governing individuals at large in the 'post-social' era. In light of this analysis, it seems that critics of the erosion of citizenship rights should be more reflective about the rhetoric of the rights of the child.

The historical research done for this book was confined to child saving in Toronto during the period from the late 1880s to the 1920s. It particularly concerned the work undertaken by the Toronto Children's Aid Society. The last few years of the 1880s witnessed the beginning of agitation for measures to protect children from cruelty and neglect. It was in Toronto that organized child-saving activities first emerged in Ontario and Canada in the late nineteenth century; the Toronto Children's Aid Society, incorporated in 1891, was the first organization of its kind in Canada. In the ensuing three decades or so, child protection, similar to many other fields of social work, existed under private auspices, relied on non-professional personnel who often volunteered their time, and emphasized affecting the moral behaviour of individuals. Since the 1920s, the emerging social sciences, professionalism, and provincial funding gradually transformed child protection away from this approach.

The research is based largely on primary sources. The first source is the records generated by the Toronto Children's Aid Society: minutes, annual reports, and case records, all of which are held at the City of

Toronto Archives. Another important source of data is the personal papers of Toronto child saver John Joseph Kelso, held at the National Archives of Canada in Ottawa. Kelso is widely recognized as the architect of the Canadian child-welfare system, particularly child protection. His papers have been a popular source of information for researchers in child welfare, juvenile justice, and social welfare in general. Andrew Jones and Leonard Rutman have made the most extensive use of Kelso's papers to reconstruct his life and work experiences.[2] What I have used most in this study are Kelso's journals of his own day-to-day child-saving activities in 1893 and 1894, his diaries, and manuscripts of his speeches, which were often stories about a particular child or family. These are not used to track Kelso's roles in various historical events, but rather to trace his thinking on child saving and juvenile delinquency. Other additional sources of information that I consulted for this book include the 1891 report of the Commission Appointed to Enquire into the Prison and Reformatory System of Ontario, the Charlotte Whitton Papers, the William Louis Scott Papers, the City of Toronto Executive Committee Fonds, the Metropolitan Toronto Police Service Fonds, and newspapers. The report of the Commission on the Prison and Reformatory System was examined because the commission played a crucial role in advancing public perception of the link between crime prevention and child saving and in envisioning the establishment of children's aid societies. Charlotte Whitton, a prominent figure in the history of Canadian social services, who started her long career as a leading social worker towards the end of the period examined, contributed her thinking about child-welfare issues, especially juvenile delinquency. W.L. Scott was president of the Ottawa Children's Aid Society and played an essential role in the passage of the 1908 Juvenile Delinquents Act, which included provisions for juvenile courts.

Although the book draws upon child saving in Toronto, it is neither a conventional history of child saving in that city, nor one of the Toronto Children's Aid Society.[3] Rather, it is a Foucauldian historical sociological study of child protection, and the discussions are guided by an analytical concern with governmental rationalities and technologies.

The Genealogy Approach

The Foucauldian genealogy approach is radically different from traditional historical studies. In his essay 'Nietzsche, Genealogy, History,'[4] Michel Foucault discusses at length the concerns of genealogy – 'emergence' and 'descent,' which are opposed to the 'origin' and 'evolution' of traditional history. Following Friedrich Nietzsche's intellectual rebellion, Foucault challenges the pursuit of the origin. For him, to believe that there is a lofty origin of things, for example, the crystallization of the aspiration to child protection in the 1880s, is to presume that there is a moment of birth when things are purest, most precious, and essential. To chase after such an origin is to buy into and participate in the careful fabrication and protection of identities of conceptions, practices, and institutions. The depiction of the origin produces the impression, either intentionally or not, that historical beginnings are the inevitable result of a long and deliberate preparation; hence the entrenchment of the inevitability of the present. By 'emergence,' Foucault makes the point that historical beginnings are lowly, contingent, and heterogeneous: '[emergence] is not the unavoidable conclusion of a long preparation, but a scene where forces are risked in the change of confrontations, where they emerge triumphant, where they can also be confiscated.'[5] Thus, a genealogical study would seek to describe 'the strength these forces wage against each other or against adverse circumstances,' as well as the 'attempt to avoid degeneration and regain strength by dividing these forces against themselves.'[6] The implication for this study is that one should not assume, for example, that there is an essential, pure, but often hidden origin of child protection, be it humanitarianism or interests of the ruling class, in the late nineteenth century waiting to be discovered by a historian. Instead, it would be more useful to document the heterogeneous forces that were at play when child abuse and neglect emerged as social problems.

Traditional history represents the evolution of things, and attempts to map out the destiny of a people, institutions, morality, knowledge, and so on. It seeks to identify the exclusive and universal characteristics by 'dissolving the singular event into an ideal continuity – as a teleological movement or a natural process.'[7] Genealogy, on the contrary, concerns an analysis of descent. The course of descent can be understood as a profusion of lost events. It suggests a complex, unpredictable, and incoherent course of things, with moments of strength and weakness. In contrast to traditional history, genealogy seeks to identify accidents, minute deviations, errors, logical inaccuracies, and miscalculations that produced things that still exist today or have been 'corrected.' It does not reduce events for the sake of analytical synthesis; rather, it maintains them in their proper dispersion. A case in point is the history of the shelter at the Toronto Children's Aid's Society. The shelter was designed to be a handmaid facility for the overall child-protection system. However, in the first decade or two of the society's existence, much to some child savers' dismay, it became a central function of the society, and worse, it was 'abused' by parents as a child care facility. These 'deviations' were gradually corrected after the 1920s, when the shelter was deliberately marginalized in the society's operation. Today it no longer exists. Although a more conventional historical study of child protection might not provide a detailed discussion of the history of the shelter, because it did not reflect the main themes of child saving, a genealogical study would privilege the story of the shelter precisely because its deviation from the main ethos of child saving and its short-lived and unintended prominence.

A Foucauldian historical sociology of child protection can contribute to a critical understanding in several ways. One is to document the genealogy of child protection, to historicize certain ideas and practices that we tend to think of as givens. For example, an examination of the history of the term 'child abuse' reveals that it is not a self-evident category. In the late nineteenth century, child abuse was understood primarily as cruelty and, thus, a moral problem on the part of parents. It is only recently that child abuse has been comprehended as a danger to a child's personal safety. Conceptions of child abuse speak more to the cultural, political, and economic conditions in a society than to the experience of the individuals to whom the term is applied. The current way of understanding child abuse is not necessarily the only possible one, and it thus can and should be contested.

In a similar vein, a genealogy of child protection documents historical contingencies and shows how things might have gone in other directions. This is useful for illuminating the differences between the present and the past, so as to make intelligible the possibilities of the present. The society's shelter was used quite frequently by parents as a resource to provide temporary care for their children without any stigmatizing result, for example. This suggests that in the late nineteenth century there were possibilities of developing child-care services for parents who were unable to care for their children for reasons of sickness or work. In the end, however, the shelter's function was deliberately and strictly restrained, and the option of providing organized child-care services was repressed. Documenting these marginalized and suppressed historical alternatives is an important way to invite history to inform today's decisions.

Understanding Child Protection as Governance

This book's analytical concern with child protection rationalities and technologies is informed by the Foucauldian governmentality approach. The concept of governmentality was first introduced by Foucault in his essay 'On Governmentality'[8] and has stimulated a rich body of writing on alternative thinking about power in Western societies. Foucault defines 'government' in general as 'the conduct of conduct.' Mitchell Dean expands this definition: 'Government is any more or less calculated and rational activity, undertaken by a multiplicity of authorities and agencies, employing a variety of techniques and forms of knowledge, that seeks to shape conduct by working through our desires, aspirations, interests and beliefs, for definite but shifting ends and with a diverse set of relatively unpredictable consequences, effects and outcomes.'[9]

While this definition appears to refer to an extremely broad range of activities, not all action is governmental. One of the most important dimensions that distinguishes governmental activity from other kinds of action is that it uses and generates knowledge. Child protection is one example of such governmental activity. As I show in the following chapters, the objective of child saving was to shape parenting conduct so that parents in turn would guide and regulate their children's conduct in proper ways. The primary objective of this particular governmental activity was to ensure that children grew up to become adults who were capable of morally regulating themselves. It rested on a theory that had emerged in Europe in the context of sixteenth-century humanism: that the way in which children were treated would affect how they would be as adults. Child protection also generates knowledge in that many of its practices are directed at collecting information on family history, parents' occupations, patterns of behaviour, habits, and the mental conditions of parents and children, for example.

There are two integrated areas of investigation in studies of governmental activities: 'political rationalities' and 'governmental technologies.'[10] Dean explains that rationalities of governance refer to relatively systematic thinking about reality, calculations, defining of purposes, and the employment of knowledge.[11] They are the ways in which programs of government are conceptualized, formulated, and articulated within broad discourses of rule.[12] The interest in analysing rationalities comes from Foucault's thesis that the actions of governing always involve some degree of thought.[13] For example, historically, child protection was premised on the thought that something could and ought to be done so that children would be rescued from becoming criminals, beggars, and prostitutes. In contrast, in the late 1990s one strong theme of thought is that child-protection services ought to be restructured so as to keep children safe and to prevent their deaths.

Foucault's notion of rationality differs from Max Weber's rationalism, in that Foucault refuses to accept that a particular form of rationalization applies to a society or a culture as a whole. Thus, he suggests that analysis of rationality be directed to specific fields, each of which is grounded in a fundamental experience (such as madness, or in the case of this book, parent-child relations). Another feature of the Foucauldian analysis of rationality is related to the use of history, as discussed earlier. Dean explains that in Foucault's view political rationality does not simply arise from the rulers' interests or 'ahistorical common sense.' Instead it arises from 'historically developed and modified forms of rationality.'[14] Hence, Foucault's argument that to understand political action it is necessary to understand the historically given forms of political rationality.[15]

Child-saving work emerged in the late nineteenth century, at the threshold of an era in Western states that was characterized by an unabashed philosophy of interventionism and accompanying expansion of governmental and societal intervention into the private sphere of family and life in general. Jacques Donzelot has called this the formation of 'the social' sector.[16] Mariana Valverde argues that, more importantly, 'the social' is a new way of conceptualizing any and all problems of the collectivity. It defines problems, which may have been seen as private or economic issues before, as *social* problems.[17]

The era of 'the social' manifested a distinctive mentality of rule invented during the eighteenth century, namely, bio-power or power over life in Foucault's terms.[18] Colin Gordon defines bio-power as 'a politics concerned with subjects as members of a *population*, in which issues of individual sexual and reproductive conduct interconnect with issues of national policy and power [original emphasis].'[19] I would broaden this definition to include individual social reproductive conduct,[20] mostly parenting conduct, as issues that are interconnected to the collective interests of the nation. As I show in the following chapters, specifically in the field of child protection, bio-power or bio-politics was manifested in a principal rationality that children should be protected from abuse and neglect, so that they would grow up to be good citizens, rather than criminals, beggars, or prostitutes.

This observation about rationalities has important implications for a critical understanding of child protection. First, analyses of rationality show that we ought to look at the very roots, the very logic of institutions such as those in child protection. If we are to resist, rebel against, or transform power, it is not enough to denounce and resist an institution's intrusiveness or biases; nor is it enough to cast the blame on ideology in general. What has to be questioned is the particular form of rationality at stake. As Foucault indicates, that is the only way to avoid having in place a new legislation, a new organization, a new structure with the same objectives and the same effects as the old ones. Second, the primacy of the citizenship-building rationality when child protection emerged illuminates that the current rationality of keeping kids safe and preventing child deaths is peculiar. It considers children as innocent victims and parents, only parents, especially poor and single mothers, as potential criminals. This is in contrast to earlier thinking, which assumed both children and parents to be guilty (or at least potentially guilty) of criminality and immorality, albeit in various degrees. Its peculiarity suggests that it is relative and specific to time and place and thus should not be taken for granted.

Technologies of governance are the means to translate rationalities, categories, and abstract programs into actual governing practices.[21] In other words, they are the means to bring power relations into being. Specifically, they refer to 'the complex of mundane programmes, calculations, techniques, apparatuses, documents and procedures through which authorities seek to embody and give effect to governmental ambitions.'[22] Reporting, case records in ledger books, family visits, warnings, temporary custody of children away from their parents at the shelter, custody of juvenile delinquents separate from adult criminals at the detention room, and foster care are all examples of child protection technologies.

To study the technologies of government is to learn how diverse forces – legal, religious, professional, administrative, financial, and moral – operate, in concert or in conflict, to achieve a state in which 'aspects of the decisions and actions of individuals, groups, organizations and population come to be understood and regulated in relation to authoritative criteria.'[23] Analysing the technology of case records illustrates this point. The Toronto Children's Aid Society kept most of its case records in ledger books during the period under examination. Typically one-half of a page was numbered and designated for each case, in which four or five handwritten notes were entered when the case was first opened and later re-opened. Information was collected on the father's occupation, parents' places of origin, birthplace of the child if not born in Canada, family history (e.g., marriage, divorce, or desertion), general behaviour of family members (e.g., mother in adulterous relationship with a man; father committed to jail, etc.), 'nativity' (i.e., whether the family were Canadian, American, or immigrants), actions taken by agencies, and the child's conduct after intervention. An analysis of case records illustrates the effects brought about by the technology of keeping case records. This technology directed attention to individual inadequacies or defects as causes of child abuse and neglect; it enabled the surveillance of the child's and parents' conduct; it documented actions to induce normalization and the result of such actions; and it also enabled the monitoring of the conduct of frontline workers by regulatory authorities, such as the board of the Toronto Children's Aid Society and the provincial office of the Superintendent of Neglected and Dependent Children.

Modes of Power

These technologies were to bring into being various kinds of power relations. Foucault put forward the notion of different modes of power, specifically sovereign power, discipline, and pastoral power.[24] Before Foucault, sovereign power, the political power exercised by the ruler of a state or by its government, was treated as the single most important power in the society in both the conventional study of politics and power and in critical theory. To many theorists, this power is created by the implicit consent of its subjects, who are in turn conceptualized as autonomous individuals. Sovereign power works primarily by means of decisions that its subjects normally accept as binding.

Foucault's contribution to contemporary Western understanding of society and politics lies with this insight: If we are to understand how we are ruled, we have to go beyond questions of sovereign power, since modern forms of (governmental) power cannot be adequately understood if we treat them basically the same as sovereign power in the classical age. Thus, rather than exploring questions of sovereign power in terms of legitimacy, right, and the autonomy of subjects, Foucault is concerned with, first, governmental power in particular, in contrast to classical sovereign power; and second, the means through which the effects of governmental power are produced.

One of the best-known contributions of Foucault is probably his analysis of discipline as a specific form of governmental power. Discipline emerged in seventeenth-century Europe and continued throughout the history of the modern West. In Foucault's view, discipline is not essentially repressive or negative; instead, it is a productive power. It aims at normalizing human individuals. It is a mode of power that is central to government. As Hindess explains, discipline 'is a power exercised over one or more individuals in order to provide them with particular skills and attributes, to develop their capacity for self-control, to promote their ability to act in concert, or render them amenable to instruction, or to mould their characters in other ways.'[25]

A crucial component of Foucault's discussion of discipline is his analysis of the 'humanist subject.' He argues that the emergence of discipline goes hand-in-hand with the invention of the humanist subject. The humanist subject is first of all a malleable creature of social conditions as set out in Locke's *Essay Concerning Human Understanding*; second, he is seen as 'endowed with a soul, consciousness, guilt, remorse, and other features of an interiority,'[26] which are in turn instruments for moulding efforts. The exercise of discipline is based on knowledge of the humanist subject, which has developed into what is known as social and behavioural sciences. When child saving emerged in the late nineteenth century, it conceptualized both parents and children as humanist subjects who could be shaped into proper parents and proper adults. In the widely used gardening metaphors, they were often compared to plants to be straightened, trained, fertilized, and placed in proper soil. Key techniques associated with discipline are observation, examination, surveillance, regimentation, and classification, all of which were utilized widely in child protection.

Pastoral power is another mode of governmental power. Foucault suggests that the mode of pastoral power was first developed in the early Christian church. It was later adopted by governments in seventeenth-century European states and still remains an influential aspect of government in the societies of the modern West. He suggests that the pastoral image of the state has played an important role in the emergence of the paternalistic welfare state in the twentieth century. Foucault used the 'shepherd-flock' metaphor to explain aspects of pastoral power: The aim of pastoral power is to promote the well-being of subjects by means of detailed and comprehensive regulation of their behaviour; the relationship between the ruler and ruled is as intimate and continuous as that between the shepherd and his flock. In contrast to discipline, pastoral power is exercised on 'individuals who can normally be relied upon to impose an appropriate rule on their own behaviour.'[27] Confession, self-examination, and guidance are key techniques of pastoral power. As it will become clear later, guidance and education were also aspects that were emphasized in child-saving work.

The System of Differentiations

Foucault's concept of the system of differentiations encompasses 'differentiations determined by the law or by traditions of status and privilege; economic differences in the appropriation of riches and goods, shifts in the process of production, linguistic or cultural differences; differences in know-how and competence, and so forth.'[28] Differentiations are conditions for every power relationship; at the same time every relationship of power puts differentiations into operation. This concept is useful for mapping power relations in child saving in relation to the differentiations between adults and children, the moral and the immoral, the child savers and the targeted parents and children, which in turn reflect the differentiations between the well-off and the poor, the civilized and the 'dangerous class,' men and women, and Protestants and others.

The class basis of child saving was clear in the social and economic credentials of leaders of the child-saving movement and the board members of the Toronto Children's Aid Society. They were mostly from the upper and middle classes, that is, capitalists, politicians, philanthropists, as well as managers and professionals such as physicians and lawyers. Class differences in beliefs and practices of parenting were central in the construction of cruelty and neglect as forms of deviance. Often, the contradictions between the ideal form of parenting and economic realities became the defining characteristic of what the child savers referred to as child abuse and neglect. For instance, domesticity for both mothers and children in the working class was a choice that virtually did not exist. Often they were forced by economic necessity to work for pay; their earnings were essential to supplement the wages of men, or were the only source of income in the case of families headed by single mothers. However, their participation in the work force was criticized, because it was seen as disrupting the moral training of children. When the child savers established and exercised their authority in investigating, documenting, and assessing working-class people's parenting conduct, and their authority in taking further actions, it again gave concrete expression to their superior economic, social, political, and moral status in the society.

While child saving was clearly a matter of middle-class reformers imposing their values on working-class communities, this did not mean that child savers intended to transform working-class children into middle- or upper-class Canadians. They did want these children to embrace middle-class culture and values that they would like to see in future citizens, but most of them never doubted that these children should be trained for typical working-class employment, for example, as domestic servants in the case of girls, and as farmers or factory workers in the case of boys. The class organization of child saving had another dimension. Child saving was at the same time also a process of creating and reaffirming the bourgeois identity, as a civilized class and one that fulfilled its citizenship duties. This aspect also applied to others who took part in the project, such as foster parents and even complainants.

The child-saving movement in Toronto was male dominated, as reflected in its leadership, management, and ideological hostility towards traditional residential institutions for children run by women.[29] However, within the movement some women were also given the possibility of acquiring a public and relatively powerful identity as board members, matrons, 'lady superintendents,' and 'lady visitors.' In her study of the social purity movement, Valverde has noted the paradox that certain middle-class women made a career out of studying ordinary women.[30] The same applied to the gender organization of child saving, as lady visitors of the Toronto Children's Aid Society, Big Sisters, and deaconesses traveled around the city, inspected the homes of working-class women, reported on their house-keeping and conduct, and gave warnings or advice.

Religious division was clearly an important dimension to child saving, but its manifestation in Toronto was different from that in cities in the United States. In Toronto, a separate St Vincent de Paul Children's Aid Society was established for the Roman Catholic community, in addition to the Toronto Children's Aid Society. This, however, did not happen without opposition. For example, when the provincial government received an application by the Roman Catholic church to operate a children's aid society under the 1893 child protection legislation, John Joseph Kelso, the provincial Superintendent of Neglected and Dependent Children, firmly recommended that the provincial secretary not approve the application.[31] When the St Vincent de Paul Children's Aid Society was established, conflicts broke out from time to time between it and the non-denominational Toronto Children's Aid Society over guardianship of the children of parents of different faiths. Nevertheless, because of the separate systems, in Toronto religious division and discrimination were not reflected in case numbers, unlike the situation in Boston, for example, where Roman Catholics, who were mostly Irish and Italian immigrants, were disproportionately over-represented in caseloads, as Linda Gordon has documented.[32]

The racial organization of child-saving work also took forms different from today's. The vast majority of cases dealt with by the Toronto Children's Aid Society involved children and families of working-class Anglo-Celtic background. Beginning in the late 1910s, there was a slight increase in the number of families from Eastern and Southern European countries. Cases involving mixed-race, 'native', Chinese, or 'black' children appeared, but quite rarely. Similarly, 'race' seldom appeared in texts on child saving or records of the Toronto Children's Aid Society. This, however, did not mean that race was an irrelevant concept, since it underlay notions such as 'nation-building' or 'national strength' – codes that denoted the Anglo-Celtic 'race'. Essentially, child-saving work at the time reflected anxiety about the size and quality of the predominant Anglo-Celtic population.

Children, Citizenship, and Child Protection

Building a useful, strong, and Christian citizenry was the main objective of child saving when it emerged in the late nineteenth century. The linkage between children and citizenship took two forms, corresponding to the two targets of the child-saving movement: cruelty and neglect. First, brutal acts, to which children often fell victim, constituted bad citizenship. This was because the use of force on the harmless, weak, and lowly, such as animals and innocent children, was now conceived as immoral. Cruel acts of individuals, mostly working-class men, were thought of as warranting organized intervention, because individual immorality was seen as corrupting the general moral tone of society at large. The second linkage of children to citizenship was that children were thought of as future citizens to be rescued. This linkage would not have been possible without the humanist conception of human beings, which assumed that individuals were products of conditions. This conception of the human being was best captured by popular gardening metaphors. Childhood was conceived as a stage when the character was most responsive to external influences. Thus, how children were parented would largely determine what kind of citizens they would become. Neglectful parenting, most often mothering, was considered a problem because it failed in building children's character and, thus, caused social and moral problems such as crime, dependency, and immorality in general.

These were the two primary political rationalities for child protection in the late nineteenth century. Although problems of cruelty and neglect concerned different aspects of citizenship, they shared some commonalities. Cruelty and neglect, in contrasting directions, deviated from emerging middle-class and English norms of parent-child relations, which featured an intimate, gentle, intelligent, and incessant parental power over children. Cruelty erred on the side of using too much force; neglect erred on the side of too little parenting. Additionally, both cruelty and neglect were defined as problems from the stance of society, rather than from the stance of children and/or families. Finally, both connected the conduct of individual parents and children in the private sphere with issues of social and national importance.

At the practical level, the work undertaken by the Toronto Children's Aid Society had two components. One was the protection of children from cruel treatment by their parents. The ideas and administration of this line of work were connected to other anti-cruelty work, specifically that with animals. A much larger part of the Toronto Children's Aid Society's work concerned neglect, which at the time was considered as a cause of social and moral problems. Thus, during the period studied the operation of the Toronto Children's Aid Society was heavily shaped by its complex relationship with the governance of juvenile delinquency. From the perspective of governmentality, one can see that child protection and juvenile correction served as fields of observation for each other; supplied each other with rationalities for existence; and shared strategies, personnel, and even facilities. The extent and forms of interweaving between child protection and juvenile correction were manifested particularly in the operation of the detention room at the Toronto Children's Aid Society and the society's involvement in the work of the Toronto Juvenile Court.

Child protection was a regime of power that regulated how parents exercised power over their children. On the one hand, child protection sought to foster ideal forms of parental power that were essentially governmental, that is, power exercised on the basis of rational calculation by working through individuals' desires, aspirations, interests, and beliefs. Parenting technologies that the child savers attempted to foster among parents were often likened to gardening. Technologies of tending to children's character were based on intimate knowledge of the children concerned, and took forms of ruling by kindness, constant oversight, guidance, and inculcation of 'proper' habits of life. On the other hand, child protection condemned forms of parental power that deviated from the ideal forms of parental power, either rule by simplistic brute force or lack of rule. What were considered to be proper forms of power of parents over children reflected what were considered to be proper forms of power over humanist subjects in general. Indeed, the child savers' power over parents and children was envisioned such that it mirrored ideal forms of parenting conduct in many ways. Child-saving strategies were designed to be principally positive, individualized, knowledge-based, and local. The most representative strategies included guidance, supervision, investigation, classification, separation, and dispersion. These were embodied in the child-saving activities of reporting, visiting, record-keeping, the operation of the shelter and the detention room, and foster care.

In contrast to the historical rationalities and technologies of child protection during the period from the 1880s to 1920s, child protection in Ontario at the turn of the twenty-first century has a very different objective and takes a very different shape. If many ideas and technologies of child protection in the early period were representative of the 'social' era, the current child-protection regime signifies profound transformations of citizenship, the conception of human identity, and modes of power for governing individuals at large in the 'post-social' era.

First, instead of being considered as 'future citizens' whose criminal tendencies must be stamped out, today children are constituted as the ideal privatized citizens, whose legitimate ethical and political claims rest on private victimization and personal innocence. In particular, the child-victim citizen discourse as it operates in the site of child protection accentuates children's rights to personal safety. If a century ago parents were condemned because they were uncivilized or because they corrupted children and made them potentially dangerous elements in society, today they are condemned as perpetrators of personal crimes against innocent child-citizens.

Second, in contrast to the historical objective of preventing crime and immorality in society, the primary objective of current child protection is 'keeping kids safe.'[33] This objective assumes that child abuse and neglect are only a matter of personal danger and harm to children. Child protection is envisioned as a project to guarantee the fulfillment of the rights of individual children to personal safety. This is an extremely narrow understanding of children's well-being, and it severely limits the kinds of collective actions that are considered.

Third, new child-protection technologies feature risk management on the one hand and criminal punishment on the other. In contrast to the humanist subject and corresponding gardening strategies, technologies at the turn of the twenty-first century assume a new conception of human identity. Individuals are divided into dichotomous groups of victims and (potential) perpetrators. Furthermore, as Nikolas Rose points out, (potential) perpetrators are defined through risk factors, but are at the same time held morally responsible for their conduct.[34] On the basis of this understanding of human subjects, child-protection practices at the provincial level are transformed primarily into information management for providing safety to children. At the same time, harsher criminal punishment of parents at the federal level is being considered seriously.

The transformations in the area of child protection fit with changes in the broader context. They exemplify a process of what Lauren Berlant calls the privatization of citizenship, wherein public discussions about rights, power, ethics, and collective actions are organized by questions of personal significance.[35] In child protection and some other sites, the personal safety of certain groups has dominated as the major criterion in considering the rights and obligations of citizenship. The monopoly of concerns with personal safety excludes structural questions about capitalism, poverty, racism, and gender inequality. The preoccupation with personal safety also confines actions to managing risks of harm and punishing criminals, and excludes other actions oriented to providing supports to marginalized groups in society.

The following study contains eight chapters. Chapter 1 addresses the context of the emergence of child saving, drawing attention to the influence of Christian missionary work and penal reform. Chapter 2 traces how child saving was thought of and deliberated when it emerged in the late nineteenth century. It argues that public concern with moral progress was the ideological framework of the English-Canadian conceptualization of child protection in the period from the 1880s to the 1920s. Chapter 3 focuses on the gardening metaphors widely used in child-saving writings. It explores the humanist model of the human subject as a malleable individual from the point of view of the child savers and the forms of power represented in the allegory of the gardener and plants and weeds. It also analyses a range of child-saving strategies targeting children's habitat, habits, and hearts. In Chapter 4, the technologies of reports, visits, and case records are discussed. Then chapters 5 and 6 provide detailed examination of the shelter and the detention room, respectively. Chapter 7 focuses on foster care. Finally, Chapter 8 turns to Ontario's Child Welfare Reform (1996–1999) and explores how historical analyses can be used to understand the present.

Chapter 1

The Emergence of Child Saving:
Influence of the Christian Mission
and the Prison-Reform Movements

For most of the nineteenth century some public and voluntary measures for certain groups of children existed in Ontario. Like Britain and the United States, Ontario had been concerned mainly with orphans, children who lost their fathers in the War of 1812, children of unmarried mothers, deaf and blind children, and mentally ill children. Measures took the form of institutional care, apprenticeships, war pensions, regulation of guardianship, and stipulations on the support for illegitimate children.[1] Evidently, formal care and support was restricted primarily to the general category of children who did not have a 'normal' family with two parents. Most of these provisions fell under the doctrine of *parens patriae*, which can be literally translated as 'parent of the nation.' This doctrine was used to provide the state and its representatives authority respecting children, which was seen as normally belonging to parents. The jurisdiction of such authority gradually expanded.[2] Towards the end of the 1880s, the state's authority was extended to children of two-parent families. The late-1880s wave of legislative actions respecting children mainly targeted parents' cruelty towards children and neglectful treatment of them.[3] For the first time, parents' cruelty and neglect were considered as major societal issues to be addressed in legislation and through organized intervention.

Brutality, Negligence, and Indulgence

Cruelty and neglect were not new problems. They had historical precedents, that is, brutality, negligence, and indulgence. Children's experiences with brute force and inflicted pain have always existed and were regulated in various ways. In early modern Europe, moderate corporal punishment was a regular and encouraged part of discipline at home, in school, and in the shops of trade masters where children received vocational training as apprentices.[4] Excessive violence against children, however, was discouraged and even condemned. The use of excessive force on children by parents, usually fathers, and its use by non-family-members such as masters and schoolteachers were dealt with differently. Masters' or teachers' brutality towards apprentices or pupils was perceived as a far greater problem than parental violence. Ralph Houlbrooke notes that masters were warned not to 'curse, and lame [apprenticed children,] cast dishes and pots at their heads, beat them, [or] put them in danger of their life.' They were also taken to court by parents. In these situations excessive and arbitrary violence against children on the part of masters and teachers was problematized mainly as damage to their fathers' property.[5]

The brutality of fathers was problematized as one form of improper parenting. Opposite to the problem of too much force was another form of improper parenting: negligent and uninformed parenting, which I argue is the predecessor of what is known today as 'child neglect.' This disagrees with the observation of many studies that child neglect was a new problem given rise by the social and economic conditions of the twentieth century. Concerns with parenting were underpinned by a particular understanding of childhood that emerged in Europe in the early modern period[6] (and persists to the twentieth century) and was radically different from earlier understandings. In the Middle Ages people believed that what the future adult would be was predetermined. The discerning eye could see such predispositions by picking out tell-tale traits in the child. Thus, childhood was important not in itself but for what it might tell about the adult to be.[7] Modern concepts of childhood,[8] in contrast, assumed that how children were reared would have direct and enormous effect on their adult future. This notion gave rise to the question of how children should be reared, and what emerged was an emphasis on instructing and disciplining children.[9]

In Europe in early modern times moderate corporal punishment was encouraged as a regular part of disciplining of children, particularly during the formative years between ages six and twelve. However, fathers' use of force was criticized when it was considered arbitrary and excessive. Although fathers were advised not to be harsh and arbitrary in disciplining children (or wives and servants), mainly because it was considered ineffective, fathers' brutality was not so much a public problem, partly because of the primary emphasis on the importance of parents' disciplining of children, and partly because of the perception of children as private property of their fathers. Writing in the American context, Linda Gordon notes that 'cruel treatment' had been dealt with by the application of community sanctions against parents. These community reactions, however, were restricted to limited and informal intervention by relatives or neighbours.[10]

In fact, what was considered to be a more serious problem, and thus warranting more action, was negligence and indulgence on the part of parents in dealing with their children. As Steven Ozment observes, an indulgent and permissive parent was thought to be worse than a harsh parent, because the former rejected the basic parental responsibility of shaping a child, while the latter appeared to take his responsibility seriously, although perhaps to an extreme.[11]

Thus, neglecting children was a worse sin than being brutal towards them. The history of neglect can be traced back to 'willful negligence and indulgence' in early modern Europe. The older category 'willful negligence and indulgence' was formulated to denote deviance from what was considered as parenting responsibility, that is, 'to instill in a child the inner virtue and qualities that will enable him to serve and survive in the world and before God.'[12] According to moralists in early modern Europe, wilful negligence and indulgence of children was not only the cardinal sin of parenting, it was also an all-too-common one.[13]

Parents from all parts of society were criticized for their negligence and indulgence of children, but the content of the criticisms and advice were class-specific. The upper classes were usually criticized for indulgence, in corrupting their children with material goods. They were often accused of negligence in ensuring their children's acquisition of the 'skills, wisdom, and cunning by which a land and people must be ruled.' In contrast, parents from 'common' backgrounds were more likely to be accused of indulgence and negligence in allowing undesirable conduct, such as letting children 'creep out idly, eating and drinking whenever they please, and casually dressed in ragged pants and jackets,' which resulted in general indiscipline and self-indulgence.[14] Furthermore, such parents were criticized for not correcting their children when they learnt from bad example to curse, swear, lie and steal; for not disciplining them when they stayed out dancing until midnight, and not waking them up on Sunday morning and taking them to church, and so on. For these children, the fear was that they might turn out to be 'mercenaries, murderers, and criminals.'[15]

In colonial North America, similar fears were reflected in the thought that 'willful negligence and indulgence' would cause children to become 'trouble and charge,' that is, criminals or paupers dependent on charity. For example, there is a record of proceedings at Watertown, Massachusetts from 1726 regarding complaints about the 'very Neady and Suffering Circumstances' of some families in town:

> Some families in Said Town ... are under very Neady & Suffering Circumstances. In which families there are Children of beth Sex's that are able to work in order to their Maintenance, and also of being Sent to School and brought to the Publick worship of God; But through the willfullness Negligence and Indulgence of their parents they are brought up in Idleness Ignorance & Ereligion, and are more Likely to prove a Trouble and Charge, then blessings in their Day and Generation if not timely prevented [sic].[16]

To sum up, brutality and negligence had always been twin problems in parenting since the early modern period. Each deviated from the ideal form of parenting, albeit in opposite directions. Parents in the West have been accused of either using too much force or not disciplining children sufficiently since the sixteenth century. Brutality was clearly a fathers' problem. While the discourse on negligence and indulgence almost always used the gender-neutral term 'parents,' in reality the guilt was most often placed on mothers, since they were supposed to assume a major role in providing instruction, guidance, and gentle discipline to children. Comparatively speaking, brutality was considered as a much less serious problem than negligence and indulgence, partly because of the emphasis that was put on parents' actions in shaping children's character, and partly because of the lack of challenge to the conception of children as their fathers' private property. As we shall see, the gender-specificity and the relative weightiness of the problem of negligence and indulgence were maintained in the child-saving movement when it emerged in the late nineteenth century.

In earlier times, brutality by fathers was regarded as a very private matter, and only informal forms of power such as advising by relatives or people with status in the community were thought of as appropriate for addressing the problem. Negligence and indulgence seemed to be problems that were more connected to the well-being of society at large, and were thus subjected to more community intervention. Still, regulation was sporadic and contained within close-knit communities. The child-saving movement in the late nineteenth century transformed early modern thinking and actions concerning improper parenting in several aspects. The use of excessive force was now problematized as cruelty (as opposed to mere brutality), testifying to the influence of the Christian concern of morality; the problem of wilful negligence and indulgence became child neglect and was mostly a working-class problem; and both cruelty and neglect were perceived as widespread social problems to be regulated by formal and bureaucratic intervention, which still relied on the community for its operation (e.g., the reliance on the community to report cases of cruelty and neglect) but was mainly undertaken by strangers.

This transformation was part and parcel of urban reform in English-speaking Canada at the turn of the twentieth century. It reflected that aspect of moral reform which sought to purify and reshape the ethical subjectivities of individuals so as to 'raise the moral tone' of Canadian society in general, and working-class communities in particular.[17] Canadian scholars have noted the various effects of industrialization and urbanization in their attempts to understand the emergence of child saving in the late nineteenth century.[18] Industrialization came relatively late in Canada, although in the 1870s and 1880s the pace of industrialization in urban centres such as Toronto began to accelerate. In the process of becoming an industrialized nation, Canada saw its urban population grow, mainly as a result of both domestic and international migration, at a speed that could hardly be sustained by the infrastructure. Rapid and largely unplanned growth resulted in deteriorating living standards in the poor areas of the cities. These were manifested in poor housing, overcrowding, lack of proper sanitary conditions, and waste disposal problems.[19] Neil Sutherland has documented the growing fears of contamination (in both physical and moral terms) and social disorder that were felt by the emerging middle class.[20] Karen Swift identifies a set of conditions that conspired to produce organizational and legislative action to protect children: homelessness and exploitation for many Canadian children of the working class; the creation of a new middle class whose standard of living rapidly increased, as did their standards of child rearing; and increased leisure for middle-class women, which provided time and energy for social change.[21] Patricia Rooke and Rodolph Schnell stressed that the child-saving movement began because of the middle-class ideology that every child should have a 'childhood.'[22] These were salient aspects that formed the background to the child-saving movement. As well, there were other important sources of influence on child saving. The Christian mission and the prison-reform movements were two earlier but long-lasting movements that particularly pertained to the surge of interest in the child-saving aspect of urban reform.

The Christian Mission Movement

The modern Christian mission movement was largely dominated by Anglo-Celtic Protestants.[23] It began in England in the 1790s and continued well into the twentieth century. In England, the movement was mainly oriented to foreign missionary work in 'heathen nations' in Africa and Asia. In North America, the first missionary activities had been chiefly concerned with carrying the gospel to 'Indians' and to settlers on the frontier. By the 1870s Canadian churches were formally committed to overseas missionary activities.[24] While the ultimate goal of missionary work was conversion, evangelizing was always accompanied by the concern for civilizing. Sometimes civilizing was even believed to be a prerequisite for conversion; more often the two were so intertwined that it is futile to try to separate one from another.[25] Among targets of civilizing work such as clothing and marriage customs, the humane sentiment was a major aspect of character that missionaries attempted to foster, so as to make heathens 'men' before making them Christians. The Englishness of the humane sentiment and the sense of superiority that it constituted was evident in stories of anti-cruelty work in other lands that were published at home. For example, a report in an American humane association journal told the story of the spreading of anti-cruelty work in China to foot-binding and ill-treatment of slave girls, largely as a result of 'the philanthropic efforts of foreign ladies.' The report attributed the spreading of philanthropy to 'education along modern lines,' and purported that the anti-cruelty work undertaken by 'China's sons' would bring about 'real progress' and 'place among the enlightened and civilized nations of the earth.'[26]

Christian missionary work was an important influence on child-saving work. For one thing, parents who used excessive force on children came to be interpreted as moral defectives who needed to be civilized. The child savers, such as Kelso, characterized parties involved in child saving, such as foster parents, as being 'inspired and directed by the Christian missionary spirit.'[27] Children were also seen as objects to be civilized through, for example, the education-oriented activities of the Band of Mercy, so that they would be humane towards 'dumb animals' and would grow up to be moral individuals. As well, the consciousness of both missionaries and the child savers was characterized by a sense that they were God's special messengers and much needed saviours for poor souls (see Illustration 1). Similarly, the 'come-over-and-help-us' theme in the missionaries' projection of their objects to be civilized was replicated in the child savers' representation of abused and neglected children, who raised their arms to hold on to their saviour and looked at him or her in an adoring and thankful way (see Illustration 2).

Christian mission work, particularly its direct evangelical and civilizing work also influenced the techniques of practical child-saving work. In Ruth Brouwer's study of Canadian Presbyterian women's missions in India at the turn of the past century, she examines many methods used by these women in their evangelizing and civilizing work: public preaching, zenana visiting (visiting privileged Indian women in their private family quarters), itinerating (camp work, village visiting, or district work), teaching by example, Bhajans (hymns), and magic lantern slides.[28] We find similar practices widely used by the child savers, such as public speeches, family visits, neighbourhood inspections, Band of Mercy hymns in child-saving work, and, not least, the famous magic-lantern slides used by Kelso when he traveled across Ontario and other provinces spreading his views on child welfare.[29]

The Prison-Reform Movement

The other movement that shaped child-saving thinking was prison reform in general, and juvenile-delinquency reform in particular. Anthony Platt's classical study from a criminology perspective of the child savers' role in the invention of delinquency provides a detailed analysis of the intertwined relations between child saving and juvenile delinquency in the United States.[30] In Canada, the crime-prevention and treatment dimension of child saving has only received limited attention. On the one hand, criminologists who write about the history of juvenile delinquency acknowledge the child savers' influence in general, but do not examine the crime-prevention and treatment work undertaken by child-saving institutions such as the Toronto Children's Aid Society. (One exception is Paula Maurutto's recent work on Catholic child saving and juvenile correction.[31]) On the other hand, historical studies of child saving occasionally note the presence of crime and juvenile delinquency components in child-saving work, but generally are not interested in exploring the influence of the broad penal reform on child saving.

Penal reform in the nineteenth century primarily aimed at producing new mechanisms that were more effective in reducing crime than the old ones. Up to that point, children who committed criminal offences were usually subjected to the same punishment as adults. Exceptions were made, such as reduced sentences, out of mercy or reason (e.g., children under the age of seven could not be punished because of their mental incapacity). However, in general, children went through essentially the same criminal trial processes as adults; they were given harsh punishments and kept in detention with adults if incarcerated.[32]

The prison reformers, however, started to see young criminals in a new light, as objects to be governed separately and differently. This view was developed on the basis of the modern belief that childhood was the most mouldable stage in the life course. In relation to prison reform, two inferences were drawn: (1) Young criminals could be influenced to become worse if they were locked up together with adult criminals. This had made the prison-based penal system a self-defeating project: Instead of turning children away from crime, it became a finishing school for criminals. (2) The criminal conduct of children was produced and moulded by external factors such as the home environment and inappropriate parenting. Thus, it would be both unfair and futile to punish children for results for which they were not responsible. Instead, energy and resources should be invested in ensuring that children grew up in a good environment and that parents governed them properly.

These reflections were translated into practices in the reform of the traditional judicial model applied to young criminals. It was a slow, uneven, resisted, but nonetheless persistent process, spanning the second half of the nineteenth century and the early twentieth century. We can roughly divide the process into two phases. The first phase was from about the 1860s to the 1880s, during which time several reformatories and industrial schools were established for the young. The second phase of penal reform involving youth – from the late 1880s to 1920s – was intertwined with the child-saving movement. This period witnessed the emergence of several other strategies designed for governing juvenile delinquents: separate detention rooms, the Juvenile Court (initially the Children's Court), probation and indeterminate sentences, and a trend to de-institutionalization that resulted in the downsizing and even dismantling of some reformatories and industrial schools established only a few decades earlier.

The initial impact of the penal reform respecting the young came from its production of knowledge beginning as early as in the 1860s. Specifically, as young criminals increasingly became a separate type of criminal, information was gathered on their family circumstances and background, which in turn became material for analysis linking neglect to crime.[33] From the late 1880s to 1920s, juvenile-delinquency reform was a major driving force behind mobilization in the voluntary sector to protect children from neglectful parents. This was evident in the significant overlap in personnel, ideas, and even facilities between juvenile correction and the child-saving movement, which I elaborate in following chapters.

The Child-Saving Movement

The economic, cultural, and legal developments that formed the background to the child-saving movement discussed here were not unique to Canada. Similar developments in the northeastern United States and in urban Britain led to child-saving movements first in the United States in the 1870s[34] and then in Britain in the early 1880s.[35] In English-speaking Canada, the child-saving movement started in Toronto in the late 1880s. It resembled those in the United States and England in several aspects: for example, its urban location, its initial connection to the prevention of cruelty to animals, and its association with other social and moral reform projects. In 1886, John Kidson Macdonald, a successful Toronto businessman and a prominent figure in local charity work, wrote to the local newspaper, the *World*, deploring the absence in the city of a society to prevent cruelty to animals.[36] His letter was handled by Kelso, who at the time was a police reporter for the *World* and who later contributed to the establishment of the Canadian child-protection system probably more than any of his contemporaries.[37] When Kelso proposed actions to establish such a society in reply to Macdonald, he expanded Macdonald's concern with animals to include prevention of cruelty against children, as well as what would be later categorized as neglect (e.g., 'vicious influences'). Kelso's vision was accepted when the Toronto Humane Society for the Prevention of Cruelty was established at a public meeting organized by Kelso and Macdonald in February 1887.

As Richard Splane observes, the Toronto Humane Society directly and indirectly influenced three highly important developments of the late 1880s and early 1890s, which in turn structured child-protection work for most of the twentieth century. The first was provincial child-protection legislation in 1888, under the title 'An Act for the Protection and Reformation of Neglected Children.' Essentially the act confirmed the authority of the courts to commit neglected children to a variety of institutions. It established public responsibility for the maintenance of neglected children in all types of children's institutions recognized by the province. However, to the child savers, one major flaw of the act was that it did not deal with the question of the Humane Society's power to remove children from their families, and in a related way the lack of recognition of the non-institutional care in which leading male child savers particularly believed. These were remedied by later child-protection legislation, specifically the 'Act for the Prevention of Cruelty to, and Better Protection of Children' in 1893 and amendments in ensuing decades.[38]

The second major development was the appointment of the Ontario Royal Commission on the Prison and Reformatory System in 1890, which in Splane's assessment was perhaps the most important single event at the time in advancing public knowledge and official action respecting child welfare. In fact, the conceptual foundation for child-saving work was solidified through the royal commission. The royal commission considered, among others, two major issues: the principal causes of crime and the rescue of children from criminal careers. The commission consulted writers of high authority on the subject of crime, judges, wardens of prisons, and reformers. The process of the commission assembled and gave authority to quasi-scientific knowledge that connected neglect of children and social and moral problems, most notably crime, drinking, prostitution, and pauperism. The commission reached a conclusion on the chief causes of crime in the community, which was claimed to be the almost universal opinion of all who gave testimony: 'the want of proper parental control; the lack of good home training and the baneful influence of bad homes, largely due to the culpable neglect and indifference of parents and the evil effects of drunkenness.'[39]

One of the recommendations of the commissioners respecting children was the establishment of an association with local boards in every important centre of the province who would take upon themselves the 'important but delicate duty' of supervising and caring for children leaving both the industrial schools and the boys' reformatory and the girls' refuge. Splane speculated that if the commissioners had been asked to suggest a descriptive name for their proposed association, they might well have suggested a term such as 'children's aid association.'[40] It is probably sound to speculate that the association that the royal commission recommended and that the Toronto Children's Aid Society was largely modeled on was an association patterned after the already existing Prisoners' Aid Association. Instead of supervising and helping adult prisoners, the new parallel association was envisioned to deal with child criminals and prisoners.

The third major development during the period was the establishment of the Toronto Children's Aid Society in 1891. Kelso had been instrumental in the organization of the Toronto Children's Aid Society in July 1891. However, his personal relation with the society was tense and even acrimonious, barring the very early years. Upon the society's incorporation in 1891, Kelso was elected its president. He was determined to be in control and to develop the society according to his vision. In their biography of Kelso, Jones and Rutman noted that Kelso's method of operation was to undertake personally the tasks that he believed necessary. While this individualist approach was effective in starting discussion about protection of animals and children, it caused strain in an organizational setting. Quickly Kelso found it difficult to dominate the society, as he was continuously questioned and challenged by other leading people in the organization, mostly notably Macdonald, who was also young, energetic, and opinionated.[41] A major difference between Kelso and Macdonald worked to Kelso's disadvantage: Macdonald was one of the establishment, while Kelso was an outsider. Kelso had come to Canada from a small town in northeastern Ireland as a child. Although his family was relatively prosperous when his father owned a starch factory in Ireland, a fire had abruptly plunged the family into economic insecurity. At the time he instigated child-saving work in Toronto, Kelso was still struggling to get himself into a financially sound position. Macdonald, however, was already well-known as the 'Canadian dry goods king,' the managing director of the Confederation Life Association Company, and one of the most respectable philanthropists in Toronto.[42] This difference in class and status was reflected in their subsequent career moves in the child-protection system. Kelso's anxiety over his own limited financial resources and his dissatisfaction with his lack of influence in the society resulted in a decision to resign from the presidency of the society after having served for only eight months. The board of the society then unanimously elected Macdonald president in February 1892, a position that he held for the following three decades.[43] Meanwhile, Kelso was appointed by the provincial government to the position of the Superintendent of Neglected and Dependent Children in Ontario in July 1893.[44] Thus, while Macdonald dominated the voluntary society as a philanthropist, Kelso, as a man without independent means, became a salaried middle-class civil servant in the growing bureaucracy.

The Toronto Children's Aid Society undertook two streams of work. One was the anti-cruelty-to-children work that had been under the auspices of the Humane Society, but was split out because of the conflicts created by the competition between child-protection work and animal-protection work.[45] The other was the supervision and caring work for neglected children who were thought of as being on their way to become delinquents as well as those who were consummated juvenile delinquents, that is, those who had been charged by the police and brought to the justice system. Although sensational cruelty cases were often widely publicized and thus tended to be better known, during the period under examination the bulk of cases involved neglect.[46] Thus, while anti-cruelty work in the humane tradition was always a part of child-saving work, the Toronto Children's Aid Society's operation during the historical period with which this book is concerned was overwhelmingly shaped by its strong, complex, and circular connection with the governance of juvenile delinquency. The child-saving system and the judicial system served each other as fields of observation for the invention of knowledge; supplied each other with reasons for existence; and shared strategies (e.g., investigation, guidance, and supervision), personnel, and even facilities (e.g., the detention room operated by the Toronto Children's Aid Society for the Toronto Juvenile Court).

Chapter 2

The Evil Twins of Cruelty and Neglect:
Seeds of Moral and Social Problems

This chapter elaborates on how child saving was thought of and deliberated among the child savers when it emerged in the late nineteenth
century. The main argument is that the theme of moral progress largely
framed the English-Canadian discussion of child saving in the period
from the 1880s to the 1920s. Child-saving initiatives were undertaken to
ensure the proper making of 'future citizens.' Experiences of violence,
deprivation, and freedom were made intelligible in a conceptual framework that by and large corresponded to the dominating concern of
moral progress. However, then, as now, the perspectives of the subjects
of these experiences, who were mostly at the margins of society, were
ignored or suppressed. The aspirations and imaginations of dominant
groups largely influenced how experiences were understood and acted
upon.

To the first generation of child-protection workers, child abuse was
mainly known as 'cruelty'; neglect was mainly understood as either the
omission of moral training, contamination, or active corruption of children. Cruelty and neglect were different in that the former was a straight-
forward moral offence in itself. It was concerned with adults' civility
more than with children's suffering. In contrast, neglect was considered
a major cause of crime, immorality, and pauperism. The objective of
regulating neglectful parents was to steer them to administer proper
moral training and discipline to children, so that they could grow up to
be useful, self-controlled, and Christian citizens. The difference between
these two categories was in turn reflected in the kinds of knowledge
involved and the forms of power developed for addressing cruelty and
neglect.

Briefly, performance of civility and moral judgment characterized knowledge of cruelty. Civility and knowledge of cruelty operated as conditions for and consequences of each other. If a person were enlightened and civilized, she would recognize cruelty; and if a person were able to identify cruelty, she must be an enlightened and civilized person. As a rule, experience or education did not distinguish anyone as an expert on cruelty. Knowledge of neglect, however, was to a significant extent accumulated through the work experience of quasi-professionals in the broad areas of charity and correction. Thus, at the time, the 'experts' on child neglect were wardens of prisons, magistrates, and charity workers. They claimed their authority on the basis of their administrative and quasi-professional knowledge[1] of neglected children, criminals, prostitutes, and beggars, as well as their observation of correlations and rudimentary statistical information. For these reasons I will discuss cruelty and neglect separately in this chapter.

Cruelty as Immorality

The anti-cruelty movement that first emerged in England considered cruelty a moral wrong. Despite concerns with fathers' brutality towards children in earlier times, children were not the initial concern of the modern organized anti-cruelty movement. In fact, the movement started with protection of animals from whatever was considered as inhumane treatment.[2] Canadian reformers, like their American and English counterparts, were first mobilized for protection of animals, and only extended their attention to children later. The establishment of the Toronto Humane Society encompassed animal protection and child protection under one organizational roof, with the overall objective of improving the moral tone of society. Animals and children (and to some extent women) were regarded as fellow victims of cruelty, who shared the characteristics of being weak, lowly, and harmless. For example, when the Toronto Humane Society was organized in February 1887, the following was laid out as the kinds of work that it would do: 'to stop cruelty to children; to rescue them from vicious influences and remedy their condition; [to prevent] the beating of animals, overloading street cars, overloading wagons, working old horses, driving galled and disabled animals; to introduce drinking fountains, better laws, better methods of horseshoeing, humane literature into schools and homes; to induce children to be humane; everybody to practice and teach kindness to animals and others.'[3]

These dual foci of the Toronto Humane Society were also represented vividly in the society's emblem. For a number of years before the split of work with animals and with children, the Toronto Humane Society's emblem featured two overlapping pictures. One depicted a horse being beaten by a driver with a club and a guardian angel who appeared from the clouds, one arm raised and the other holding a sword. The other picture depicted three or four small children being beaten by a man with a club and a goddess-like figure who intervened to protect the children with a shield and represented the high morality of anti-cruelty workers (see Illustration 3).

In the documents produced by the Toronto Humane Society, the similarity between animals and children was built through emphasizing their 'sameness' as victims of cruelty. Specifically, their 'sameness' was characterized in the aspects of weakness, lowliness, and innocence. In humane discourse 'the weak' was a generic category for animals, children, and women, who were perceived as defenseless by moral reformers. In a letter to the editor of the *World*, Kelso, in the capacity of the Secretary of the Toronto Humane Society, expressed his appreciation to the public for suggesting the kind of protection work for the Humane Society. He also described the Humane Society's work plan, ranging from looking after cattle in transit, to improving laws respecting cruelty to children and erecting a shelter for separating arrested women and children from hardened criminals while awaiting and during trial. He pleaded for financial contributions and explained that 'all who believe in the principle of helping and protecting the weak are eligible as members.'[4] Similarly, animals to be protected from cruelty were often referred to as 'the lower creatures' or 'dumb animals.' Although children were usually not described in these terms directly, they had nevertheless a low status and were at the receiving end of charity and governance.

The educational literature produced by the Toronto Humane Society instructed people to be kind, not to just any creature, but to 'harmless creatures,' in other words innocent and non-threatening beings. The characteristic of innocence was evident in the kinds of animals that were commonly featured in protection work: working beasts such as horses and cattle, pets such as dogs and cats, and wild birds. Animals that were customarily regarded as dangerous and evil, for example wolves, were not listed as worthy of anti-cruelty sentiment. As for children, their worthiness of protection was defined in moral terms and in relation to the interests of society. Honest and obedient children were worthy of protection. However, for wayward children, the use of physical force was justified and was categorized as corporal punishment, not cruelty. The notion of innocence therefore reveals the limits of anti-cruelty work and the fact that even though it involved humane sentiment, those who participated in it did not indiscriminately shower everyone with humane love. In the end, it was a rational project, and its members were conscious of the boundaries and objectives of their work.

Thus, instead of viewing protection of children from cruel treatment by parents as a self-explanatory step in human progress, we should understand the critique of cruelty in the larger context of urban reform in general, and moral regeneration in particular, occurring at that time. In this sense, the anti-cruelty sentiment and activities were part of a broad-scale reflection on how 'we' ought to relate to subordinate groups in society – that is, animals, children, pupils, prisoners, and so on. Certainly the child savers were concerned with children suffering violence, but they were concerned not so much because it was an issue of personal rights to safety (as it is today) as because they believed that society's moral strength was at stake when relations with children were characterized with violence. That they were primarily interested in society's morals was further illustrated in their efforts to mould children into subjects of civility by encouraging them to establish appropriate relations with animals and to be merciful towards them.

'Cruelty' was a historically specific category. In comparison with the earlier category of 'brutality,' 'cruelty' had a quite precise boundary, in that it only applied to acts of one person towards a being that was subordinate, weak, non-threatening, and usually innocent. In contrast, a person could be brutal not only towards his subordinates, but also towards his equals. 'Cruelty' also differs from the modern category of 'child abuse.' 'Child abuse,' even though it maintains a moral connotation, integrates knowledge from a variety of social-scientific disciplines. For most of the twentieth century, child abuse has been explained mainly as a symptom of problems with a parent's mind. Wini Breines and Linda Gordon have provided a critical discussion of how child abuse has been explained and diagnosed since the 1920s by using a variety of psychological and psychiatric concepts,[5] for example, 'feeble-mindedness,' 'confusion' with gender roles, 'role reversal,'[6] 'cycle of abuse,'[7] and 'maternal bonding and attachment' theory.[8] Child abuse has also been explained by some as, at least partly, a symptom of the society's structural problems, using sociological concepts such as 'triggering context' and 'the interaction between structural considerations (e.g., unemployment) and personal factors (e.g., stress).'[9] The most recent intellectual shift is a reconceptualization of child abuse as a threat to children's safety. Along with the reconceptualization of child abuse as danger, problems with either the mind (e.g., lack of maternal bonding) or society (e.g., poverty) are refashioned into risk factors, which tend to be accepted as pre-existing givens rather than issues to be addressed.

In contrast to all these social scientific theories and concepts, the understanding of 'cruelty' rested on the moral concept of 'the heart.' Cruelty was explained as a problem with 'the heart,' usually of a working-class man. For example, parents who beat their children were often described as 'heartless parents,'[10] or 'a cruel-hearted man.'[11] At the same time, cruelty was to be discerned by a civilized heart. It did not require a pair of trained eyes, or evidence such as an X-ray of a fractured bone, or statistical information on factors, correlations, and probabilities to determine cruelty. Instead, it required a civilized heart to know what cruelty was.

Of course, this is not to say that in reality only those with civilized hearts knew what was cruelty. Indeed, some children claimed their knowledge of cruelty on the basis of their personal experiences. For example, on 6 April 1892, Grace Garland, age 14, took shelter at 9 p.m., and 'told a story of cruelty by parents.'[12] Similarly, a few days later Eva Gray, age 9, took refuge at 8 p.m., and 'said she had been cruelly beaten by her father with a strap with a buckle on it.'[13] However, children's knowledge of cruelty was typically treated with suspicion. The child savers were wary about the possibility of children manipulating the authority of the Children's Aid Society to their advantage by manufacturing a story of cruelty. In the case of Grace, her story of her parents' cruelty was found to be 'untrue,' and she was returned to her home next day. As for Eva, she was undressed and 'her body bore sorry evidence of the truth of her statement.' Although her parents denied that they had treated her cruelly, her story was accepted as the true one.

It seemed that in dealing with children's allegations of cruelty, the benefit of doubt was usually given to those accused who were associated with or identified with the child-saving movement, such as foster parents and industrial schools. For example, Kelso dismissed charges of cruelty laid by inmates of a reform school against the institution. He thought that the investigating committee had made a mistake in 'privately interviewing the inmates and accepting as true the fanciful stories that were told them.' This was because, he argued, 'It is well known that the average boy or girl, especially those who find their way into a reform school, will tell a story just as big as the capacity of the listener to receive and absorb it.' He defended the head of the reform school by saying that 'the head of a reform institution is always in danger from charges of cruelty to inmates, because he is dealing with unwilling people and he is likely to get the worst of it in any public discussion however good or efficient he may be.'[14]

Other knowers of cruelty recognized a cruel act with their civilized, that is, Christian, hearts. Presumably, they had achieved a sufficient level of civility and were thus able to tell what were the right or wrong ways to treat children. They could be grandparents, uncles and aunts, neighbours, the clergy, or the police. Their complaints of cruelty to the Toronto Children's Aid Society were treated as rudimentary knowledge. This was to be digested, sorted, verified, and developed by the child savers, who were in a position of higher authority in the chain of knowledge production. The authority of the child savers mainly drew upon presumed greater civility. The reasoning was that a civilized person cared about how children were treated, and if he cared enough to devote himself to the cause of child saving, he must be more civilized than the average.

Cruelty was conditional on a child's innocence. A slap on the face of an innocent child would be cruelty, but would be proper discipline if the child were judged to have been wayward. In this sense, the child savers determined cruelty in different ways. When a child did not do anything wrong, the simple use of force was cruelty. In situations where a child had done wrong, cruelty existed only if the use of force was excessive. Thus, the child savers' first task was to determine whether a child had done anything 'bad.' If he had not, then the task was to verify whether acts of beating, thrashing, and so on had occurred or not. However, sometimes children were found guilty of running away, stealing, or being disobedient. For example, on 5 March 1903, Reverend P.C. Parker complained to the Toronto Children's Aid Society that a young girl, Edith Donnelly, had been cruelly thrashed by her father on Dundas Street until the blood ran down her back.[15] The inspector of the society visited the family and reported on Edith and her father. He learnt that the father kept a stationery store. The girl, in company with another, had run away from her house and got herself a domestic job on Euclid Avenue. She admitted to the inspector that 'she deserved whipping.' In cases such as this, the inspector typically would then gather information to determine whether the child had been punished with 'inhuman severity,'[16] and whether the parent was in the habit of doing it, both of which were rather subjective judgments. The inspector checked Edith's back and found that blood had not been drawn, although there were marks left there. Apparently, he felt ambivalent about the situation. In the end, he decided to just warn both the parents and the girl.

Knowledge of cruelty was intertwined with morality in several ways. The credible knowers were people with civilized hearts. The higher one's moral status (e.g., the child savers or the clergy), the more authority one held. Since morality was defined from the perspectives of Anglo-Celtic middle-class adults, the views of the working-class, immigrants, and children as to what counted as cruelty were in effect discounted. Cruelty was also relative to the innocence or guilt of the object of violence. Thus, knowledge of cruelty was of a qualitative kind, in that it was situation-specific.

Neglect and the Criminal Bud

The development of the understanding of neglect in the late nineteenth century had roots in the legacy of 'willful negligence and indulgence,' but it flourished in the context of social and moral reforms, when the problems of crime, immorality, and pauperism seemed to loom particularly large, and solutions were sought for more eagerly than ever. Although the correlation between neglect and pauperism and dependency was discussed, the discourse on neglect seemed to have been most closely tied to discussions of delinquency and crime. The neglect, delinquency, and crime connection is a rich site for examining the linkage between neglect of individual children and broader problems in society. In the following pages, I discuss how the protection of neglected children became recognized as the best way to prevent crime, by 'reaching children before they have become altogether corrupt.'[17] As an alternative thinking that existed in the past, it highlights the temporal specificity of present thinking, which considers protection of neglected children as a project of guarding children's rights to personal safety.

The proliferation of knowledge of child neglect and delinquency started as soon as young criminals were thought of as a separate group in the 1830s, and particularly increased when they were physically segregated from adults from the 1860s on. This new object – 'unperceived until then'[18] – stimulated fresh questions and observations. New knowledge was developed, accumulated, tested, and transformed. For example, in D. Owen Carrigan's historical study of juvenile delinquency in Canada, he noted a consistent emergence of records of family problems in youth institutions in the 1860s. His examination of the records of the Penetanguishene Reformatory showed the compilation of statistics on the boys' parents – how many boys' fathers and mothers were deceased or were heavy drinkers.[19] The growth of knowledge on neglect and delinquency was remarkable, both in quantity and in variety. In contrast to the earlier authorities on negligence and indulgence of children, who were mostly clergymen and scholars, the late nineteenth-century generation of experts on neglect and delinquency established their authority on the basis of their experiences in dealing with delinquents. Knowledge was disseminated, exchanged, and consolidated through various gatherings, formal conferences, and writings, as well as authorized knowledge production mechanisms such as the Royal Commission on the Prison and Reformatory System in Ontario in 1890.

There were two major themes to this body of knowledge, which were often expressed in gardening metaphors. First, crime or delinquency was more than just an act in and of itself; it was the 'offspring' of evil seeds, cultivated by inappropriate parenting conduct. Second, crime was not merely a matter of a definite time period during which the criminal act was committed. Instead, it was a development or a process that extended well back into the months or even years before the act; it was 'a growth' from evil seeds to defective seedlings and finally to a poisonous plant. These concepts of evil seeds, cultivation, and a growth process were essential to the imagination and rationalization of child saving. Drawing upon these concepts, child saving was seen, first of all, as a true solution to delinquency and crime, since it addressed the roots of the problem. Equally important, child saving was also seen as smart, feasible, and economical, because it was intervention at an early stage and with a target relatively small in comparison with full-fledged crime.

I provide an overview of the causes of delinquency identified by the reformers and discuss how these were linked to the production of child-saving knowledge. Social reformers of the time came up with a variety of diagnoses of sources (or causes, correlated factors) of delinquency and crime. I discuss these diagnoses of sources of delinquency one by one, but this does not mean that they were necessarily thought of as disparate factors or competing theories by contemporaries. Quite the contrary – most social reformers, based on their hands-on experience or driven by pragmatic concerns, subscribed to an eclectic combination of explanations, rather than chaining themselves to any particular theory. It was not uncommon to find syntheses like this one: 'police and gaol officers will agree that the majority of criminals are *weak and mentally unbalanced* men, who *as children were neglected and abandoned* and who simply drifted into professional criminality through *association* with others like themselves (emphasis added).'[20] This also shows that it would be pointless to try to sort out which factor was considered the most important by reformers, since to them all factors were interlinked and slippage from one seemingly disparate factor to another was a characteristic of the discourse.

The sources or causes of juvenile delinquency for which reformers such as Kelso searched were diverse. They generally fell into three groups: predisposing causes, or evil seeds – age, heredity, and feeble-mindedness; environmental factors, which were often compared to poisonous soil, air, or darkness – jails, urban slums, and home conditions; and factors that pointed to problematic parenting – child labour and bad companions.

Predisposing Causes

One essentialist explanation of why children, particularly boys, went wrong assumed that some innate characteristics made them do so. However, discussions of predisposing factors were typically tempered with the admission that the reformers could not fully explain why children went wrong. Colonel Farewell, crown attorney and county clerk of Whitby, gave an address at the seventh Annual Canadian Conference of Charities and Correction in 1904, in which he explained that bad boys were like a certain class of lobsters – they must swim backwards! As this was an argument that could potentially threaten the raison d'être of any effort in doing anything with juvenile delinquents, it could not be pushed too far. Thus, notwithstanding the deterministic explanation, immediately after the lobster comment Farewell also argued that something should be done to prevent boys from swimming backwards.[21] Similarly, Kelso argued that a boy would naturally do wrong things such as lying. However, at this stage his 'nature' was still malleable, and adults should be forgiving and patient in helping him overcome his fault.[22]

Heredity was considered to cause juvenile delinquency.[23] There is, however, evidence that at the beginning the reformers were cautious about not putting too much emphasis on heredity. For example, in 1909, along with other leading child savers such as W.L. Scott, Kelso argued that crime 'is generally the result of bad surroundings, poor education, defective physique, false ideals, lack of employment arising from lack of training; it is rarely due wholly to heredity.'[24] The reason for such caution was the same as in the case of arguing that some boys were naturally deviant: A strict adherence to an essentialist explanation could negate any possible role for social reformers in preventing or curing juvenile delinquency.

Feeble-mindedness was not identified as an explanation for juvenile delinquency until the 1910s and the 1920s. It is curious that in 1922 Kelso claimed that he had been 'constantly writing and speaking about the feeble minded from 1894 on.'[25] In fact, the term 'feeble-mindedness' was not in the language of social reformers in the late nineteenth century. In any event, since the 1910s, feeble-mindedness seemed to have become accepted as the root cause of almost all major social problems: alcoholism, pauperism, as well as crime. In 1912, Dr Henry H. Goddard, director of research in the Vineland Institution for the Feeble-minded at New Jersey, addressed the Canadian Conference of Charities and Corrections. He explained that 'people of this sort either became pauper or criminal, according to the temperament – if nervous and iritable [sic], the latter; if phlegmatic, the former.'[26] In 1922, Kelso wrote a letter to the editor of the *Mail and Empire* to defend this attention to the subject of feeble-mindedness. He wrote 'Those who are in daily contact with social problems ... understand how large the feeble-minded person looms up in juvenile courts, police court, jails, reformatories and penitentiaries.'[27] The social reformers' embrace of feeble-mindedness as an explanation for social problems, including juvenile delinquency, was in contrast to their previous ambivalence towards heredity. In Kelso's writings in this period, two kinds of narratives seemed to reappear in tandem with the theme of feeble-mindedness. One kind of narrative was about admitting and explaining failed attempts to reform juvenile delinquents, as was evident in recidivism. The other kind of narrative concerned the proposal for segregated institutionalization of this class and imagining how satisfactory this strategy would be to everyone, even the feeble-minded.[28]

Environmental Factors

The environmental approach emphasized problems such as the mixing of the young and adults in jail, crowded urban slums, poor housing, and improper home life. The jail as a 'crime-breeder' was probably the first problem that was raised regarding the surroundings of the young. Although jail was still mentioned by some as a problem as late as in the 1920s,[29] its relative importance seemed to have been surpassed by other factors in reformers' discussions of juvenile delinquency. This is partly a result of the gradual implementation of remedial measures such as separate detention facilities for youth. Housing problems were also thought of as resulting in juvenile delinquency. Kelso, when attending an annual meeting of the Working Boys' Home, joined the discussion on the subject of juvenile crime and claimed that there would never be much improvement in the conduct or morals of the boys until the 'Home' was moved to a cleaner healthier neighborhood uptown – good surroundings would have a marked effect in refining the boys.[30]

Parenting Problems

Parenting was criticized in three aspects: omission – lack of moral training by parents and lack of discipline and control; contamination – unfit impressions left on children's minds by parents or by examples children encountered; and commission – that is, parents actively and explicitly teaching, encouraging, or coercing children to do wrongful things.

In the 1910s and the 1920s, there was evidence that some rethinking had taken place. Home conditions seem to have become 'the great outstanding cause of juvenile delinquency,'[31] even though other factors had not been eliminated from the discourse. This conceptual shift is perhaps best captured by a cartoon that originally appeared in the *Chicago Daily Tribune* in the 1920s and was used by Kelso (see Illustration 4). The cartoon portrayed a man holding the shotgun of Juvenile Reform, who was determined to 'track down the real cause of my children's ill conduct.' After much tracking and poking at suspicious-looking bushes that represented various takes on what led to juvenile delinquency, the man ended up facing his own house. He realized with shock that the real cause of his children's problem lay inside his house. The inscription on the roof of the house read 'Neglected Home Training.'[32]

We find another expression of this conceptual shift in the writings of Charlotte Whitton, who at the time examined in this study had just started articulating her conservative understanding of social problems, an analysis that was to become very influential in the field of social services in later decades.[33] In the year of 1919 or 1920, Whitton mentioned in her lectures a variety of contributors to juvenile delinquency, some of which had been aggravated by the war: 'youth's tempestuous blood and wayward instincts,' relaxing of discipline and restraint, the atmosphere of romance and adventure, child labour, and the spare time of children. Nevertheless, she claimed that 'after a careful digest of all available information it is safe to say, that the great outstanding cause of juvenile delinquency is wrong conditions in the home.'[34] A close reading

of her analysis makes clear that 'home conditions' was a highly comprehensive concept that summarized an eclectic mixture of things: bad
heredity, especially mental; incompetent and/or immoral parents; partial disruption of the home resulting from desertion, divorce, or the
death of either parent; bad housing; and poverty.

Parents were held responsible for their children's bad companions.
They were criticized for failing to watch them and ensure that they were
not contaminated and led astray. Similarly, child labour was blamed on
parents as well. Child labour was one of the first identified sources of
juvenile delinquency. In the late nineteenth century, criticism of child
labour was more about *where* children worked than about child labour
itself. Kelso argued in the late 1880s that certain forms of child labour,
such as selling newspapers, pencils, and shoelaces on the street, were
occupations that produced the criminal class. Working on the street
brought children in direct contact with all kinds of evil lurking in urban
areas, particularly when 'they lived where they pleased.' Children could
not on the street learn a trade that they could be employed in later.
Worse, many boys were trained to be thieves and girls were lured to
become prostitutes.[35] In the beginning decades of the twentieth century,
however, children's work itself became problematized, and, thus, child
labour in almost all situations was condemned. This shift is best demonstrated by how the links between child labour and juvenile delinquency
were constructed differently later. Soon after the First World War broke
out, Canada reported a significant increase in young offenders. Whitton
listed increasing child labour as a contributor to the problem. To Whitton,
child labour led to juvenile delinquency in two ways. First, 'the child had
been exploited by the overtaxing of his nervous system and physique,
the inevitable reaction results in a lowered tone.' Second, 'the child may
have free use of his wages, may be taking the place of an older man or
woman and may develop a false independence and "swagger," as the
result of the sudden change in his circumstances. This sudden acquisition of importance may have disastrous results as the boy attempts to
play the man.'[36]

It becomes clear that among the causes of juvenile delinquency identified by reformers, many were directly related to parents and their bad
parenting conduct. This was true even with environmental explanations,
since there was little doubt in reformers' minds that it was primarily the
responsibility of parents to provide proper housing in a good district. It
was also their responsibility to maintain home conditions in such a way
that children were not exposed to drinking, swearing, or general immo-

rality. For example, Judge Emerson Coatsworth asserted that the 'pure, clean, earnest, honest, cheerful, and attractive' atmosphere of the home 'must be created and maintained by parents.'[37] Child labour was also blamed on problematic parenting. Although children were the subjects of agency to a certain extent in at least some situations, they were almost always presented by the reformers as involuntary and passive. The typical image of a child labourer was that of an exhausted, frightened, vulnerable, and miserable child who was encouraged or coerced by adults, most likely his parents, to work on the street or in a factory. The point is not whether these children were coerced and exploited or not; rather, the point is that in instances where working children exercised their agency by ridiculing and rebelling against attempts to regulate their working on the street, these never made their way to the dominant discourse. The gender-neutral term parenting, however, is misleading, because most criticism was targeted at mothers or other women. Kelso believed that 'in 99 cases out of 100 it is either the want of a good woman's influence or the influence of a bad woman that has brought the child within the meshes of the law.'[38] In short, the knowledge on juvenile delinquency and child neglect examined above effectively individualized the causes of societal problems and put most of the burden of guilt on mothers. The protection of children from neglect by their mothers was thus thought of as a remedy to bad housing, immoral home conditions, child labour, and bad companions, and in the end as a solution to juvenile delinquency.

The view that child saving was a smart, practical, and economical way of addressing delinquency was based on the concept of delinquency and crime as a process. As I argued earlier, the conviction that crime was not a single fact but a process, which started with delinquency, was a theme underlying turn-of-the-twentieth-century knowledge of juvenile delinquency and child neglect. Metaphors of gardening – seeds, plants, soil – came in handy to social reformers in explaining this truth and at the same time lending support to it, as we can see from Judge Emerson Coatsworth's speech: 'Crime does not come into the life of a person fully developed at once. It is a growth, the seed of evil thoughts is planted and if in fertile soil gradually develops until finally it is a full grown poisonous plant which can be eradicated from the character and person only with great difficulty and perseverance.'[39]

In addition to the theme of gardening, several other metaphors or expressions were often used to denote the process from juvenile delinquents to criminals: the rotting of apples,[40] rivers flowing into the ocean,[41] 'finally become criminals,'[42] and 'going wrong,'[43] and so on. On the one hand, the concept of process differentiated juvenile delinquency from crime. When offences committed by children, such as stealing, shop breaking, disorderly conduct, trespassing, malicious injury to property, and vagrancy, were compared to a defect in a young seedling, a small decay, or a drop of polluted water, what was accentuated was their small scale, lack of threat, and helplessness – characteristics that inspired empathy and called for forgiveness.

On the other hand, the concept of process linked juvenile delinquency to crime. If no action were taken, a tender defective seedling would finally grow into an evil plant, a small decay on a apple would finally result in the rotting of not just one apple but the whole barrel, and small drops of delinquency would finally create the ocean of crime. The evil was in motion and cumulative. Reformers hoped to do something with juvenile delinquency, since to rehabilitate a juvenile delinquent would be an undertaking as manageable as to straighten a tender stem, to cut off a decaying spot from an apple, and to purify a drop of water. This in turn strengthened the legitimacy of rescuing juvenile delinquents who were going off in the wrong direction and setting them on the correct path, because it would be much easier, much less costly, and more effective in controlling crime.

The late nineteenth-century analysis of delinquency as a process starting with neglect was applied to boys and girls in different ways, reflecting and reinforcing constructions of masculinity and femininity. Generally, the concept of a process implied great optimism in rehabilitating boys. Kelso even went so far as to say that a 'bad boy turned into the right course, often makes the best kind of man. His badness or willfulness frequently arises from the vigorous animalism that is also essential to true manliness: physical perfection is a grand incentive to moral courage.'[44] To girls, the concept of delinquency as a process, however, did not necessarily imply hope. To reformers like Kelso, once she had fallen, a girl's 'degeneration' was but 'an awful descent' beyond full redemption.[45]

Thinking about child neglect in the framework of crime prevention was to constitute parents and children in a particular way. Although the new ways of understanding criminal offences committed by children characteristically put the blame on parents, this did not mean that children were always seen as innocent and free from culpability. Children's freedom from culpability was seen as in inverse proportion to their age. Age indicated levels of command of will, moral knowledge, and a sense of personal responsibility. The conception of a scale of responsibility became apparent and more specific towards the end of the period that I examine. Whitton laid out a scale in this way: Up to eight years of age, the child could not be held responsible for his acts – his parents were really to be blamed for his delinquency; from nine to thirteen years of age, his parents were still largely responsible for his behaviour; from the age of twelve or thirteen to seventeen years of age, 'the delinquencies ... gradually shift from the parent to the child, and the parents' responsibility will gradually merge into the consideration of what preparation was given the child in the preceding years.'[46]

The conceptualized continuum of responsibility implied a continuum of identity, from neglected children, to juvenile delinquents, and to criminals. In this sense, the identity of juvenile delinquent was not an independent and disparate one. It existed in between the identity of neglected child and that of the criminal, but at the same time tried to be somewhat distinct from them. A juvenile delinquent was one who was neither totally a neglected child nor totally a criminal. Similarly, a neglected child was not simply a neglected child; he was, at the minimum, a potential juvenile delinquent (see Illustration 5). This ambivalent and fluid conceptual situation may explain blurs and even confusions in practices. For example, the two terms neglected children and juvenile delinquents were used interchangeably in child protection legislation[47] and juvenile delinquents detained in the Toronto Children's Aid Society shelter were routinely called prisoners.[48]

During the period from the 1880s to 1920s, the thinking of the child savers linked cruelty and neglect to societal and national issues. Specifically, the objective of child saving was articulated with the civilizing imperative. Children assumed the identity of 'future citizens,' and the overarching concern of child saving was to ensure that they were parented properly so that they became useful adult citizens with Christian virtues and capacity for self-control. The use of force on children was criticized because it was considered as an uncivilized way to treat children, and equally importantly, an ineffective way to cure children's weaknesses. Child neglect was identified as a major problem because, instead of making children good citizens, neglectful parents turned them into criminals, prostitutes, and beggars through failure to provide their children a proper home, to watch over them, and to keep them away from the morally dangerous street. The very emergence of a child-protection system through the child-saving movement testified to the fact that the overarching rationality of the interests of society was a forceful argument for collective actions. That raises questions about the implications of today's rationality centred around the individual child's interest in personal safety.

Chapter 3

'Cultivate Children as You Would Valuable Plants:' The Gardening Governmentality of Parenting and Child Saving[1]

Cruelty to and neglect of children in the late nineteenth century were problematizations from the standpoint of producing good adult citizens. Reformers at the time believed that both the use of excessive force on children (cruelty) and the lack of discipline (neglect) would hamper and damage the development of children's character, which would then lead to persistent social and moral problems in the society. How, then, should a parent raise a child so that she would 'develop into an honest, useful and industrious citizen?'[2] And more importantly to the child savers, what should be done when parents failed in doing so?

This chapter focuses on some influential thoughts around these questions, especially the child-saving strategies modeled on gardening. Child saving did not always follow the gardening approach in all its aspects. For example, concerns about 'moral contagion' or the architectural design of the building used as the shelter, and the popularization of foster care were much shaped by the medical model of disease and disease control. The gardening logic and strategies, however, although much less-discussed than the medical model, also had an important place in the imagining of proper parental power and the corresponding regulatory mechanism of child saving, and as such is the focus of this chapter.

Gardening, or sometimes farming, allegories were narrative devices that were widely used by Kelso and other reformers in their writings and speeches. Seeds, tender slips, and tough branches captured the conception of the individual in the view of the child savers. They represented human subjects at different stages of life, with varying degrees of moral plasticity and potential for successful reform. Poisoned soil or diseased parent stock, in contrast to sunlight, fresh air, and healthy plants, came in handy for the child savers to describe bad or good home environments and parents. The relation between the gardener and plants and weeds was used to illustrate the desirable mode of power in child rearing and child saving. Careful and regular watering, gentle but firm weeding, appropriate pruning, and calculated bending provided images of both good parenting and child-saving activities.

The prevalence of this gardening imagery in child saving should not be dismissed as mere rhetoric, because governance on the site of child saving was indeed often organized like gardening. In many ways gardening is a fitting allegory for the 'bio-power' referred to in the Introduction. Both aim at making lives flourish in a controlled way. Its usefulness for illustrating and naturalizing strategies of bio-power assembled on the site of child saving lay precisely in the fact that gardening was a common and taken-for-granted practice that at least the middle class could very easily relate to. Moreover, gardening metaphors were particularly useful for representing three elements of the mechanisms of bio-power: the child savers' conception of the malleable humanist subject; the key objects of child-saving actions; and strategies of governance in child saving.

The first section that follows is a note on English gardening's class, economic, cultural, and gender dimensions, and English gardening's influence on Canada so as to contextualize subsequent discussions.[3] The subsequent section is an overview of gardening allegories and their effects on the conceptualization of the child. This is followed by an analysis of the representation of the mode of power that was considered desirable and effective by the child savers. Specifically, it discusses how gardening metaphors illustrate a disciplinary power and its objects – habitat, habits, and hearts of children. It also discusses the system of multiple rulers and the ruled as signified by gardening metaphors. The final section outlines several major child-saving strategies in practice – guidance, supervision, investigation, classification, separation, and dispersion – and the underlying gardening logic and techniques. These strategies were designed to regulate parenting and to provide supplementary or substitute governing of children when parents were considered to have failed. The child savers promoted and sought to implement these strategies through legislation and the establishment of new types of institutions such as children's aid societies, which in turn administered reporting of cases, visits, case records, the shelter, the detention room, and foster care.

The main argument of this chapter is that the child-saving movement attempted to install a mode of 'proper parental control'[4] that was primarily positive and productive (albeit without excluding repressive elements), individualized, intelligent, and localized — what I term gardening strategies. The gardening mode of parental power and its constitutive strategies were posed as desirable alternatives to the dual (and opposite) problems in parenting, the excessive use of force and the lack of discipline.

Gardening and Gardening Metaphors

Studies of the history of gardening show that gardening has always been more than just a hobby. Given its requirements for money, land, leisure, and taste, gardening had various class, economic, cultural, and gender functions. Joan Bassin observed that in eighteenth-century England landscape parks, which came to be known as 'English gardens,' showed off their aristocratic owners' unquestionable wealth and leisure, provided visual pleasure and investment, brought about political influence, and 'offered acres of protection, psychological as much as physical' from the realities of the changing and possibly threatening world around them.[5] Starting at the end of the eighteenth century and the beginning of the nineteenth century, gardening also became an important element in the making of the middle-class family in England. Leonore Davidoff and Catherine Hall have documented that gardening was a rather notable economic and cultural symbol in the making of the middle class. It expressed the anti-urban, romantic but rational middle-class sensibilities; it also provided 'strong visual confirmation of the middle-class ideal' – particularly order, intelligence, civility, taste, and an appreciation of nature in a controlled environment.[6] Martin Gaskell's study showed that in increasingly industrialized and urbanized Victorian England, gardens were promoted by the middle class to provide 'rational recreation' for the working classes.[7] This was for the interlinked purposes of fostering habits of leisure compatible with efficient and orderly production, educating the working classes in the social values of the middle class, and preventing disturbances and alienation. In England, such paternalistic encouragement of rational recreation started with a small number of factory masters, such as mill owners, providing labouring families with small gardens in the 1830s and 1840s. Propaganda advocating gardens was later incorporated into the housing-reform movement that peaked in the 1870s; it drew attention to physical and moral benefits of a less-crowded layout of houses and gardens. As well, this was an integral part of the civic beautification movement.[8] Canadian social historians, most notably Edwinna von Baeyer, have written about similar class-specific gardening movements in the midst of the reforming zeal from the late 1800s up to the 1920s; gardening was seen as morally uplifting and purifying. Urban reformers promoted building railway gardens on station grounds and school gardens, landscaping urban areas, and starting home gardens.[9]

Despite its physical proximity to domestic life, the garden was not merely considered to be a proper and desirable space for men; it was dominated by them. Indeed, the garden was thought of as 'the place of a new kind of heroism, the heroic struggle between man and nature.'[10] As Bell observed of the gendered history of the eighteenth-century English garden, the 'names of great garden and landscape designers fall male.'[11] Of course, women have always participated in various aspects of gardening. Women's participation, however, tended to be restricted to and/or gravitate to flowers and shrubs, as opposed to the overall design and the hallmark of the landscape garden – judiciously planted trees, small woods, lakes, and architectural structures such as bridges. Consequently, women have been relegated to invisibility in much contemporary and historical garden literature.[12] This dominance of the male in gardening was also reflected in the horticultural societies organized by middle-class men in the nineteenth and twentieth centuries. Von Baeyer, writing about the Canadian case, noted that horticultural societies were organized by men interested in amateur and commercial growing of fruits, vegetables, and ornamentals. Although the societies did have women members, some of whom were highly accomplished gardeners and gardening writers, men almost always occupied the official positions up to the 1920s.[13]

If to male gardeners gardening was 'the heroic struggle between man and nature,'[14] to male reformers social gardening, such as child saving, was similarly a 'heroic struggle' between man and society, waged for the sake of the nation. Parallel to the gendered division of labour in the history of gardening as observed by Bell and von Baeyer,[15] in child saving men dominated the visible aspects of social gardening, such as designing the layout of the field, plotting spatial arrangements for children, conducting investigations to generate knowledge, administering guidance in public arenas (e.g., in the figure of the Juvenile Court Judge), and occupying executive positions. The presence of female social gardeners was in frontline work and administrative support, work that was essential for the operation but seldom recognized. As for the objects of gardening, mothers were mostly targeted as the parties to be taught proper parental control.

Perhaps because of its status as an English institution with class and cultural inscriptions, the garden has been a quite common source of inspiration for metaphors. For example, long before child saving was represented as gardening, Horace Walpole wrote about the modernization of gardening as a way of making political commentary.[16] Richard Quaintance described Walpole's and some even earlier commentators' genre of infusing gardening with political belief as 'hortipolitical';[17] we can perhaps describe the reform era at the turn of the twentieth century as a 'hortisocial' phase that incorporated not only movements promoting gardening activities, but also gardening language in social and moral reform.

Studies of the hortisocial phase tend to be restricted to those of actual gardening activities in the reform era. However, gardening's possible conceptual and technological relevance to reform overall has not been looked at from the other direction: How might non-gardening movements such as child saving have incorporated gardening thinking? In a similar vein, gardening in the metaphorical sense, as some reformers imagined their work in horticultural terms, has not received much attention either. One case of interest, however, was Valverde's analysis of the 'jungle' metaphor – the apparent opposite of the rational, civilized, and tasteful English garden. Examining the connection between imperial travel writing and social reform writing, Valverde argued that the metaphor of the 'jungle' was used in abundance to describe urban slums.[18] The African rainforest was described as exotic, female, primitive, and above all, untampered. It was a ruthless 'dark' power, threatening 'to silently engulf and destroy patriarchs of both nature and civilisation.'[19] This vision of the jungle was then imported into the discourse on urban problems as an already established knowledge, with the effect of making the urban poor at home a different and inferior breed to be civilized.[20] The civilizing mission, including child saving, was thus analogous to turning jungles (both foreign and home-grown) into gardens that were rationally designed, but more importantly under gentle but firm control.

What follows examines gardening metaphors in writings about child saving, which give important clues to popular ideas among the child savers about how children should be governed. The analysis also has broader implications. It shows that the concern of social and moral reformers was not limited to bringing the actual garden and its associated values to the working class. Metaphorically, they imagined the working class as their horticultural objects – flowers, trees, or weeds – to work on, saved children as well-cultivated plants or harvested produce (see Illustration 6), and themselves as social gardeners or gardeners of the nation. Furthermore, analysis of the power mechanisms embodied in gardening suggests that those might account for the widespread interest in promoting gardening activities and using gardening allegories. Social and moral reform was concerned with effective and civilized discipline of others and self, which was precisely the mode of power between the gardener and the gardening objects.

Saving 'The Delicate Plant of Humanity'[21]

This section addresses how the humanist model of the individual was concretized by the allegory of the human subject as a plant that requires governance (gardening) and is at the same time governable (gardenable). It also discusses how gardening metaphors effectively illustrated the strategic importance of childhood in the humanist model of the individual.

The invention of the humanist subject was fundamental to reformers' deliberations on how children should be governed. The notion of the humanist subject was a 'conception of the human individual as endowed with a soul, consciousness, guilt, remorse, and other features of an interiority that can be worked on by other agents.'[22] Gardening imagery worked well to concretize the thought that human beings, particularly children, could be induced to behave in certain ways, just as plants could be trained to stand straight, to trail, and to blossom profusely through nurturing when they were young. This was a large conceptual shift from the Medieval model, in which the individual's character was thought to be innate.

It would be a mistake to assume that to the reformers this emphasis on the importance of nurture meant the banishment of natural determinism. Even the most enthusiastic advocates of reform, like Kelso, seemed to think that vice was hereditary on some occasions. For example, Kelso confided in his diary after a visit to the Infants' Home that he 'saw all the [baby] inmates, very low type,'[23] as if these babies bore visible bodily imprints of moral inferiority. As well, he had no difficulty spotting the 'inherited seeds of vice' on the faces of some Barnardo girls.[24] Thus, it would be more accurate to understand the late nineteenth-century reformers' model of the individual as a conceptual adjustment between nature (pre-existing conditions, most notably heredity) and human agency. If the reformers rejected anything, it was the dichotomy of heredity and environment. Indeed, the gardening imagery was a very useful conceptual tool for deconstructing this dichotomy: While seeds were important, careful watering, weeding, pruning, and bending were also indispensable in the making of straight trees or blooming plants. As Douglas Chambers observed, 'under cultivation trees will change their character, thereby raising questions about the relation of art and nature,'[25] questions that were practical to reformers.

The following poem, found in Kelso's diary in 1888 or 1889, is an example of acknowledging both heredity and environment as relevant factors in determining a child's future character, drawing upon gardening imagery:

> As plants while tender
> Bend which way you please
> And are though crooked first
> Made straight with ease;
> But if neglected till they grow in years,
> And each ... [illegible] parent –
> Their dear darling spares,
> Error becomes habitual and we find
> 'Tis then hard labour to reform the wind.[26]

Evidently the relevance of nature was understood to follow the Christian doctrine of original sin. However, since human subjects were living beings responsive to surrounding conditions and possessing peculiar traits such as habits and will, if the seed of evil would develop was uncertain. This uncertainty was precisely the hope of reform. Thus, the effect of the conception of the human individual as comparable to a plant was to provide a rationale for human intervention, given that people, and in particular children, were susceptible to good influences, even if people were inherently evil.

Certain practical implications flowed from this understanding of humans as living beings susceptible to external forces. One such implication was that the early stage of life became more important than others, because living beings tended to be more yielding to external forces at the beginning of life. Thus, childhood was pronounced 'the strategic time in life,'[27] a period during which a person, like a tender plant, could be easily and permanently influenced more than at any other time. In contrast, adults were like rigid tree trunks or branches that were formed long ago, and they thus bore little hope of reform.

Reformers put forward two types of arguments for taking childhood seriously: One concerned effectiveness, the other economics. The effectiveness argument drew upon the apparently common-sense belief that direct effort with the beginning of things was almost certain of reward.[28] Often this had to do with the formation of habits: 'The impression received, the habits formed by children in their first ten years, mould them through life for better or worse.'[29] Later, psychologists would lend their authority to the view that childhood should be taken seriously. For example, psychologist H. Addington Bruce stated in 1916 that 'as any modern psychologist will tell you, habits are formed early, and the impressions made on the mind in childhood are the most lasting of all impressions and the most difficult to blot out.'[30]

The economic argument for focusing reform efforts on the early stage of life was established through a comparison between the cost of the perceived relatively easy work of reforming children and the cost of dealing with hardened criminals, beggars, and prostitutes. Kelso expressed his observation this way: 'If the government would pay more attention to [child-saving work], and check the evil in the bud which springs from this low class of people, there would be no need of building so many prisons, reformatories, or the like.'[31] Thus, it would be a good investment 'to withdraw every effort for adults and bend over the cradles of the world.'[32]

In practice, these thoughts were embodied in the early-intervention approach.[33] Child saving in itself was an enactment of this approach, and to many reformers the merit and even superiority of child saving lay precisely with the fact that it tackled the beginning years. Thus, Kelso characterized child saving as a work that was full of hope, 'for it has to do with the beginning of things where well directed effort is almost certain of reward. It offers an unlimited field of pleasant and profitable employment to the volunteer workers who realize the possibilities of good in the saving and reclamation of unfortunate children, and it means to the community relief from the burden of pauperism and criminality that is the sure outcome of indifference toward neglected childhood.'[34]

Tending the Habitat, Habit, and Heart

Gardening metaphors were not only helpful for establishing the truth of the individual as a living being, who was capable of responding to external forces. They also confirmed certain desirable modes of power exercised over the individual, particularly when he was at an early stage of life. Gardening imagery nicely captured the ethos of ideal modern

Western child-rearing practices – calculated and continuous caring for and watching over children, the craft of combining gentle coaching with occasional firm action, and even the cherishing and rewarding sentiments that were internal to the relation. What was involved in these practices was primarily a disciplinary mode of power.

Gardening provided a vivid contrast to, and thus a critique of, cruelty and neglect: Just as no garden could flourish if the gardener were either irrational, rough, or indifferent, no child could be turned into a good citizen by either force or neglect. For example, neglected and indulged children were often compared to a jungle, as in the following poem:

As plants raised with tenderness are seldom strong
Man's coltish disposition asks the thong;
And without discipline, the favorite child
Like a neglected forest, runs wild[35]

Much discussion of how to cultivate a child focused on the habitat of the 'delicate plant of humanity.'[36] Habit, which was considered partially the product of surrounding influences, was also a popular subject in child-saving writing. While habitat and habit exemplified the parallel between plants and children, the other equally notable object of knowledge and power involved in child saving – the heart of the child – did not draw upon the commonsense authority of gardening concepts. To the reformers, the heart or the soul was the one thing that distinguished human beings from other life forms. As Kelso remarked, 'but with human beings there is a soul to be reckoned with and an ever-present tendency to higher and nobler living.'[37] These aspects of a child – habitat, habits, and heart – were identified as key objects with which parenting and child-saving work should be concerned. Although they derived from seemingly varied conceptual sources, habitat, habit, and heart shared some significant commonality: They all appeared as alternatives to heredity; and they were consistent in underlining the truth of the live individual, who was capable of responding to conditions of his habitat and forming habits through everyday living, and who was capable of feelings and desires that could be manipulated to certain ends. The following is a sketch of how these three aspects of the individual's existence were thought of by those interested in practical action as worthy objects to be known and to be ruled, what reformers hoped to achieve by focusing resources, intellectual processes, and action on them, and how reformers intended to know and regulate them.

To most reformers the habitat for children, like the garden for plants, referred to specific spaces where children lived, rather than broader social, economic and political structures, as socialists would interpret it. Kelso thought that 'the impressions and surroundings of childhood mould the character for better or worse and the evil example of parents, idleness, dissipation are the factors responsible for criminal conduct.'[38] Since the unfortunate, the immoral, and the criminal were creatures of their environment, reformers reasoned that as environment improved, so too would the standard of social morality.[39] Jails, courts, and poor houses where children were mixed indiscriminately with adult criminals, beggars, prostitutes, and the mad were among the first problematic spaces identified. The street was seen as inappropriate space for 'newsies' as well as other children, because it brought them in direct contact with all kinds of evil. Above all, undesirable homes were regarded as most detrimental to the development of children's character, since parents' bad characters and slum conditions constituted 'the poisoned atmosphere ... where obscenity, vulgarity and profanity blight [a child's] life.'[40] Good homes, in contrast, were seen as fundamental to the making of citizens. For example, Kelso commented that 'if one lives on a nice street it is impossible to resist the refining influence of association.'[41] Thus, one piece of advice he gave to those dealing with wayward boys was that 'if necessary for the child's good, insist on possible changes, such as moving into a better neighbourhood,'[42] which unfortunately would be impossible for impoverished parents to follow. It is worth noting that one common characteristic of these spaces – jail, court, street, and home – was that they had fairly definitive physical and administrative boundaries, just as gardens had unambiguous boundaries. Therefore, reforms targeting such spaces could be easily contained, without much threat to the overall system.

Scholars such as Valverde have shown that the concept of habits was a key technique in lay and expert technologies of ethical reform.[43] The featuring of habits in social reform writing in general, and in child saving in this case, reveals the influence of pragmatist philosophical thinking. Valverde observes that to pragmatist philosophers such as William James, good and bad habits are equivalent to virtue and vice itself, because virtue and vice are not made up of individual 'sins' (willed acts, as sins are understood in Christianity) but are the product of small everyday habits. Kelso certainly agreed with such thinking when he wrote: 'It is a well-known fact that decency of life and conduct is a matter of enforced habit – a tribute of respect to those around us.'[44] Habits made reforms imaginable, because habits are neither totally automatic nor unchange-able. In child-saving literature, habits often appeared as the 'other' of heredity.[45] Anything hereditary was something over which humans could have little or no control; in contrast, habits were seen to be the product of surrounding influences and daily routines, and they could therefore be reversed or modified by changing the habit-forming factors. Reform-ing a child's habits started with knowing his habits. Thus, Kelso in-structed those engaged in saving delinquent boys: 'Make a study of his habits, likes and dislikes.'[46] Another example of the preoccupation with knowing habits can be found in many inspectors' notes of their annual visits to foster homes.

As to how to encourage good habits in children and prevent bad ones from forming, Kelso and many other reformers shared the view that 'the moral sentiments in children [should] be cultivated until they pass into habits. The habits of doing right actions will be formed by the constant repetition of single acts. Hence the importance of one untruthful asser-tion, the one profane word, the one wrong act. – Let these be repeated and the bad habit is formed. So also the one act of self-denial, the one act of justice or benevolence; let these be repeated and the good habit is formed.'[47]

Thus, every single word uttered and every single act taken by the child was now considered an organic part of the child's character; it could grow or it could perish. What was implied in practice was that parents and reformers had to be vigilant about every detail of the child's life all the time. The expectation was that once good habits had been formed through the diligent work of those responsible for a child, she would grow up to be an individual who could regulate herself more or less automatically; doing so would be second nature.

A large amount of child-saving writing was also devoted to explaining why child-saving work should focus on the heart of a child. In contrast to the concept of habits and its embedded pragmatism, discussion of the heart or the soul typically involved spiritual arguments. For example, Kelso invoked divinity in an attempt to convince his contemporaries of the superiority of being aware of and working with the heart: 'men judge by outward acts. God reads the heart and considers the motive, as well as the degree of temptation.'[48] Narratives on the superiority and even nobleness of heart-focused governing were anchored in the inner being versus acts, and the related heart-versus-body oppositions. Many reform-ers argued that, first, it was inadequate to be only concerned with acts (e.g., stealing, drinking, and lying), as acts were only symptoms of the inner being. Thus, instead of punishing acts, the subjects of such acts should be the primary object of ruling. Second, the classical approach to punishment and deterrence of undesirable acts through inflicting physical pain, or depriving bodily comfort, was brutal and pointless so far as children were concerned. Kelso compared punishing, scolding, and threatening a child to trying to force a baby to go to sleep by beating it.[49] He argued that instead of using hand one should use head and heart in shaping up a child,[50] which produced 'the power that conquers.'[51] This was because 'genuine reformation is brought about by moral suasion – by kindly influences subduing a rebellious and stubborn will.'[52] He went on explaining that 'this is the principle on which the Children's Aid work is founded and success will come in proportion to the patience and personality that is exerted.'[53] To Kelso, success would come at least partially when 'the bolts and bars are placed in the child's heart, the restraints are made part of his own conscience.'[54]

Punishment with physical force was also criticized for not being capable of positively building up the child's character. The constructive work was important, because as Kelso observed, 'when our hearts are set upon what is high and noble we become active agents in bringing about the steady diminution of crime, with all its baneful consequences.'[55] However, at its best, the use of force achieved only the repression of bad thoughts and conduct, but nothing more. Kelso reasoned that 'fear may be readily implanted through severity and harshness but refraining from doing something through fear of punishment is not productive of the fine character that we admire and desire in children. Greater than corporal, or any other kind of punishment, is the awakening of a sense of honor in the mind of a child – that moral sensitiveness which will instinctively cause a turning away from a questionable thing even when no one is looking.'[56]

Thus, to reformers the heart was an important site in the production of self-regulating individuals. The purpose of governing the heart was to induce change 'in the inner man so that the desire to do wrong will be taken away'[57] and to instil the desire for the good. The ruling would be successful when there was no longer a need for external rulers, when subjects had internalized restraints and yearnings for the good to rule themselves.

In order to work on a child's heart, workers first had to have an intimate knowledge of the child's heart. Kelso compared knowing the heart to opening a lock. He offered the advice that 'a master key is required to unlock the heart. The keys most likely to turn the lock are faith and perseverance.'[58] The heart could only be known and worked upon when there was 'mutual understanding and appreciation'[59] between the child and the parent or the child saver. Those who were entrusted with working the child's heart were advised that 'moral virtues never flourish when forced.'[60] Human nature was such that 'they [children] resent being driven but are glad to be led.'[61] Thus, it was not force but love that would govern the heart.[62] It should be noted, however, that 'love' here was not used in the romantic and more general affectionate sense, but in the sense of 'agape,' Christian love. It is worthwhile to consider how Kelso distinguished the reformers' love from cruelty on the one hand and sentimentalism on the other. To Kelso, the reformers' love of the people they sought to reform was compassion; it was different from cruelty in that compassion was a sign of civility. As for the difference between the reformers' love and sentimentality, he remarked that there was as great a difference as there was 'between night and day,' because the former was an intelligent and practical sentiment.[63] It was intelligent because it was sentiment based on an understanding of human nature; it was practical because it had very rational, specific, and worldly aims. The ability to reform parents and children through this kind of calculated compassion was precisely the 'special ability' that was called for in the child savers. Equipped with the 'special ability' to exercise calculated compassion, the child savers were expected to use their hearts to win over children's hearts, to exert the 'magnetic influence of one soul reacting upon another.'[64] One way to achieve this was to manipulate the rapport established between two hearts: 'If we earnestly desire the reformation of a child, and let the child feel and know that we have such a desire, the response will in almost every instance be prompt and sincere.'[65]

The child's heart could be trained to form habits, for example the 'habit of being kind.'[66] Even though the heart or the soul of the child did not have an obvious equivalent in plants, it could nevertheless be susceptible to gardening strategies characterized by individual attention, gentle but firm action, specific goals, and patience. Thus, Kelso suggested a way of stimulating a child to form such habits: 'Why not ask children to "try" to be kind, to "try" to do some nice thing every day, and though they may fail sometimes they will gradually be forming a habit that will last through life.'[67] The heart of the child could be trained to be kind, just as a young plant can be trained to stand straight.

So far I have discussed the child's habitat, habits, and the heart separately for analytical purposes. It should be noted that these three key objects of knowledge and power were often inter-related in the child-savers' analysis of specific problems. One example was the problem of children's activities on the street. To reformers, the street, a quintessential symbol of urbanity, was one of the most morally dangerous spaces, because it was anonymous and unsupervised. These features were even more accentuated at night. Kelso spoke for many reformers when he remarked that 'there can hardly be two opinions of the evil of young children being on the streets after nightfall. Moral contagion, or soul-poisoning, begins its deadly work, or rather comes more boldly out into the open, with the gathering darkness.'[68] Habits came into play when children became 'accustomed to wander at night through the tough districts and haunt the saloons, brothels and theatres, sometimes but not always under the guise of selling newspapers.'[69] Their hearts were contaminated as their experiences on the streets destroyed their modesty and undermined their purity of life and conduct. Thus, children who were left alone to play and wander on the street in the dark would very likely be led by devious paths to the juvenile court, the reformatory, and the brothel. Even if they escaped these criminal paths, reformers such as Kelso firmly believed that the stories children would hear on the street, the scenes that they would witness with repetition would kill or blight 'that aspiration for a noble, self-controlling and Christian citizenship, on which all that is best in life is founded.'[70]

In addition to suggesting discipline as the ideal mode of power and suitable objects of that power, gardening metaphors were also used to signify a system of multiple rulers and the ruled. Specifically, the system or the web of ruling consisted of several sets of interlocking power relations: the child savers as gardeners ruled parents and children, parents as gardeners ruled children, and children as gardeners ruled themselves. The first set of relations was evident when a child deemed in need of rescue was compared to the young part of a crooked or sick tree. In this imagery, the child savers were portrayed as gardeners of human beings. They were compared to the horticulturist who carefully bent straight a young branch or engrafted a delicate slip from one tree to another.[71] The metaphor of parent-child as 'tree-slip' visualized and naturalized the conviction that parents were to be blamed as the source of their children's moral problems. However, this particular version of gardening imagery was less helpful for reformers who intended to make parents take up the responsibility of shaping their children. The comparison of parents and children to tree and tree slip rendered them both passive objects of the gardeners' power, and thus tended to exclude them as internal players in the web of ruling.

Other versions of gardening metaphors, however, portrayed parents and children themselves as simultaneously the ruled and agents of the enterprise of making good citizens. For example, some gardening metaphors presented parents as gardeners and compared children to plants in the garden of family. The famed plant breeder Luther Burbank was quoted as saying, 'grow your children as you grow your flowers, and you will push evil out of the world, and make a generation which will make this world a wonderful, beautiful place.'[72] On still other occasions, children were depicted as gardens, and their thoughts and behaviours as either flowers or weeds. In these instances, parents and even children themselves were assigned the responsibility and power of gardeners. The story 'The Weeds that Bothered Dora,' originating in Chicago's Juvenile Court but used by Kelso, was a good example in this regard. The story compared dishonesty, bad temper, 'kickin the door,' 'screamin' and slappin' back' as weeds that would not only choke out 'the dear little lovable flowers' of good character, but also prick everybody else.[73] It started with a casual conversation about weeds between the girl Dora and her neighbour in a garden. Dora asked how weeds came about and the neighbour said 'very much like the bad thoughts and ways that come into our hearts – just spring right up and grow and grow and grow – if we don't pull them out, until all the dear little lovable flowers are quite choken out.' Hence the transition from real gardening to moral education. The subsequent dialogue began with the neighbour claiming that 'truth is a beautiful little flower,' then she or he posed a question 'what would a falsehood be?' to Dora to establish the dichotomy between truth (good) and falsehood (bad), just like flower and weeds. Dora was thus guided to think of her bad behaviours as weeds, which naturally needed to be eradicated, as common sense about gardening would suggest. In this case, Dora the little girl was made aware of her responsibility to be a gardener of her own mind.

Late nineteenth-century child saving identified the child's space, habits, and heart as major objects of discipline, to be disciplined by parents and the child savers, as well as the child herself. Gardening imagery was used to illustrate these ideas. Its use was a deployment of what Valverde has named 'the dialectic of the familiar and the unfamiliar,' a common and effective cultural device for rendering something or somebody, such as children, governable in a novel way.[74] The dynamic began from an established everyday knowledge – of growing flowers and removing weeds – and then proceeded to use that to construct a particular form of knowledge of and practical engagement with the question of how to develop children's character. The effect was to make real the reformers' convictions that the individual was primarily a creature of conditioning, and that parents (mostly mothers) and the child savers should watch carefully to cultivate the good and eradicate the evil in children.

Gardening Strategies of Child Saving

Child-saving strategies to govern children's habitats, habits, and hearts were formed in the late nineteenth century and continued to be used in most of the twentieth century. They fell into several general categories: guidance, supervision, investigation, spatial distribution featuring classification, separation, and dispersion. These typical child-saving strategies derived from the humanist understanding of the individual as the product of conditioning, and many were easily captured by gardening metaphors. They were promoted as effective, economical, and civil ways of rescuing children from the path to crime, dependence and prostitution. What follows is an outline of the reasoning behind each strategy and its main components.

Guidance

Guidance usually appeared as an alternative to the negative approach of punishment. Because the individual was seen as largely a creature of environment and habits, the idea was that it would be unfair to punish children for being immoral, since they had not been taught to be moral in the first place: 'it is wrong to punish children for offences they but faintly understand, and to which they have been trained or driven by immoral parents or guardians, or lack of guardianship. What such children need is Christian home influence.'[75]

To educate children when they went wrong was thus to give them an opportunity to redeem their ways and to be taught proper conduct in life.[76] The principle that morality had to be constructed in an individual was also applied to adults in many circumstances. For example, in their activities aimed at preventing cruelty to animals and children, most often the reformers took the approach of 'reasoning with drivers [of horse-drawn wagons] and others'; prosecution and punishment was only a secondary option when it became necessary.[77] Reformers like Kelso also believed that prosecution should not be the preferred way in dealing with parents of a family in which 'the children are destitute and unable to attend school, hearing constantly oaths and blasphemy, and witnessing scenes of immoral living.'[78] Instead, a reformer's duty was 'to bring to the attention of such people in a kindly way the wrongs under which their children suffer, and persuade them by friendly advice, and not infrequently by practical help, that they can and should do better, rather than take chances on losing their most precious possessions, the boys and girls of the family.'[79] It should be pointed out, however, that despite the emphasis on education, persuasion, and the leverage of practical help, repressive power also had a position in child saving. A small number of parents, when viewed as beyond redemption, were punished by having their children removed from them and even prosecuted in some rare cases. Mrs Julia E. Work, a child saver in Indiana, offered an advice to her fellow workers: 'experience proves conclusively the wisdom of removing the comparatively healthy slip from the diseased parent stock and transplanting to new and more productive soil.'[80] This experienced wisdom of 'transplanting' in child saving illustrates how such a seemingly contradictory approach was actually accepted as justified among the child savers.

Guidance strategy emphasized treating the helped as individuals, and doing so with personal touches, similar to a gardener giving each individual plant care, help, and direction. Kelso's list of the ingredients of 'friendly visiting' included the cordiality of the greeting, the pressure of the hand, the sympathetic advice given in a kindly but firm manner, and practical suggestions on how to repair broken fortunes.[81] The 'friendly' and 'personal' elements were old inheritances from Christianity. As Kelso once commented, 'Christianity whether acknowledged or not, is the inspiration of neighborly service.'[82] Teaching by example was another important way of providing guidance. This was exemplified by the social-settlement movement. In Kelso's view, the idea of a social settlement, which first originated among university people in Britain and spread to Toronto in 1910,[83] was based on a belief in the potency of education and culture in solving some of the intricate social problems that affected the daily life of the poor. Seeing themselves as examples of civilized and purposeful living, the 'little group of educated workers of high vision and purpose' sought to influence the poor by taking up residence with them. It was hoped that their way of living would 'inspire even the lowliest to an effort at self-improvement.'[84]

Supervision

Supervision was seen as a plausible strategy largely because the making of an individual was now understood as a process. As budding and blooming never happened overnight, the character of an individual was not determined by his or her heredity, nor was it formed in a snap of the fingers. Instead, it was a product of influences over time. For example, Kelso explained:

> It is not a sudden fall after years of good living that brings men and women to the prison door. It is a neglected childhood, the absence of proper guidance and control, the repetition of numerous small acts of disobedience, theft, deceit and falsehood, the gradual hardening of character, the absence of self-control and industry, culminating ultimately in the abandonment of all restraint. It is in the child of nine and ten years of age that the seeds of crime take root, to reach fruition at fifteen or sixteen. This surely indicates the pressing needs for closer watchfulness and control of young children, so that they may early learn the better way.[85]

Thus, by definition, supervision was a strategy with specific temporal dimensions: It was regular and tended to be long term. Proper parenting must put children 'under the watchful eye of parent or guardian, so that children would not hear inappropriate stories, not witness inappropriate scenes with repetition.'[86] The centrality of the strategy of supervision was evident in that the Toronto Children's Aid Society was established following a recommendation of the Royal Commission on the Prison and Reformatory in 1891 that an association be formed to take up 'the important but delicate duty' of judiciously exercising supervision and care over discharged, paroled, or apprenticed children.[87]

Investigation

The strategy of investigation sought to address what was seen as the earlier judicial model's perceived failure in reducing recidivism. As a contemporary writer criticized, 'the old way of dealing with juvenile criminals was to treat them with severity without inquiring very much into their surroundings or early training.' A boy was quoted to have expressed his unhappiness that the magistrate did not bother to ask him anything: The magistrate listened to the police's description of what the boy did, and 'Den de guy on de high bench sends me up widout given' me a chanct to say a woid [*sic*].'[88] This model became problematic. In the late nineteenth century it became accepted by more people that delinquency and crime were largely caused by bad influences and defective moral training, and that the objective of governing was not to punish, but to correct through taking action on the root causes of delinquency. The belief in correction was gradually institutionalized. Judge H.S. Mott, who later presided over the Juvenile Court in Toronto, commented in 1930: 'The old conception of punishment was merely vindictive. We punished one person as an example to another, in order to protect the other person. The modern conception of punishment, particularly in Children's Court, is more of a corrective nature ... [In order to correct a child, one] must diagnose the condition, find the cause and remedy the same.'[89]

Unlike traditional punishment, which did not require any intimate knowledge of the criminal, correction had to start with that knowledge. It required knowledge of what exactly were the bad influences and what exactly the child's early life was like, since correction could only be effective if sanctions could be tailored to individual circumstances. The objective of investigation, then, was to unearth and accumulate such knowledge. For example, the agents of the Toronto Children's Aid Society were instructed to find out particulars of theft cases and investigate the homes of the children accused of theft.[90]

Separation and Dispersion

The strategies of separation and dispersion were similar in that they were concerned with the spatial arrangement of classified groups of children, similar to designing a garden to achieve ideals of aesthetics, plant health, and efficiency. The idea of separation was to physically segregate children from adult criminals, paupers, prostitutes, and even undesirable parents. The objective was to prevent children from being influenced by these adults. It was primarily from this standpoint that many reformers mounted their criticism of traditional practices of trying and punishing children and adults in the same facilities. For example, Kelso protested that 'if it is desirable to correct impure or criminal tendencies, surely the place to do so is not in the midst of corrupting influences or criminal associations, and yet this is the system in vogue at the present time!' He believed that 'no child should be locked up in a police station or committed to a gaol, while there is a hope of preserving in him or her the qualities of honest citizenship.'[91] It was against this background that separate detention facilities,[92] a separate court system, and a separate record system and personnel were promoted and gradually became established.

Dispersion, in contrast to assembly, was regarded as a desirable strategy for several reasons. First, it was feared that when a group of bad, or potentially bad, children were put together, such as in a reformatory, they were likely to contaminate each other. This was evident in Kelso's belief that in an ideal reform school, 'the influence of one pupil upon another should be carefully noted ... Pupils of low morals should not be allowed to form friendships or to be together in class or dormitory.'[93] However, the size of such assemblies of children usually made these intentions impractical. Second, it was also cautioned that when children were put together, they could band together and resist. This idea was reflected in Kelso's diagnosis of the defects of the reform-school system: 'One frequently hears the charge that reform schools do not reform. This is not due to any fault on the part of the institution or the officials so much as to the friendships formed among lads who encourage each other to resist moral influences and afterwards bound themselves together to continue the old life of idleness and crime.'[94]

The third reason that the dispersion of children appeared more favourable than assembly was the belief that the best approach to shaping a child's character was to treat the child as an individual and through personal touches, which would always be limited in an institution. These were the main considerations underlying the arguments of many late nineteenth-century reformers for de-institutionalization. Thus, instead of sending children to a reformatory, it was thought that a better way was to have no more than twelve or fifteen boys on a small farm. It would be best, however, to place them in good foster homes to secure personalized rehabilitation.[95] In a similar vein, Kelso insisted that the children's aid shelter should be a facility for transplanting children to foster homes, rather than a facility to provide institutional care.

The child-saving strategies discussed above – guidance, supervision, investigation, separation, and dispersion – shared several common characteristics. These strategies were positive, in that they sought to exercise power through constructive means of teaching and encouragement, rather than suppression and deterrence. They were individualized, in that they treated a child as an individual with his own peculiarities and required interpersonal exchange and mutual commitment between the authority and the ruled. They were intelligent, in that they were informed by intimate knowledge of a child, for example, her life history, surroundings, habits, likes, and dislikes. Finally, these strategies were local, in that the sources of power were dispersed at the grassroots level, as opposed to centralized within the state.

These characteristics certainly distinguished the new brand of strategies from the older tradition of crude, direct, and simplistic sovereign power and from today's technologies of risk management and criminal punishment. In actual practice, some traditional measures such as the prohibitive curfew law were gradually replaced by child-saving strategies. Some others, such as corporal punishment, persisted and continued to exist side-by-side with child saving. An analysis of the unsystematic transition from one model of ruling to another and the associated incongruent elements can shed some light on child-saving strategies, particularly with respect to their primary objective of effectively governing children. For this purpose, I shall briefly look at two examples of more traditional ways of exercising power – the curfew law and bodily punishment – and their varied relations to child-saving strategies. The demise of the curfew justified child saving as an effective approach to governing children. Corporal punishment co-existed with child-saving strategies as a necessary supplement, despite their incompatible logic.

The debates around the curfew law can serve as an illuminating example of the persistent but gradually outdated prohibition approach. In the search for a remedy for the 'great and manifold evils' on the street, particularly after nightfall, the reformers initially did not turn to any of the typical child-saving strategies discussed above. Instead, many regarded a curfew as a plausible method. A curfew would ban the presence of all children on the street in the evening, regardless of their social and economic status, religion, or gender. It promised to be the most direct, most certain, and most efficient way of protecting children from corrupting influences lurking on the street in the dark. Soon after the curfew law was put in place, however, it became clear that the results fell short of expectations. As Kelso remarked after the fact: 'the Curfew Law does not fill the bill and has not anywhere ... stood the practical test for any length of time.'[96]

Resistance against the curfew law developed as soon as it was passed, but to reformers the most compelling resistance came from 'highly respectable and Christian parents.'[97] One of the problems with the curfew law lay with the fact that it was a totalizing strategy, in that it was indiscriminate and treated all children as the same. Those 'highly respectable and Christian parents' did not wish to see their children and themselves being put in the same category with the 'lowly.' They found that it was unfair to conclude categorically that 'all children [were] on the streets after nightfall for evil purposes or that they must necessarily be acquiring evil habits or thoughts.'[98] They asserted that they could see no harm in their children playing for a short time on the street near their homes after night set in. Another related problem with the curfew law was that it was a top-down strategy. Moral regulation, however, essentially relied on public opinion and grassroots participation. The objection and resistance of the respectable masses no doubt rendered authoritarian and non-participatory laws such as the curfew law irrelevant in real life. From his experience with the failed curfew law, Kelso made the observation that 'the moral growth of the children might be protected without the passing of a stringent or unpopular law.' He advised, 'Do not bother with the Curfew but try to reach the evil in some other ways less open to objection and opposition.'[99] Kelso recommended a range of alternatives, among them the use of probation officers to watch over children who came before the juvenile court and the enlargement of the statutory definition of a neglected child (e.g., to include children who were habitually on the streets) so that the presence of children on the street could be regulated through the law protecting neglected children.[100]

The curfew law failed not just because it was prohibitive, but also because it was indiscriminate. In contrast, child-saving strategies were 'less open to objection and opposition' by the influential class, religious, and ethnic segments of the public, largely because it was not totalizing and was only concerned with a newly invented category of humans, that is, abused and neglected children. Despite the differences in strategies, it was evident that child saving was not that different from the measures that it replaced, in that they shared the objective of seeking to govern children effectively.

The story of corporal punishment, however, is different. While there was a clear paradigm shift away from the focus on the body, the body as an object of discipline was never totally excluded. Parental discipline and control was considered so fundamental by the child savers that it even rationalized physical punishment of children in certain situations. Kelso recalled an incident in which a complaint was made to him about a farmer who was cruel in his treatment of an English boy. Kelso's investigation proved that apparently there was a certain amount of truth in the charge. The man had given the boy a 'thoroughly good thrashing,' but he had done so with the explicit approval of an agent of the society that placed the English boy. Kelso also found out that this was not the first time that the farmer had done so.

Obviously, whenever there was a ward whom no one else could manage, the child was placed under the charge of this farmer. It was claimed that 'in the course of two or three years he had brought under control and made good citizens of a dozen boys who had been given up in despair by others.' Instead of being condemned as a serial child abuser, this farmer was regarded as 'a public benefactor' – 'a stern but kindly disciplinarian.' Kelso himself felt compelled to acknowledge that he was doing a fine service for boys and for the country at large. Cruelty to children was justified by the observation that it 'is well known that many young fellows find their way to prison through lack of guidance and control – never taught obedience or submission to the recognized discipline of life.'[101]

It is clear from examining ideas about corporal punishment that the primary concern of child saving was to turn children into good citizens. With some children, only bodily pain seemed to be effective, even if it ran counter to the ideal of proper technologies for child rearing, and it would be condoned. In the 1930s, when the debate on the merit of whipping juvenile offenders was revived, even Kelso conceded that spanking had a place in moral training, because it was at least 'better than the prison.'[102]

Drawing attention to the prevalent use of gardening imagery in child-saving writings, I have examined gardening metaphors and the 'gardening governmentality' of child saving, that is, the conception of the individual as largely the product of conditioning, the mode of disciplinary power and its key objects, and practical strategies of child-saving governance. The gardening governmentality was posed as a desirable alternative to the two opposite problems in parenting, the excessive use of force and the lack of discipline.

It would be naïve to take these gentler and more constructive strategies as an enactment of transparent humanitarianism and progression. As I have shown, the primary objective of these strategies was to govern children properly, so that they grow up to be self-regulating individuals. Furthermore, while the child savers embraced the gardening governmentality, they did not exclude repressive forms of power such as forced separation of children and parents. Indeed, even gardening imagery allowed the use of extreme force such as 'weeding' and 'transplanting.' Nevertheless, it would be unfair to say that the reformers' call for compassion, knowledge, and local participation was a mere smokescreen for some more sinister and hidden agenda of oppression; to the reformers these elements were internal to the effective operation of power. Certainly, 'gardening strategies' were ways through which power was exercised in relations with poor families, single mothers, new immigrants, and wayward children. They were ways through which these segments of the population were normalized for the sake of the interests of society as defined by the privileged. Today, similar images of children and/or plants, such as a carrot or a seedling with a child's face, can sometimes be found in the early-development discourse.[103] In present-day child protection, however, children seem to be seen not so much as plants to be properly grown but as subjects to be kept safe physically, sexually, and emotionally, through risk management and criminal punishment of those adults who threaten children's safety. In contrast to the current bureaucratic and punitive strategies in child protection, the 'gardening strategies' at least were more positive, as opposed to repressive, and were more consonant with consideration of available resources.

Chapter 4

Reports, Visits, and Case Records: Processes of Establishing Power/Knowledge

In this chapter and the following ones, I turn to child-saving technologies that were supposed to implement the 'gardening' strategies and thus connect authorities and subjects in ways that by and large resembled the relation between the gardener and plants and weeds. These mainly included the reporting mechanism, record-keeping, visits, the shelter, the detention room, and foster care, which embodied strategies of guidance, supervision, investigation, classification, separation, and dispersion. Foucault commented that 'the exercise of power is not a naked fact, an institutional right, nor is it a structure which holds out or is smashed: it is elaborated, transformed, organized; it endows itself with processes which are more or less adjusted to the situation.'[1] To analyse these child-saving technologies is to understand the processes through which power relations were established, with particular effects on people's lives.

Technologies took different apparatuses – some were informal (e.g., reporting), some were dispersed (e.g., foster care), and some were highly institutionalized (e.g., separate custody of children at the shelter and the detention room). Consequently, they were documented un-evenly. For example, there is a relative wealth of information on the operation of the shelter and the detention room, including the meeting minutes of the shelter committee, the shelter committee's reports to the board, rules and regulations at the shelter, as well as the complaint books. Towards the end of the period under examination foster care had gradually become an important method of child-saving work, but, its very dispersed, individualized, and private nature shielded it from a close examination in a document-dependent historical sociological study. Similarly, although the technology of reporting was an equally important component of the child-saving operation as, say, the detention room and the shelter, what one can learn about it is limited to only the brief mentions of complaints in case records. In this chapter I focus on three child-saving technologies: reports, visits, and case records, which emerged during the period examined and continue to be deployed in today's child-protection work.

Reports

Children's aid societies worked partly because the neighbourhood, or the community, was given the power to report on families in which children were 'not being properly cared for.' The technology of reporting was established in legislation and was made known to the community at large through deliberate efforts. One way of disseminating information about the existence of the reporting mechanism was by circular letters. For example, the Toronto Children's Aid Society issued circular letters to ministers, doctors, and school principals, asking for their cooperation and help in reporting cases 'where the service of the Society would be of use in reforming the homes of vicious or neglectful parents.'[2] Exposure in major secular newspapers as well as denominational newsletters was also effective in introducing the reporting technology. In addition, the child-savers' intervention itself would stir up publicity about the new form of power.

The technique of anonymity, although optional, was crucial in encouraging reporting, because complainants usually had relatively close relations with those they complained about. The society did not require complainants to have expert knowledge about what constituted neglect or cruelty. This worked to maximize the democratic potential at the reporting stage of child-saving work, thus involving the general public. Complaints were laid in a wide range of situations: by police, missionary workers, the clergy, and neighbours against neglectful mothers, abusive fathers, or 'annoying children,' by family relatives,[3] by parents against incorrigible children, by mothers against abusive fathers, by fathers against mothers who had drinking problems or were living with other men, by people against organizations such as an industrial school or an opera house, and by children against foster parents.

The language, which termed reporting as 'laying complaints,' suggested an adversarial relation between the complainants and those complained about. In this adversarial relation, complainants were assumed to be on the side of the children's aid society and society at large, while the parties complained against were construed as being at fault. Thus, one major effect was that the situation tended to be understood as a moral issue of right or wrong, rather than a lack of social and economic resources. This constructed nature of the situation was illuminated when parents came to the society because they could not care for their children as a result of sickness or other life exigencies and when friends took poor mothers to the society asking for help. In such cases, there were no complaints against individual parents; if there were any, it was a complaint against society at large.

At present, reporting is no longer termed 'complaint.' Instead, more neutral words – referral and self-referral – are used. Although the term 'referral' holds out the promise of addressing needs, the legacy of moral regulation remains largely unchallenged as long as child neglect continues to be defined as a personal rather than a social problem.[4]

Visits

Visits to homes were conducted for investigative and supervisory purposes. The personnel at the society who did the actual field visits were the agent and later the inspector. Investigations of homes were usually made after complaints regarding neglected children or cruelty to children, although the agent or inspector might make inquires without complaints. Visits to homes were also made to ensure that home life be improved for children. In addition, the agent or inspector attended the Children's Court and later the Juvenile Court from day to day, paying attention to the children who came before it.[5] The agent or inspector was expected to keep full and complete records of cases investigated and dealt with by him for filing and for entry in the record books. The scant recorded information, particularly in the column of report of investigation in the complaint books that I will discuss in the next section, perhaps suggests a discrepancy between actual mundane practice and grand vision of thorough investigation that would produce comprehensive knowledge and then allow intelligent governance of children. This might be a case of inertia, explicit resistance, or a lack of human and financial resources. The last problem was made apparent in 1905, when the inspector of the society, the only staff member undertaking field work, said in one of his reports that so much of his time was taken up by the Children's Court that he found it difficult to keep up with the investigative work.[6]

Nonetheless, the agent or inspector did generate knowledge of individual children and families and transmit it to the board to inform decision-making. He was asked to present reports to the board at its regular meetings on the specifics of cases and what was done if any action had been taken.[7] Based on what was known about the cases from the agent or inspector's report, the board then discussed the cases and made decisions on what to do with them. The minutes of the board meetings mostly recorded that the agent's or inspector's report was read and cases were discussed and commented on. Where details were recorded, the cases often involved more intrusive actions. On 16 April 1896, the agent's report on a boy named Frank was read and discussed. Then the board resolved to make him a ward of the society and to hand him over to the superintendent of the Working Boys' Home to be trained.[8]

The position of the agent and later the inspector was a male-only position, and at the beginning it was taken up by men of some means and social status as a part-time job. The first agent appointed by the board of the society in 1892 was the Reverend John Edward Starr. His was a part-time position with an initial remuneration of $500 per annum.[9] Starr was an ordained Methodist minister and was an active member of the board, especially on the legislation committee and the shelter committee. Given the intertwined relation between child saving and juvenile delinquency, it is not surprising that he later served as the first Commissioner for the Juvenile Court in Toronto in 1911. In 1895 Starr resigned, and Alderman John J. Graham was appointed as his successor at a salary of $1,000 per annum.[10] In 1900, Graham was appointed inspector, instead of agent, and stayed in that position until 1903.[11] After some interim turnovers, in 1906 William Duncan was appointed the full-time inspector and superintendent of the shelter and his wife the lady superintendent of the shelter, salaried at the rate of $800 and $400 annually respectively, with board and apartments in the shelter.[12] They stayed in these positions throughout the rest of the period studied.

While the inspector was a position occupied by males only, starting in 1908 the society hired women to work as lady visitors or lady inspectors to 'look after' children who received suspended sentences from the Children's Court. The Children's Court was opened in Toronto in 1888 in response to the child savers' advocacy of separating children from adult criminals during court hearings. The Toronto Children's Aid Society's involvement in the day-to-day operation of the Children's Court was largely limited to detaining accused juvenile delinquents at the society's detention room and accompanying them to court for hearings, since its initial concern was primarily with the separation of children from adult criminals. Towards the end of the 1910s, however, the society started to participate in the administration of suspended sentences and, thus, rehabilitation work. Suspended sentences were seen to be a solution to the problems associated with the old-fashioned institution-based punishment. Institutionalized punishment was criticized for failing to reduce crime. Worse, it turned out more and hardened criminals, because when they were imprisoned together juvenile delinquents were contaminated by adult criminals and by each other. Suspended sentences were intended to avoid that trap. During the time of the Children's Court, suspended sentences did not involve mandatory supervision. The Toronto Children's Aid Society, however, strongly believed in the importance of supervision and assigned itself the responsibility of supervising children on suspended sentences. In 1903, the society's inspector recommended to the board a committee of teachers and mission workers 'who would take up the work of visiting the homes of the children who have come before the Magistrate, thus being helpful to such children.' The board was favourable to the recommendation and left the matter of invitations to join such a committee to the inspector.[13] There is no evidence suggesting that progress was made in that direction until 1907, when the board passed a similar resolution. The resolution stated that since so many boys were left by the police magistrate to go on suspended sentences, there was an evident necessity of these boys 'being looked after'; thus, 'one or more capable women would be engaged to follow up these boys for the purpose of influencing them for good, and so preventing their reappearance before the Magistrate.'[14] In 1908 a lady visitor, Mrs Hamilton, was hired.[15] Additional lady visitors were hired in subsequent years. At one board meeting Macdonald stated his view that 'these women, with the love of the Saviour and of children in their hearts, will find entrance into homes where it would not be possible for men inspectors to get in.'[16] Despite the belief that lady visitors would be more effective, their salary was much lower than that of the male inspector; for example, when Mrs Hamilton was hired in 1908 her salary was only $400 per annum. At the same time, the Toronto Children's Aid Society also approached organizations connected with churches, such as St Andrew's Prebyterian, to ask for their cooperation in 'looking after' and 'taking an interest' in the children who were given suspended sentences by the magistrates.[17]

The society's conviction of the importance of supervisory visits was corroborated by influential reformers such as Dr Bruce Smith. At the Conference of Charities and Correction in 1908, Dr Smith, the retiring president of the conference, stated that 'the suspended sentence without having a local probation officer as a guardian has too often proved futile.' Emphasizing that in Britain the Probation of Offenders Law came in force the previous year, he concluded that probation with indeterminate sentence would be the right system. 'There can be no doubt that if many first offenders were given a reasonable time to make restitution, in cases of various forms of larceny, they would not only do so, but would also repent of their folly at the same time.'[18] The society's initiatives in supervision were also endorsed by the 1908 Dominion Juvenile Delinquents Act, which owed its passage partly to the determined lobbying of the child savers. Under the act, agents of children's aid societies were given the powers of court officials, and their job was officially described as supervising the child's home life, keeping the child under constant oversight, and reporting to the court from time to time as to the child's progress.[19]

Complying with the Dominion Juvenile Delinquents Act, the Juvenile Court Act was passed by the Ontario Legislature in 1910. This act established juvenile courts that, in contrast to the Children's Court, provided truly separate trials of children and, more importantly, aimed at accumulating knowledge of each child and administering treatment on the basis of that knowledge.[20] After the establishment of the Juvenile Court, the Children's Aid Society hired more lady visitors, who were now formally recognized by law as probation officers. These positions greatly interested young women, as was made obvious by the forty-one applicants who responded to an advertisement for three lady visitor positions at a starting salary of $400 per annum.[21]

Volunteers from the Big Sister and Big Brother associations were also involved in probation work. In the case of the Big Sister Association, the personal work among the little sisters, most of whom were girls appearing in the Juvenile Court, was carried on by a general secretary and two field secretaries. In cases of girls whose charges were not serious, the field secretary would investigate the cases. That would involve visiting and investigating the girls' homes, whether they were their parents' homes or boarding houses. If conditions were found to be unsatisfactory, the Big Sisters would make efforts to get the girls into proper homes. They would also try to arrange places of work for the girls. In cases of families with girls who were sentenced to industrial schools, often the Big Sisters would 'take care of' other sisters to prevent them following in the footsteps of the wrong-doers.[22]

Case Records

That record-keeping was taken seriously in child-saving work was evident in Kelso's numerous mentions in his diary, as well as in the society's minute books,[23] of activities related to the design and creation of the record-keeping system. Kelso firmly believed that 'the fullest possible records should be kept of children dealt with by the Children's Aid Societies.'[24] In the same vein, he also commented that 'the Juvenile Court should have a system of records, which should be "clear, complete and showing results."'[25] Kelso had taken the lead in creating a variety of forms and registers for various aspects of child-saving work. These included complaint books, a register of children waiting for foster homes, a register of people wanting foster children, forms of application for parties wanting foster children, agreement forms between the society and foster parents, and so on.

What follows is an analysis of how record-keeping was organized and with what effects. In the past several years, more and more historians have become interested in case-file research or in collecting and using records that bear similarities with case files, as represented by Franca Iacovetta and Wendy Mitchinson's edited volume, *On the Case: Explorations in Social History*.[26] For many, case files are a particularly useful source of information for analysing mechanisms of knowledge and power, political contestation, and their outcomes at the local level. I focus on the complaint books, mainly because they represent the largest and best-preserved source of case records in the society's archival collection. I have sampled records kept in complaint books from the following years: 1892, 1893, 1898, 1903, 1908, and 1913. Complaint books were ledger books (as opposed to file folders),[27] and they followed the same format from 1892 to 1917.

When the ledger books are opened, these columns extend from left to right across both pages: No. of Case, Children's Court No., Date of Complaint, No. of Children Concerned, Name and Address, Age, Particulars of Case, Previous Complaints, Report of Investigation, and Result. This layout was designed to structure child-saving work as a mode of knowledge-based governance. Immediately after the columns of basic information, came four columns corresponding to the steps that ought to be taken in work, namely, Particulars of Case, Previous Complaints, Report of Investigation, and Result. 'Particulars of Case' documented background information on the child and his immediate surroundings, such as his parents and religion. 'Previous Complaints' traced the known history of the child and family. 'Report of Investigation' recorded all other information that might be related to the case, and 'Result' documented what had been done with the child and the effects of intervention.

Entries in the complaint books were generally rather skimpy. What one can know about a particular case is very limited, except for some cases in the 1910s, when the staff pasted press clippings concerning a particular child in his page (or section of the page); the clippings allow a few more glimpses into the story. Information that was entered in handwriting, no matter how scanty, changed over the years. The general pattern was a shift from basic information to increasing detail, and then back to fewer details around 1913. Qualitatively, the changes in case records over the years show certain patterns that reflect broader trends. For example, the increasing importance of case history was reflected in the 1898 records, where 'Previous Occurrences' of child abuse and neglect started to be more systematically documented.

As a technology of power, record-keeping had various effects on the regulated population. One example of the effects of record-keeping on individual experience can be found in the case of two boys. In June 1905 it was reported that two boys in the care of the society aged fifteen had run away from their foster homes. Macdonald, president of the society, expressed his opinion that if the boys came into the custody of the society once more they should be sent to the Victoria Industrial School.[28] This action would not have been possible if the boys' names and histories had not been documented in the case records.

Record-keeping was crucial to knowledge-based governance of both parents and children, particularly when it came to the temporalization and spatialization of regulation. Temporally, record-keeping not only made it possible to bring in the historical dimension of what could be known about an individual, it also enabled continuous regulation (e.g., in the case of supervising foster parents and children). Spatially, case records, for example, entries made in the complaint books about information gathered from the police, the school, and missionary workers about a particular family, not only centralized 'a number of disparate case histories into one textual site,'[29] but also served as a knowledge conduit to facilitate simultaneous regulation of a single family or an individual in different locations.

Reports, or complaints, investigative and supervisory visits, and case records were technologies that the child savers deployed in their day-to-day work. They were means that brought the power of the child savers into being. Through establishing the reporting mechanism, criteria for investigation and supervision, and categories of information in case records, these technologies brought together a state in which parental conduct and children's experience come to be understood and regulated according to the beliefs of the child savers.

Chapter 5

The Shelter: A Locus of Organizing and Transforming Power Relations

This chapter and the following one focus on the operation of the Toronto Children's Aid Society's shelter and the detention room. The detailed examination is made possible by the relatively richer information on the shelter, but also encouraged by the Foucauldian notion of strategic, critical, and effective histories. The historical accounts of the shelter and the detention room privilege certain dimensions of the past that I consider most relevant and useful for 'an illumination of present reality.'[1] For example, the shelter chapter brings into focus historical contestation about the purpose of the shelter – whether it was intended to help parents and children or to undermine parents so as to protect children. Thus, this analysis can potentially strengthen criticisms of the punitive and anti-parent approaches endorsed in the recent Child Welfare Reform in Ontario. My deliberate highlighting of the work at the shelter strives to destablize the status of better-known and more widely used methods in child protection, such as foster care. It attempts to revive interest in community alternatives such as residential care for children and even families, which may be more useful in addressing needs defined from the perspective of parents.

According to Kelso's well-publicized and generally accepted story, the idea of a children's shelter started one cold night in 1887, when he found two youngsters standing in a doorway on Yonge Street at about 11:00 o'clock. Kelso learnt from the two children that they had been sent out to beg and as they had been unsuccessful they were afraid of a beating if they went home. To justify his subsequent action, Kelso added that the children's parents were known to the police as 'habitual drunkards' who used their children to collect money from charitable people to keep up their 'vicious mode of living.' Several alternative actions were possible – Kelso could have taken the children to their home and tried to persuade their parents not to beat them and not to send them out begging again. He could have also taken the children to a relative or a neighbour, and he could even have taken the children to his own home for the night. Had Kelso followed any of these routes, perhaps the idea of a shelter would not have occurred to him. We cannot know for certain how he considered the situation, but in the end he decided to take the children to one, and in the end several, of the city's orphanages. Much to his dismay, however, none of the orphanages would take the children without a preliminary application and examination that would require their parents' consent. Failing that, he went to a lodging house for men and finally was able to secure admission for the children on his own. He wrote up the story and advocated a children's refuge or temporary shelter where any needy child could at once be admitted and cared for.[2]

There was, however, another source of the idea of the shelter, which was also accounted for by Kelso. In March 1887, Kelso wrote to the editor of the *World* describing the work that the Toronto Humane Society intended to undertake. Among the list of tasks such as investigating cases of cruelty to horses, cattle, and children, erecting drinking fountains 'suitable for man or beast,' and regulating the overcrowding of horse-drawn streetcars, he mentioned the necessity for 'the erection of a temporary home in connection with the Police Department for the reception of women and children whom it may not be desirable to confine with hardened criminals during trial.'[3] Similarly, in December 1889, Kelso was reported to have urged that 'there should be a Children's Shelter for the temporary confinement of children [apart from adults].'[4] Such evidence points out that another vision of the shelter was to provide segregated judicial custody to children who had been caught up in the justice system.

This double vision attested to the fundamental linkage between child saving and crime prevention in the late nineteenth-century child-saving thinking. In practice, this was translated into the shelter for neglected, abused, and other categories of children, and the detention room for juvenile delinquents who came to the court and were either in remand awaiting court appearances or waiting to be sent to reformatories or industrial schools. The shelter was opened at 32 Centre Avenue in 1892, soon after the Toronto Children's Aid Society was incorporated. The detention room was opened in the basement of the shelter in 1894. The two facilities had a quite ambiguous relation during the period from the mid-1890s to the early 1920s. The shelter and the detention room were connected, in that they were housed in the same building, they shared the same staff, and records of children in both places were kept in the same ledger in a mixed way. And yet they were separate, in that juvenile delinquent boys were not allowed to be in contact with boys at the shelter (girls were not segregated into two groups as a result of a lack of space), because juvenile delinquents were thought to be more damaged and evil and thus would morally contaminate the shelter children. Furthermore, to many board members as well as staff of the society, the detention room was simply not as dear to their hearts as the shelter. This was reflected in the much poorer conditions in the former. These inconsistent and even contradictory practices mirrored the ambiguous identity continuum from neglected and abused children to juvenile delinquents. At one level, the two groups of children were considered essentially the same subjects, as far as crime prevention was concerned, because they were all seen to be on the path leading to eventual crime. This idea was made real by actually housing neglected and abused children together with juvenile delinquents in one building, and by mixing their records in ledger books. At the same time, however, intellectual instruments employed by reformers, such as the concept of crime as a gradual growth process and the idea that delinquency was learnt, also worked to suggest stages or degrees of corruption, and thus to distinguish juvenile delinquents from neglected and abused children.

The focus of this chapter is on the shelter and how various power relations were organized and sometimes transformed on this site. The first section examines how as a technology the shelter undercut, produced, or reinforced power relations among parents, children, and the society in both intended and unintended ways. The second section analyses the relations between the society and external authorities, mainly the city of Toronto board of control, which oversaw the sizeable annual grant to the Children's Aid Society, the city's medical health officer, and the provincial superintendent's office, which was brought into being largely through the operation of the shelter. The third section provides a descriptive analysis of the hierarchical structure that positioned the staff, the shelter committee, and the board of the society at different points of power at the shelter, with an emphasis on the uneven gendered division of authorities. It then discusses how women were marginalized into the caring work at the shelter, but also how they in turn took control of the shelter and used it as a springboard for increasing their influence in the society. The main theme of this chapter is the organization and transformation of power. The argument is that a technology like the shelter constituted and shaped not only a web of relations among the society, parents, and children, but also relations within the society itself, and relations between the society and external authorities. How a technology would work could never be fully foreseen. The history of the shelter shows that it was possible to challenge its originally defined purpose. It also shows that the society, as an authority to parents and children, was neither monolithic nor autonomous.

Contesting the Objective of the Shelter

The shelter, as Kelso envisioned in his story of the two children he helped on one cold night in the late 1880s, was different from the charitable institutions for children that had emerged in Ontario in the 1830s and dominated as the major way to provide for dependent children for most of the nineteenth century.[5] The shelter was distinct in two aspects. First, the ideal shelter was a facility that was hostile towards parents (it was not for the convenience of parents who relinquished their children or who could not care for them temporarily, as child residential institutions and sometimes orphanages were, for example). This was evident in the administrative and philosophical distinction between the shelter and charitable institutions for children: The shelter did not require parental consent while orphanges did. The absence of this requirement can be seen as a bypass technology, which side-stepped parents' authority and made it possible for the society to take coercive actions against their wishes. Second, the ideal shelter was a subordinate facility that supported the primary objective of ensuring that children were properly governed by adults in a home setting. In other words, its temporary custody function was intended to support regulative actions (e.g., investigation, education, and discipline) aimed at reforming parents, or to support activities of finding a proper substitute home to rear a child. In either situation, the shelter was designed to be, again, different from classical institutions for children, in that it was meant to enforce proper parenting, not relieve parents from any parenting work. Technologically, this vision was put in practice by deliberately limiting the length of time that a child could stay at the shelter.

The process through which these ideas about the objectives and technologies of the shelter were put to practice by the Toronto Children's

Aid Society was gradual and contested. When the society opened its shelter in 1892, apparently many board members, including those of the shelter committee, were unclear about what the shelter was supposed to do. Thus, the shelter committee asked the society to retroactively define 'just what work the Shelter was intended to do.'[6] The minutes showed that 'there seemed to be the general sense of the [board] meeting that the Shelter was intended to give temporary Shelter to children until they could be otherwise provided for.'[7] Apparently, this opinion was too vague to be of use to differentiate the shelter from other residential institutions and to guide practical work. A special committee with Kelso as a leading member was thus formed to deliberate on the exact objective of the shelter. Two months later, the special committee reported its carefully detailed opinion on the work of the shelter, which was almost identical to Kelso's original vision. Specifically, the view was that

> the greatest care should be taken to prevent the idea getting abroad that the Children's Shelter is in any sense a permanent home for Children. It was established as a temporary shelter for abused, neglected and deserted children, to be open to this class night and day, without fee of any kind, but only affording shelter and protection until the children can be suitably disposed, either by compelling parents to do their duty towards their offspring or securing for homeless children, or those whom the courts decide should be removed from parental control – admittance to one of the public institutions provided for such cases.
>
> It is therefore not desirable – that any child should be kept in the shelter longer than one month, except for very special reasons, and, as result, ten days should suffice to provide for a proper disposal of any child.'[8]

As I have argued in earlier chapters, the child savers sought to bring into practice a system of interlocking power relations among the society, parents, and children, which can be summarized as a system in which the society had the authority to ensure that parents properly exercised their authority over children. The technology of the shelter brought the system into operation in several ways. First, by coercively taking children to the shelter or by accepting children who sought shelter on their own, the society upset certain ways that parents related to their children. The problematic relationships between parents and child that the society was most intent on undermining were those in which parents failed to exercise their authority over their children (neglect) and, to a lesser extent, those in which parents used excessive force (cruelty or abuse).

The technique that made this possible was the separation of children from their parents.

Another pivotal way in which the shelter brought power relations into play has rarely been recognized and discussed in child welfare literature. The shelter's existence made it possible for the society to be calculating and to attempt to shape aspects of parents' behaviour according to particular norms, so that they could in turn 'properly' execute their power in parenting. This was because through the shelter and the practice of separating (or even just the threat of separating) parents and their children, emotional pains, fears, and desires could be produced and manipulated by the society for specific ends. How Mrs Newman was regulated by the society through the fear of losing her children is a case in point. On 22 January 1913, a visitor of the society called upon Mrs Newman at her home and found her 'slightly under influence of drink.' Even though her house and children were found 'neat & clean,' Mrs Newman was threatened that her children might be put in the shelter if she continued to neglect them, in her case, through drinking. According to the society's records, 'she was terrified that Visitor would take children away, begged that some place in country where she could not get drink might be found for her to go. Promised not to drink again.' The next day, the visitor called again and was satisfied that Mrs Newman 'was perfectly sober & house nice and clean.'[9] Governing through desire and fear did not always produce the anticipated results. For example, when the society's visitor called again at Mrs Newman's a week later, she found that Mrs Newman had locked herself and children in the house and that she 'had been drinking again.'[10] Such a reaction often led the child savers to conclude that the mother was so 'bad' that she was not governable, which in turn justified the use of the most severe sanction in family law, the removal of a child.

Although the shelter was designed by the child savers as a means to the end of ensuring proper parenting at home, records show that in reality this definition of the shelter's purpose and status was quite contested. Especially in the earlier years of the society, a significant number of parents attempted to use the shelter as a resource for meeting their needs for child care, similar to parents who later used the Juvenile Court as a solution to economic difficulties and for the education and discipline of children.[11] Although it is doubtful that these parents deliberately picked a fight with the society, their actions did amount to a serious challenge. An examination of records shows that in many early cases children were admitted to the shelter upon requests of one or both parents for a variety of reasons. In 1893, Mr and Mrs Thompson were both ill and thus could not care for their five children aged from two to eight. All five children were then admitted to the shelter and stayed there until almost three months later, when their parents had recovered. The records show that the eldest daughter was taken home by her mother first; then the youngest son; and finally the other three children.[12] In another case, Lilli and Dorothy Oliver were taken to the shelter by their mother one evening. All three sought shelter from a father and husband 'enraged with drink.' A few days later, their mother took them away.[13] In yet another case, a mother brought her children to the shelter because of 'father's immoral conduct towards herself and children.'[14] About a third of all the cases in the first year of the shelter's existence were those in which parents voluntarily came to the society for assistance because circumstances such as sickness, destitution, desertion, family violence, or the break-up of homes made it very difficult, if not impossible, for them to take care of their children. Thus, it is apparent that the shelter was perceived and used by these parents as a facility providing emergency and short-term child care, which resembled such use of orphanages or children's residential institutions. It can be said that, contrary to the original vision of the society, the shelter was situationaly transformed by these parents into a resource for coping with life exigencies, without stigma or unwelcome intervention. By willingly sending their children to the shelter and requesting custody, these parents reversed the power relation between them and the society, in that they made the society provide caring services to meet their needs. Most interestingly, they rationalized their actions in no other terms but those of the crucial importance of proper parenting.

These cases occurred on a fairly frequent basis for a few more years, so much so that people like Kelso felt it necessary to write a story about such cases with the purpose of showing that the shelter was unfairly taken advantage of by parents who regarded the shelter as a resource and used it willingly. In the story of Emily, Kelso portrayed her as an immature and irresponsible wife who wanted to use the shelter for her children so that she could break up her family. The story started with Emily being unhappy with the fact that her husband came home late. 'She burst out with a torrent of abuse' when he got inside the door. The shouting match quickly escalated into physical violence. Then Emily pondered leaving her husband and going to her mother's place. The only problem, however, was what to do with the two babies, since Emily 'could hardly impose the two babies on her mother.' Suddenly, a 'happy thought' occurred to her – 'She would put them in the care of the Children's society'! She was very sure of getting sympathetic help from 'Mr Kelso.' Much to her surprise, however, instead of referring to the Children's Aid's shelter, 'Mr Kelso' gave her a lecture on how to properly conduct herself as a wife. Contrary to trying to make the shelter take care of her children so that she could go to her mother's, she should 'always be a peace-maker, always patient, forgiving and hopeful'; she should meet her husband on the doorstep 'with a smile and an embrace and a little speech'; she should 'beg for his forgiveness' and 'resolve in future to keep peace at all costs.'[15] Kelso's narrative, in effect, brushed aside women's suffering of family violence, blamed them for not being good wives, and also insinuated that if the shelter were made available upon parents' request, it would assist in breaking up families (and challenging patriarchal order).

Since the beginning of the twentieth century, proportionately fewer and fewer children were admitted to the shelter on the ground that their parents needed child care help for this or that reason. The definition of needs was increasingly systemized in such a way that parents' expressions of need were dismissed. For example, Richard Cassidy's mother deserted the family and left him with his stepfather, who did not want to keep Richard for long because he did not think of Richard as his child. The society declined his request to send the boy to the shelter, saying that he was 'not deserving.'[16]

Contestation over the purpose of the shelter was also evident in parents' using the shelter to discipline their children. John Beatty was one of the children sent to the shelter because his father and step-mother said that he was 'incorrigible' and they could do nothing with him.[17] Katie Snowdon was brought to the shelter for the same reason. Katie, who was an illegitimate child, as the society noted in her records, had been working at Mrs Walter's. In August 1902, Miss White of the YWCA requested that she be taken to the shelter for discipline. Although her mother felt that she did not have any major problems and that 'with proper training [she would] turn out all right,' the society staff noted that her actions at the shelter proved she was stubborn and hard to manage. Apparently, Katie was kept at the shelter for several months for discipline and was not released until February of the next year.[18] Sometimes children were not taken to the shelter but were warned that they would be brought to the shelter for a while unless they did better.[19] In these situations, the shelter became a resource for parents to assist them in the governance of their children. This way of using the shelter was accepted as appropriate. It was allowed to continue during the period studied, because it was compatible with the fundamental objective of child protection, that is, ensuring that children were governed by their parents (or employers) properly.

The Shelter as a Locus for External Regulatory Power

This section shows how the shelter brought the Toronto Children's Aid Society into particular relations with various external authorities, most notably the city of Toronto's board of control, the city's medical health officer, and the provincial superintendent's office. The society was not autonomous in function. So far as the shelter was concerned, it had to negotiate with, concede to, or fight with other authorities, as these were determined by law, possession of economic recourses, or medical-scientific knowledge.

The relationship between the Toronto Children's Aid Society and the city primarily concerned funding for the Shelter. The provision of funds to the operation of the shelter was stipulated in the child protection legislation. The society applied for grants according to the legislation, but it is apparent from the records that the city council treated the society's demands with reluctance. For example, in 1894 a sub-committee of the society's board waited on the executive committee of the city council. The society 'offered to accept $2,500 for the first year.' They did not ask for more than this modest amount because, first, 'the new Shelter was largely an experiment, [and] that they did not wish to unnecessarily burden the City'; and second, 'they did not wish to check the flow of voluntary contributions to the funds of the Society.' However, the executive committee of the city council refused to give more than $2,000. Macdonald, the president of the society, felt it necessary to 'most distinctly' tell the executive committee that 'they must not consider that $2,000 a finality for the year as according to the law they were obliged to provide funds to carry out the work of the Shelter.'[20] Although the grant from the city was only one source of revenue for the society, it was nevertheless an important one, because it was statutory and thus relatively steady.

In addition to its dependence on the city for financial support, the society also found itself under constraint by Toronto's medical health officer. A common reason for the medical health officer to interfere in the society's business was the frequent outbreaks of infectious diseases at the shelter and the detention room. During the period under examina-

tion, before the invention of effective medications and medical practices, epidemics of scarlet fever, diphtheria, scabies, measles, and chicken
pox regularly attacked children and disrupted the work of the shelter.
For example, 1904 alone witnessed several outbreaks of diphtheria. The
first outbreak was noted on the 24th of January. Infected children had to
be segregated from others and some sent to the isolation hospital.
Rooms had to be disinfected. From the beginning of May, fresh cases
developed; and in the middle of July another outbreak took place. Many
of these epidemics seemed to have been started by children freshly
admitted, who as the shelter committee put it, 'had apparently brought
the seeds of the disease in with them.'[21] When these diseases broke out,
the society would request the medical health officer to visit. He then
would examine all children in the shelter, divide them into groups, and
often put the buildings under quarantine.

In the early years in the history of the society, surgical operations were
performed at the shelter by visiting doctors, that is, medical doctors who
were members of the board. In 1898, the medical health officer of the
time, Dr Charles Sheard, found out about surgical operations at the
shelter by accident. As a result of an outbreak of scarlet fever, Dr Sheard
came to examine the children in the shelter and divide them into
groups. It happened that he saw a little boy upstairs who had been
operated on. According to Mr Samuel Wotton, the superintendent of
the shelter, Dr Sheard then said in a 'very emphatic' manner that 'I do
not know that the Shelter is the place for operations; there are enough
hospitals around for that purpose.'[22] When Dr Sheard's objection to
surgery at the shelter was brought to the board, considerable discussion
followed. The matter became confused when Dr Oldright, a member of
the board and a visiting doctor at the shelter, contradicted the secretary's
report of Dr Sheard's opinion and said that he had seen Dr Sheard, who
denied having made the statement attributed to him, saying that it was a
matter for the medical staff at the shelter and none of his business. At that
meeting, the board decided to express its 'utmost confidence' in the
medical staff of the shelter and permit them to use their own judgment in
dealing with all cases including operations, without instructions from the
board.[23] Still, the board thought it necessary for the president to make
enquiry himself as to what exactly Dr Sheard said at the shelter on this
particular occasion. Macdonald's report confirmed that Dr Sheard had
expressed his objection to surgical operations at the shelter.[24] It was not
clear whether the board's earlier resolution of 'utmost confidence' in
the medical staff performing surgery was reversed. However, that such

an enquiry took place shows that to the society the medical health officer represented an important authority, one whose opinion on the operation of the shelter mattered. What happened in 1902 when the shelter was moved to a new location was another example of the medical health officer's power over the society. In planning alterations to an existing building to suit the needs of the shelter, the society had to involve the medical health officer so that quarantine could be easily put in place. The society instructed its architect to confer with the medical health officer. According to the architect's report, he consulted with the medical health officer and prepared alterations to the plan of the basement in such a way that they 'would obviate the quarantine difficulty.'[25]

The strength of the regulatory muscles of the medical health officer, along with other city branches, such as the city relief officer and the staff inspector of police, was painfully felt by the society in an incident in 1901. Instructed by the city board of control, Dr Sheard, the medical health officer, Mr Edward Taylor, the city relief officer, and the staff inspector of police jointly prepared a report on the work of the Toronto Children's Aid Society. The report drew very negative conclusions about the management of the society. Acting on that report, the board of control notified the society that it had reduced the funding to the society.[26] The board of the society was shocked by the disastrous report and the action of the board of control. It moved quickly to prepare a formal statement denouncing the report as 'the most impish' of documents, reflecting total ignorance of the working of the society. The society charged that 'it purport[ed] to be a report after investigation, but [bore] evidence of being a report of foregone conclusions. No officers of the Society was notified of the investigation or information asked of anyone except the Matron at the Shelter.' The board 'indignantly resent[ed] the imputation put upon it by [the report] and regret[ed] the great injury the good work of the Society [was] likely to sustain by [the report] and the publicity given to it.'[27] Macdonald went on to request an interview with the city board of control. Apparently, the board of control was not convinced by the society's arguments; worse, it made even more charges against the society at the meeting with the society. In June 1901, the society decided to form an ad hoc committee to conduct an investigation of all matters connected with the charges made in the devastating report, as well as the fresh charges made by the board of control. This probably could be interpreted as a partial concession on the part of the society. There was no further mention of this incident in the society's records until about six months later. In

January 1902, the special committee presented its report to the board, following which some re-arrangement of the staff at the Shelter took place.[28] This incident demonstrates the extent of the power the city had over the society, as well as the higher status of medicine over social work.

In comparison with the city, the provincial Office of the Superintendent of Neglected and Dependent Children appeared to hold more power over the society, at least as defined by the child protection legislation. However, unlike the city, the Office of the Superintendent had very little leverage to put its legal power to practical use. Additionally, the appointment of Kelso to the position of superintendent in 1893, which he retained for four decades until 1934, did not help to make the society willing to accept direction from the provincial Office of Superintendent. The relation between the society and the provincial Office of Superintendent was distant at best and outright hostile during the 1910s and 1920s. Disputes often played out with Kelso raising problems with the work of the society. The issue of 'adoption by resolution' was one example. In the first few years, the society had the practice of taking guardianship of children (or in other words making a child ward of the society)[29] through resolution of the board instead of through court procedures. For example, the minutes of 15 February 1894 recorded the following resolution:

> Board takes guardianship of [Fred B., Harry, William G., Laura W., & Norman N.].
> Moved by C.J. Atkinson, seconded by R.S. Baird. That whereas the following named children, viz
> Fred B., aged 7 ...
> Have been deserted by their respective parents and are now or have been maintained by the Children's Aid Society of Toronto. Resolved that pursuant to Section 17 (1) of the Act for the Prevention of Cruelty to and Better Protection of Children, that the said Children shall from this date – the 15th day of February 1894 – until they reach the age of 21 years be under the control of the said Children's Aid Society.[30]

In December 1894 the society received a letter from Kelso claiming that the adoption of children by resolution of the board was illegal.[31] After some internal discussion and consultation with the society's lawyer, the board continued with this practice for some time despite Kelso's objection. For example, the minutes of the board show that as late as

May 1896 children were still made wards of the society by resolution of the board.[32] Although the minutes do not document such practice of adoption by resolution of the board in later years, it seems that as late as in 1912 this was still an issue between Kelso and the society.[33] The dismissive attitude of the society towards Kelso was also blatantly clear in many other confrontations. It was obvious that Kelso lacked the leverage to make the society listen to or even consider his opinions, because the society did not receive any funds from the provincial government. In February 1906, Kelso informed the society that he had recommended to the provincial government that a grant at the same rate as the orphanages', namely two cents per day for each inmate at the shelter, be given to the society. At the board meeting, Macdonald commented that the granting of such aid would involve 'undesirable interference' with the society's work by government officials. He offered to draft a letter of reply declining the grant and was able to secure the board's support.[34]

Frustrated that he could not get the society to listen to him, Kelso felt compelled to resort to other power mechanisms, for example, the media, and attempted to embarrass the society into what he considered proper practices. As well, Kelso would build alliances with other organizations, such as the Woman's Christian Temperance Union (WCTU), and let them mount direct challenges against the society.

The dispute over conditions at the shelter and the detention room, which started in 1912 and carried on until 1916, is an example of the confrontation between Kelso and the society. Kelso had always been adamant about the 'proper' use of the shelter as he had originally envisioned it. In addition to cautioning against the shelter being abused by parents, as he did in the story of Emily referred to earlier, he also took issue with the society because he thought that children had been kept in the shelter for too long. In March 1912, he wrote a letter to the society about this concern. The secretary of the Toronto Children's Aid Society was instructed to reply to Kelso saying that 'the Society would be pleased if he would relieve us of the syphilis cases, and cases of mental defectives, that it is impossible to get [foster] homes for [sic].'[35] Having failed in making any difference in the situation at the shelter, in 1916 Kelso made his complaint to Mayor Church of the city of Toronto; it was then publicized in the newspapers. Among his seven charges, Kelso stated that 'the shelter has practically developed into an institution, and the necessity has almost arisen for another shelter to do the work originally contemplated.'[36] I will discuss this conflict in more detail in the next

chapter, because most of the allegations were actually about the conditions at the detention room. For now it will suffice to say that even with
the assistance of newspapers and the WCTU, Kelso was not successful in
compelling the society to do anything about the shelter and the detention room.

The Shelter as a Resource for Challenging Gendered Hierarchy

In addition to various effects of the existence of the shelter on relations
among the society, parents, and children, and relations between the
society and external authorities, the technology of the shelter also had a
bearing on the dynamics within the society. In this section I will first
discuss the uneven division of authority between men and women at the
shelter and in the society at large. Then, I will demonstrate how the
shelter was used as a resource by women, particularly the 'ladies' of
the board, to challenge the gendered hierarchy of the society.

The shelter was operated by a staff who reported to the shelter committee, which in turn worked under the board. In the first few years after
its opening, a matron was in charge of the shelter. The matron, who was
usually either a young single woman or a widow (at least one matron had
a daughter with her), was offered boarding in the same building as the
shelter, similar to arrangements in traditional residential care facilities.[37]
According to the Children's Shelter Rules and Regulations in 1892, the
matron conducted religious services morning and evening. She en-
sured that 'the utmost cleanliness' was observed, not only for the
house and its furnishings, but also for children and their clothing. She
was responsible for keeping a written record of the children, including
their names, ages, parents, causes of neglect or destitution, and any
other remarks that might be of interest. When the position of the
superintendent was created several years later, the matron's authority
was significantly reduced. Her duties were confined to female children
and the supervision of domestic work in the shelter, that is, cooking,
laundry, and pressing.

Shelter superintendent was a position reserved for men only. The
superintendent was the executive officer in the shelter. He resided in
separate quarters of the shelter building, sometimes with his family. He
assumed 'full charge and control' of the shelter under the board and the
shelter committee. His main duties included removing children to and
from the court, passing through every part of the shelter and seeing
every child daily (accompanied by the matron when visiting female

children), carefully inspecting the locks on doors, windows, gratings, chimneys, and any other openings regularly so as to prevent escapes, and keeping a variety of records on children, daily occurrences, donations, visitors, requisitions, and accounts.[38] There is little information on the relationship between the matron and the superintendent. Evidence about other similar situations, such as at the Toronto Newsboys' Home, suggests that there could have been struggles over the division of authority. For example, in his diary, Kelso made note of a discussion regarding friction between the superintendent of the Newsboys' Home and the matron at a board meeting. On that occasion, Kelso 'advocated strongly the placing of all authority in the hands of the [superintendent and the] reducing the position of matron to that of working housekeeping [sic].' His view was adopted by the board of directors of the Newsboy's Home.[39]

In addition to the superintendent and the matron, the staff of the shelter also included a visiting physician, who was usually a member of the board, a nurse or nurse assistant, a teacher assigned to the shelter by the school board, a porter, and a cook.

A major reorganization of the staff occurred in 1906, which resulted in the hiring of couples as superintendent and lady superintendent of the shelter; their presence made the shelter resemble a heterosexual nuclear family. This reorganization seems to have been triggered by the resignation of the secretary of the society. In July 1906, at initiative of two female members of the board, a decision was made to ask the long-serving secretary, Mr J. Stuart Coleman, to tender his resignation.[40] After his resignation, the office of secretary was discontinued. A new position of 'inspector and superintendent of the shelter' was created with full charge of the working staff of the society. The lady superintendent, who was the wife of inspector and superintendent, had authority over general caring work in the shelter. Additionally, a male clerk would assist the inspector and superintendent with clerical work; a housekeeper and a cook would perform the actual housekeeping activities under the oversight of the lady superintendent.

These two positions were filled briefly by Mr and Mrs Lee Williams and then by Mr and Mrs William Duncan until the end of the period discussed in this book. The transformation of the position of shelter matron to the lady superintendent had mixed implications for women. When she was hired as the lady superintendent, Mrs Duncan enjoyed many professional development opportunities, unlike previous matrons. For example, in the summer of 1909 she was sent to visit the National Society for the Prevention of Cruelty to Children and the Ragged School in London, England. Again in 1915, she and her husband attended the National Conference of Charities and Corrections at Baltimore, Maryland, and visited various institutions in Philadelphia and New York. On both occasions, she was asked to address the board on her return.[41] Her capacity for learning about similar lines of work in other places and making connections to the society's own work, rather than her maternal qualities alone, was appreciated by the board. However, if the position of lady superintendent provided women like Mrs Duncan an opportunity to turn themselves into professionals with more power and prestige, it also restrictively attached their career development to marriage. Unlike the matron, who had been hired as an individual, the lady superintendent depended on her husband for her employment.

The superintendent reported to the shelter committee, which in turn brought to the board matters relevant to the operation of the shelter. The matron and later the lady superintendent reported on their work through the female members of the shelter committee. Like the shelter staff, the shelter committee was also concerned with the operation in both the shelter and the detention room. At the beginning, the shelter committee consisted of about twelve members, which increased to around twenty over the years. The shelter committee was one of only two committees that included female members, comparable to a House of Industry's ladies committee, which took care of children.[42] Others, such as the legislation committee and the finance committee consisted of male members only, as did ad hoc committees such as the shelter property committee, which was set up to look into possible purchase of a property for a shelter,[43] and the ad hoc committee that considered a complaint of the secretary regarding the agent's inefficiency.[44] The shelter committee was chaired by a male member for most of the period concerned. Given the connection between child saving and criminal justice, it was not surprising that one of earliest chairmen of the shelter committee was James Massie, warden of the Central Prison.[45] The 'ladies' of the board were by default members of the shelter committee.[46] Usually the number of women was equal to or slightly higher than the number of male members. Many women were wives of board members or other prominent, powerful, and wealthy men. Usually only five or six people would attend the monthly meetings; other than the chairman, most of those who attended meetings were women. During each meeting, the superintendent gave a report on the operation of the shelter in the previous month, such as the number of admissions and discharges, the number of children in the shelter on the last day of the month, the total number of child-days in the shelter, itemized expenses, and also per capita expenses. The superintendent might raise emerging issues to the shelter committee. For example, in the meeting on 14 May 1903, the superintendent asked for the shelter committee's opinion about the visiting of children by their parents and friends. The committee instructed that the arrangement for visiting should remain the same, namely, that visiting would be allowed each Wednesday from 3:00 to 5:00 in the afternoon, but it also granted the superintendent discretion in some special cases. In the same meeting, the superintendent also called attention to the necessity of sodding the yard and the need for sheets, towels, and cupboards for storing the clothes worn by children when they entered the shelter.[47]

Like many other women involved in various aspects of social and moral reform in urban Canada around the turn of the twentieth century, women on the board of the Toronto Children's Aid Society generally identified with 'maternal feminism,' in that they believed in the right of women to an increased public role because of their special nurturing talents in the redemption of 'mankind.'[48] Operating in a male-dominated organization, the activism of women in the Toronto Children's Aid Society took the form of expanding their share of authority in agenda-setting and decision-making, advocacy of better compensation and working conditions for female staff, and advocacy of what they believed were in the interests of girls in the shelter and the detention room. The minutes of board meetings and shelter committee meetings provide ample evidence of such activism. At board meetings, female members of the shelter committee regularly put forward motions for consideration of an increase in the salary of the matron and other female staff of the society, such as the 'lady visitors' to families that came to the attention of the society.[49] Their concern with the interests of the female staff was again evident when in 1912 Mrs Rutter and Mrs Van Norman proposed that a telephone be installed on the second floor of the shelter building for the convenience of the lady superintendent.[50]

Other than being advocates for female employees of the society on some occasions, female board members attempted to manoeuvre their way into the mainstream business of the society. For example, in 1907 the board decided to form a deputation to persuade the board of control of the city to visit the shelter and to judge for themselves the work done by the society, in view of getting additional financial support from the city. Mrs Sheppard supported the motion, but also suggested that ladies be part of the deputation.[51] The shelter proved to be a very useful and convenient arena for these women to make themselves part of the decision-making process. Assertion on the part of women often took the form of advocacy for children in the shelter and detention room, mirroring the general pattern of Victorian women getting involved in social and moral reform in the name of children.[52] For example, in April 1905, Mrs Rutter and Mrs Sheppard put forward a motion that the superintendent of the shelter be instructed by the board to provide milk for the children at tea.[53] Another case in point concerned female members' visits to the shelter. Female members of the board, in their function as members of the shelter committee, started visiting the shelter regularly very early on.[54] For about two decades, these visits seem to have been a formality and not to have had any impact on how the shelter was operated. In 1917, however, soon after a well-publicized row with Kelso over the latter's allegation of scandalous conditions at the shelter and the detention room, Mrs Rutter proposed that the 'ladies' of the board make a report to the board about their business visits to the shelter. This provided a formal and effective channel for women's opinions to be heard at the board meetings.[55] The subsequent months witnessed a series of recommendations put forward by women to the rest of the board, that is, the male members. For example, in March 1917, Mrs Rutter and Mrs McClelland presented the report of their inspection of the shelter and the detention room, which also contained recommendations regarding the two facilities.[56] In May 1917, Mrs Lillie presented the ladies' report, which raised the need for clothes and boots for the children, noted 'the brightness of the Shelter [in comparison] to the gloom of the Detention Home,' and suggested that a few pictures be obtained for the latter place.[57] A few months later, Mrs Jarvis and Mrs Hincks emphasized in their report that a kindergarten class should be started in the shelter school and suggested that the Board of Education be approached on the matter.[58]

In November 1917, Dr Millman, who was chairman of the shelter committee at the time, proposed that the shelter committee be composed solely of the 'lady members' of the board.[59] It is probably sound to speculate that this was connected to women's agitation for various changes in the shelter in the preceding months. When Dr Millman's proposal was adopted, the ladies reorganized the shelter committee in an earnest way. The reformed committee had its first meeting in January 1918. Mrs Rutter was elected the president of the committee, Mrs Lovering the vice-president, Mrs Bullock the treasurer, and Mrs Hincks the secretary.[60] After the change to an all-female committee, it started to give written reports to the board. As well, instead of meeting once a month, the new committee decided to meet twice a month at the shelter or detention home 'in order to be able to go through these buildings, and keep in close touch with conditions and needs there.'[61] True to this goal, in the subsequent months the shelter committee brought a range of everyday difficulties or inadequacies at the shelter and the detention home to the attention of the board and pressured the board to take prompt action. For example, in June 1918, the shelter committee informed the board that it had voted unanimously that the children in the shelter and the detention home should be given butter at least once a day, as it was thought that fat of some kind was essential to their health.[62] The shelter committee was also very concerned with issues concerning older girls. In its report dated 17 September 1918, it stated that the committee spent a morning discussing with Mrs Duncan, the lady superintendent, the 'welfare and interests of the older girls who come into the Shelter. It was felt that they were of an age at which they should be more encouraged to take pride in their personal appearance and manners.' The ladies made three recommendations in this regard:

1 That we attempt to clothe these girls better, and to make them more careful of their clothes;
2 That six lockers be built for the six oldest girls ... so that [they] may feel that they have a place of their own for their personal belongings.
3 That plated forks and spoons be bought for these girls to replace the awkward utensils now in use.[63]

The female members' emphasis on keeping in close touch with day-to-day operations was again apparent when on 20 February 1919, Mrs Lovering and Mrs Ryrie proposed that the society employ and pay 'our own visitors for own foster homes, as we feel that we should be in close touch with the children after they leave the Shelter.'[64]

The most assertive actions of the lady members came in October 1919 when the shelter committee placed a number of 'findings' before the board. According to the report, these 'findings' resulted from a discussion at length about what reforms were necessary for the 'betterment of conditions at the Shelter.' The tone of the overall report was sternly critical. For example, the first finding was: 'The accommodation in the present building is utterly inadequate, the equipment not at all what it should be nor does it seem wise to attempt to remodel the premises.' Related to this was the opinion that 'an *entirely new* building with modern appliances is sorely needed' (original emphasis), which should have enough space so that the office staff could, for example, conduct an interview with some privacy, and juvenile delinquent girls could be segregated from other girls. The shelter committee found that 'the condition of things is most discouraging and disheartening and has lasted long enough.' It pointed out that it had made suggestions of providing older girls with lockers for their privacy in September 1918, which however, had not been acted upon more than a year later.[65] It raised the need for a room for teaching girls domestic science, and that the room should be equipped with modern appliances.

Another issue that women sharply criticized was the society's country property in Bronte. The Bronte property had been purchased to be used as a cottage for taking the children of poor urban families, and sometimes their mothers, to the country for a few weeks in the summer. As the minutes of the board show, Macdonald had found inspiration for this line of work from New York societies when he visited them in 1911.[66] The purchase of the property in Bronte was more based on the notion of the romance of the country than on practical considerations. It was a questionable decision; one could argue, as women of the board did, that it would have made more sense to use the society's limited resources to finance the badly needed renovation of the shelter and the detention room. The shelter committee's report downright stated that 'the Bronte property is a bill of expense.' The report went on to say in direct terms that after full deliberation the committee recommended the disposal of the Bronte property and also of the 229 Simcoe Street property that had housed the shelter since 1902. They recommended that 'a suitable site be secured, and a building such as is required, in which to carry on the work which has so tremendously grown, to be erected. And *that* at the very earliest possible moment' (original emphasis).[67]

These findings and recommendations were referred to the all-male finance committee. Given the formality of the report from the shelter committee, the finance committee produced a formally written item-by-item response. The finance committee conceded that the shelter building was not an up-to-date one for the purpose of the society's work, but thought that it was not altogether inadequate. It suggested that it would be difficult to buy a new building because of the high cost of wages and building materials. The committee also stated that that time might not be an advantageous one to offer the property for sale, but it promised to consider the proposal carefully. In response to the declared need of a room for domestic science, the finance committee replied that 'under present conditions there is no space in the building for teaching the girls domestic science. The girls who are old enough and who are in the kitchen are taught by the cook what is possible under the circumstances.'[68]

Despite the finance committee's attempt to brush off the issue, the all-female shelter committee was determined to arrange formal domestic science education for the girls at the shelter. This was but one example which showed that the all-female shelter committee was particularly concerned with the girls at the shelter. Although the interests of the girls were certainly defined from the perspective of the 'ladies' with class and gender overtones, it was unmistakable that the 'ladies' tried hard, often against the male members of the board, to guard the girls' perceived interests. In the instance of arranging formal domestic science education for the girls, against the finance committee's suggestion that all that could be done had been done, the 'ladies' persuaded the board to ask lady superintendent to arrange with the nurses to take the girls to the nearest domestic science classes held in the public schools.[69] In the subsequent months, female members of the board persisted on this matter. In January 1920, Mrs Bullock was deputed to look into the matter and found that a nearby school was equipped with a domestic science plant and an 'instructress' held classes every day. She reported that it was only necessary to arrange for a convenient time for the girls in the shelter to attend.[70] Finally, in February of the same year, it was reported that arrangements for the shelter girls to take such lessons had been made.[71]

Other issues on which the all-female shelter committee disputed with male members of the board included an argument about where to have the board's monthly meeting. This argument is another example of gendered contestation within the board; furthermore, it also reveals the disparity between different approaches to child-saving work. From as early as in 1892, when Macdonald was elected president of the society, the board's monthly meetings had been held in the building of the Confederation Life Association Company where he was the managing director, which was quite a distance from the shelter. The all-female shelter committee gradually formed the view that the meetings should be held in the society's building where the shelter was located, not in the Confederation Life building. Although the society's own building was more cramped, humble, and generally not as pleasant as the Confederation Life's boardroom, these women thought it was more important to be close to where actual work took place. Thus, on 19 Febrary 1920, Mrs

Hincks, secretary of the shelter committee communicated a resolution of the committee to the board that 'all monthly meetings [of the board] be held in future at the Society's Building 229 Simcoe St.' In the discussion Mr Campbell proposed to have at least four quarterly meetings at the shelter. In the end, a compromise was reached: The meetings would be held alternatively at the shelter and in the boardroom of the Confederation Life Association Company.[72]

The society women's use of the shelter to forge their way exemplified the paradox of the maternal feminists' claim to power on the basis of their reproductive and nurturing capacities. The 'ladies' of the board made themselves relevant to the operation of the society by taking charge of the 'domestic' caring work at the shelter. By doing so, however, they also confined themselves to subordinate roles.

In this chapter, I have shown that the shelter constituted a web of relations between the society, parents, and children. The existence of the shelter also shaped relations within the society. Further, I have sketched a few major external sources of constraint that the society had to cope with largely because of the existence of the shelter. Starting in the 1930s, the shelter was gradually reduced to a very minor role. The reluctance to provide any form of collective residential care is such that today no equivalent of the shelter any longer exists in the child-protection system. Children who are considered to need apprehension because of abuse and neglect, even in emergency situations, are mostly placed in community homes[73] or foster homes.[74] The shelter, as it existed in the early history of the Toronto Children's Aid Society, was not without its limitations. Nonetheless, for families who were not able to care for their children for various reasons, it was a facility that could be made to work for them. That possibility was also lost with the elimination of the shelter.

The configuration of regulatory mechanisms outlined in this chapter shifted significantly over the course of the twentieth century, reflecting changes in the structure of child-protection work. Shifts in power relations usually come in tandem with changes to funding formulae. First, most funding of the Toronto Children's Aid Society ceased to be tied to the operation of the shelter, but was allotted to case work. As well, since the 1920s the Government of Ontario has gradually become more and more involved in financing the operation of the society. In 1998, the provincial government introduced a new funding framework in which it alone provides 100 per cent funding of all children's aid societies in the province.[75] This move stood out amidst the general neo-liberal trend of downloading financial responsibilities to municipalities in the areas of social policy and social services. If in the past the society found itself constrained by the city and its various branches because it partially relied on the city's grants for running its shelter, the funding and regulatory scheme at the turn of the twenty-first century suggests that the society may find the province's monopolized regulation even more single-minded and confining.

Knowledge is another important factor in the configuration of relations between the Children's Aid Society and external authorities. In its early history, the shelter and its regular outbreaks of infectious diseases apparently subjected the society to the authority of the city's medical health officer. In a similar vein, the current focus on child deaths elevates the importance of agencies like the coroner's office and privileges its views of child abuse and neglect issues.

Chapter 6

The Detention Room: A Jail under Children's Aid Auspices?

In Toronto, the detention room[1] was opened in 1894 as a custody facility for juvenile delinquents who were on arrest or on remand from the court. As a custody facility exclusively for children, the detention room resembled the reformatories and industrial schools established three or four decades earlier, in that it was intended to implement the principle of separating juvenile delinquents from adult criminals. Reformatories and industrial schools segregated children from adults after court processes; detention rooms segregated them prior to and during court hearings.

When the Toronto city council was pressured by child welfare lobbyists to find a way to separate children from adult criminals in custody awaiting trial the first possibility that was considered was to renovate part of the No. 1 Police Station at 8 Court Street.[2] When the property committee of the city council expunged from their estimates an item of $600 to provide this proposed separate accommodation at No. 1 Police Station, the Toronto Children's Aid Society's board decided that action needed to be taken to persuade city council to take the item back into their estimates. The Reverend J.E. Starr, Dr Harley Smith, and the secretary were requested by the board to wait upon the executive committee of the city council.[3] While the lobbying was going on, the society already had at least one juvenile delinquent brought to its shelter. In April 1892, Lizzie Cornwall had been arrested for 'supposed attempted larceny.' According to the society's records, she was taken out of the hands of a policeman and brought to the shelter by an unidentified Miss Hamilton, who obviously thought that the child savers were more appropriate than the police in dealing with juvenile delinquents. Lizzie was found in a terribly filthy condition. Apparently she was kept in the shelter with other children overnight. The next day, her parents, who were both intoxicated, came to the shelter bearing an order for Lizzie from Staff Inspector Archibald. People at the shelter tried to reason with them about their treatment of the child, but the parents said that her filthy state was her own fault. Even though the society did not believe that was the case, Lizzie was released to her parents.[4]

Several months later, in early October 1892, the Toronto Children's Aid Society learnt from the chief constable that nothing had yet been done towards constructing separate rooms for children at the police station, although at the same time the mayor informed them that he had asked Commissioner Coatsworth to look into matters.[5] Less than two weeks later, a letter from the mayor stated that an architect had been authorized alterations of No. 1 Police Station to provide separate facilities for children in detention there.[6] Despite that, a satisfactory solution apparently was still elusive. In November 1893, Edward Jones, nine years old, was taken out of the Police Court dock, where he had been charged with larceny, and taken to the shelter. There is not enough information to know what exactly happened to him, but the society's frustration with the situation is apparent from the note, which read 'for want of place of safety to detain him, can do nothing.'[7]

In early 1894 the Toronto Children's Aid Society agreed to offer the basement of its shelter as a detention room, out of sympathy for the desperate situation. For nearly three decades the society operated the detention room for the city, until in 1920 the city reluctantly took over the operation on the society's insistence. Despite the fact that the Toronto Children's Aid Society's involvement in the operation of the detention room began as an arrangement of convenience, and an act of charity on the part of the society, it became generally accepted as a logical and practical model. For example, at the tenth Canadian Conference of Charities and Correction held in Toronto in 1909, W.L. Scott, the president of the Ottawa Children's Aid Society and a leader in the juvenile correction system reform, urged the establishment of separate detention homes for juvenile delinquents in order to meet the conditions for implementation of the Juvenile Delinquents Act passed in the previous year. He advised that one way to easily meet the need for detention homes could be to use existing children's shelters operated by Children's Aid Societies.[8] This part of the intertwined history of child saving and juvenile justice has not been examined in the existing literature in either social work or criminology. By focusing on the operation of the detention room, this chapter contributes to an understanding of the crime-prevention objectives of child saving in Toronto, as well as of the emergence of the 'child welfare approach' in juvenile justice. It also serves to show the historical specificity of the focus of current child protection practices on innocent young children.

Throughout the period examined, despite some leading opinion favouring locating detention rooms at children's aid societies, the Toronto Children's Aid Society was ambivalent, if not regretful, about its involvement in the operation of the detention room. It maintained its stance that 'while the Children's Aid Society had great sympathy in the work of caring for the Juvenile Delinquents, they were not bound to do the work that should be done by the City.'[9] The society's sympathy reached its end when the city repeatedly declined to assume its financial responsibility for juvenile delinquents as defined in child-protection legislation. In practice, the limits of the society's sympathy towards juvenile delinquents were manifested in the much poorer conditions at the detention room in comparison with those in the shelter, its ultimatums to the city to take over the operation after failed attempts to get the city to pay the expenses, and, in the end, the closing of the detention room altogether in 1920. Partly, this was attributable to legislative definition of the city's responsibility for juvenile delinquents. However, it should also be pointed out that another factor was the child-savers' view that juvenile delinquents were more damaged and, thus, morally inferior to 'Shelter children.' The history of the detention room is therefore an illustration that the child-savers' compassion was proportionate to perceived degrees of innocence of the children involved.

The first section of this chapter describes the conflicts between the Toronto Children's Aid Society and the city, and to some extent the provincial government, over financial responsibility for the detention room. It shows that the state was reluctant to provide for whatever could be left to the voluntary sector. It also shows that as the years passed the Toronto Children's Aid Society became less committed to direct involvement with juvenile delinquents, who were seen as less deserving than more innocent abused and neglected children who had not yet committed criminal acts. The second section examines day-to-day operations at the detention room while it was a part of the Toronto Children's Aid Society. The initial vision of the detention room was a place 'in the hands of enthusiastic people,' where juvenile delinquents were to be treated as erring children, not criminals, where they would be separated from each other, and where individualized guidance and constant, varied occupation of an interesting character were to be the main criteria of work.[10]

Towards the end of the period examined in this book, in addition to the above the detention room was increasingly seen as an 'observation centre' to assist the Juvenile Court judge to make an intelligent disposal of the case. It will become clear in the following pages that it was only in the last two or three years of the period examined that the detention room came remotely close to these visions. The gulf between realities and the ideals of careful segregation, correction, and observation preoccupied idealistic critics like Kelso and haunted those who were responsible for running the place, the staff and board members of the Toronto Children's Aid Society.

Sympathy within Limits

Within the Toronto Children's Aid Society, the detention room was the poor cousin of the shelter. It was an operation undesired by either the city or the society. To the city, it was an unnecessary bill of expense. Even though provincial child-protection laws stipulated that it was the responsibility of municipalities to provide detention rooms, this duty was not taken seriously by either the city or the provincial government. To the Toronto Children's Aid Society, the detention room was a less-deserving cause than saving other, less-damaged children. The escalation of the society's involvement with the detention room was primarily the result of the pressure of the situation. As an emergency solution to the frustrating lack of progress in opening an exclusive custody facility on the part of the city, the society offered its space and staff. But the board of the society never accepted that the operation of the detention room was a voluntary work of charity on their part, at least not totally. The society had always expected the city to share part of the expenses of the detention room. Conflict arose when the city was unwilling to see matters in this light and refused to acknowledge its responsibility.

The sheer number of juvenile delinquents in custody further challenged the society's willingness to operate the detention room. According to its records, from the very beginning of the society, juvenile offenders were frequently put into its custody.[11] Through most of the period when the detention room was housed in the shelter, the number of juvenile delinquents kept increasing, and they generally accounted for one-third to one-half of all children in the building. The operation of the detention room was to a large extent characterized by a chronic lack of space, repeated attempts by the staff to draw attention to the problem, and the ever-worse situation resulting from the reluctance of both the Toronto Children's Aid Society and the city of Toronto to contribute funds.

As early as in 1906, the pressure of the number of juvenile delinquents led to consideration of getting increased accommodation for the 'prisoners.'[12] At a board meeting, Macdonald suggested that this matter be left to a meeting of the male members of the board.[13] There is no evidence that anyone suggested any concrete solution to the problem. In October 1907, it was brought up again that the shelter and the detention room, especially the latter, were very crowded. An unusual number of cases had been received from the Police Court and the detention room, which was but a basement room, at one time held twenty-one juvenile offenders.[14] A suggestion was put forward to build an addition to the shelter. Then a discussion arose as to how to raise funds for the proposed addition. It was thought that the city should help the society, because the number of juvenile delinquents had increased so much of late. Subsequently, a committee of male members was appointed to wait on the board of control of the city to ask that they supply the society with $6,500 as half of the cost of the proposed additions. The board also decided to see the police commissioners to get their sympathy and recommendation to the city. The subsequent report on the interviews with the city treasurer and the board of police commissioners stated that all were quite in sympathy with the proposal.[15] The matter was carried over to 1908. In a board meeting in May 1908, Alderman J.J. Graham, a board member and a former inspector of the society, spoke about the application for the grant for building an addition to the shelter. According to him, the city board of control was trying to arrange an increased grant of $6,500 as a special charity grant.[16] Obviously, the city was avoiding establishing its long-term responsibility for the expenses of housing juvenile delinquents.

The problem persisted and when it was brought up again in 1913, some members of the board of the Toronto Children's Aid Society started to consider giving up its responsibility for juvenile delinquents. The shelter committee reported that the month of April held the record since the inception of the society, having the highest number of children ever in custody, averaging about sixty-three. Out of these children, twenty were juvenile delinquents, who were confined to the detention room in the basement. The chronic crowding in the detention room and pressure on the staff, who also had to deal with the increasing number of children at the shelter prompted Dr Millman, the chairman of the shelter committee, to suggest that the society ask the city to provide accommodation itself for the juvenile delinquents held in the detention room. After some consideration, it was thought that on account of the state of general financial stress then, the time did not appear opportune to ask the city to do that.[17] However, the idea was not given up and was raised again by the board at a meeting with Judge Edward W. Boyd of the Juvenile Court in November 1914. According to the minutes of the board, Judge Boyd concurred with the society in approaching the city and urging obtaining or erecting a building for a proper detention home for juvenile delinquents.[18] Apparently, all these efforts were of no avail. Much to the dismay of the Toronto Children's Aid Society, the proposal was simply dismissed by the city, which had been unhappy about the increased expenses incurred by the new ways of handling juvenile delinquency, for example, investigation, separate custody, and supervision.

In October 1915, the need for additional room for juvenile delinquents was raised yet again with even more urgency, largely because of the greater number of remands that Judge Boyd ordered in comparison to his predecessor Commissioner Starr. Dr Hincks, a well-known mental health specialist who joined the board in 1915,[19] spoke at the board meeting with regard to the inadequate housing of the juvenile delinquents coming from the Juvenile Court. He reported that sometimes as many as twenty-two were in the detention room, which had only one bath tub. He spoke of 'their conditions physically, mentally, and morally, strongly emphasizing the latter.' As a partial remedy, Hincks offered the use of the central YMCA shower baths and gymnasium. Another thought raised at the meeting was to add another storey over the schoolroom. Later on, however, the board decided to rent a house in the neighbourhood.[20] In November, the next house south of the shelter was looked into by a committee. According to the committee, it could be made suitable with some alterations. The board decided to go before the board of control and made it clear that while the society had great sympathy in the work of caring for the juvenile delinquents, it was not obliged do the work that should be done by the city.[21] This did not make the city change its mind. However, undeterred by the rejection, the society decided to appear before the board of control again and requested an immediate reply.[22] This time, an agreement was reached between the Toronto Children's Aid Society and the board of control that the society would rent a house for juvenile delinquents as a two-year temporary provision, at the end of which the society would no longer be responsible for detention work.

In February 1916, the Toronto Children's Aid Society rented a house at 226 Simcoe Street for juvenile delinquents entirely at its own expense, with a rent of $45 per month and $1,750 spent on alterations and sanitary improvements.[23] Of twelve rooms in the house, four were designated as sleeping rooms for juvenile delinquents, with four or five cots in each.[24] Most of the rest of the house was used as the society's offices. From then on, the detention room became the detention home. However, even the newly rented house did not seem sufficient to cope with the number of juvenile delinquents staying in the detention home. In 1917, the society sought to cut down, or more realistically to postpone, the flow of at least some juvenile delinquents to the detention home. The society went to see the Chief of Police, Colonel Grasett, and tried to persuade him that many children charged with theft, disorderly conduct, truancy, or trespassing did not need to be brought to the detention home. In the majority of cases they might be summoned to appear at the Juvenile Court instead of being arrested. In reply Colonel Grasett promised to give due consideration to the matter.[25] This certainly compromised the belief that juvenile delinquents should be held in custody and observed in order to find out what was wrong with their lives.

In late 1918, several months past the deadline of February to which the city had agreed, there was still no sign that the city was willing to either take over the detention home or to pay the Toronto Children's Aid Society for its expenses. In September 1918, the board decided to appoint a committee to present the financial standing of the society to the mayor privately, or to the board of control, emphasizing especially the necessity of the city paying the expenses of running the detention home.[26]

Within the board of the Toronto Children's Aid Society, there was increasing internal pressure from others on Macdonald, who seemed to take a softer position on this issue. At a board meeting, Mr Van Norman pursued the issue by asking if the matter of the takeover of the detention home by the city had been determined. Macdonald replied that he expected the mayor to be in the chair at the society's twenty-seventh annual meeting, and special prominence would be given the matter in the report.[27] Indeed at the annual meeting of the society, Macdonald publicly stated that the responsibility for dealing with juvenile delinquents must rest with the city, and he criticized the city for not taking it up. Controller Robbins, who was at the time on the board of the society and was chairing the annual meeting in place of the mayor, expressed his sympathy and promised to use his influence to have a grant made by the city. However, Hon. Mr McPherson, the provincial secretary, took a different position. He counselled the members not to be too severe in their criticism of the city council, which had many financial burdens and problems to meet. He continued to say that it would be a matter for regret if the society should decide to abdicate its functions and place the affairs of the organization into other hands.[28]

Without any sign of the city taking the matter seriously, in December 1918 the Toronto Children's Aid Society board attended a city council meeting. It announced to the council the policy of the society that it would not carry on the detention home after 31 March 1919, and that the whole expense after that date was to be borne by the municipality. Despite its firm stance on the timeframe, the society still offered to cooperate with the city in running the detention home until the end of March 1919.[29] The city reacted with silence. This lack of response from the city made it necessary for Macdonald to again go before the board of control in January 1919. He expressed his wish that the whole of the society's board attend, especially the 'ladies.' Many female members of the board, like Mrs Rutter, argued vehemently that the work of the detention home should not be undertaken by the society. The city's indifference to this matter was evident; only with less than forty days away from 31 March 1919 did a letter from Mr E. Dickie, secretary of Toronto's social service commission, reach the board of the Toronto Children's Aid Society. The letter was not substantive and mainly inquired about the probable cost of a workable plan in connection with the detention home. Macdonald replied to the letter and made it clear that the society was not seeking to have charge of the detention home. It would only do so if no better means were available. Even if the society were to operate the detention home, it would only do so on condition that the city pay the entire cost.[30] The month of March passed, and the city took no action.

In April 1919, Macdonald was called on by representatives of the social service commission. At the meeting, he was asked if the Toronto Children's Aid Society would take on the detention home for the month of April, which he promised to do. Macdonald explained to the board later that he knew it was the wish of the board.[31] This turned out to be a promise that the board regretted; the agreement to run the detention home for the month of April resulted in the society being stuck with the detention home for another eleven months. In February 1920, a replay of 1919 would have taken place, had it not been for the determination of board members, particularly the female members, to put a clearcut end to the matter. In response to the society's second ultimatum that after 31st March 1920 the care of delinquent boys and girls would be discontinued by the society, Mr Chisholm, commissioner of property at city hall sent a letter to the Toronto Children's Aid Society, asking it to care for the juvenile delinquents during April. Most members of the board were insistent that the society not get into the same situation again. At a board meeting, Mrs Rutter moved, seconded by Dr Millman, that the society did not concur in extending the time to 30 April in caring for delinquent boys and girls. After some discussion Macdonald said that although the city had not given the society's work much consideration, it would be courteous to offer to carry on the detention home work until the end of April. In the end, however, opinion was in favour of Mrs Rutter's motion, and the chairman of the board so ruled – a rarity because the board seldom made decisions contradicting Macdonald's views. The Toronto Children's Aid Society informed the city of its firm position, and the detention home was finally taken over by a reluctant and annoyed City of Toronto.[32]

A Child Welfare Facility or a Jail?

This section turns to the daily operation of the detention room while it was under the auspices of the Toronto Children's Aid Society. The new system of governing juvenile delinquents, of which the detention room for children was a component, is often characterized as the 'child-welfare approach' in criminology literature.[33] However, an examination of day-to-day operations at the detention room suggests that in reality the child-welfare approach was not a singular way of doing things. It would be accurate to say that on the site of the detention room several modes of power coexisted – the old punitive and despotic tradition of dealing with 'infant criminals,' discipline based on the identity of juvenile delinquent, and pastoral power over 'erring children.' The very name of the place – 'detention room' and other prison terminology such as 'cell,' 'prisoners,' and 'criminals' were used frequently by the staff and board members of the Toronto Children's Aid Society. At the same time, other terms such as 'dormitory,' 'school-room,' 'juvenile delinquents,' and 'boys' and 'girls' were often used in an interchangeable way with the prison terminology. Different models of governance, however, did not just coexist relatively peacefully in language. Sometimes a model dominated practice no matter how diverse the language might be, and sometimes the clashes among different approaches developed into nasty fights.

For most of the period under examination, particularly the nearly two decades before the establishment of the Juvenile Court in 1911, the operation of the detention room inherited a great deal from the prison tradition. Let us start with a look of its architectural characteristics, which included the following: iron gratings on windows[34]; in the basement, two iron bar doors, one for the 'cell corridor' and one for the dormitory[35]; heavy fine-mesh wire screens on five outside windows facing University Avenue to prevent outsiders from handing anything to the juvenile delinquents[36]; on the ground floor, outside iron bars with ornamental tops on the lower half of the schoolroom windows to prevent escapes[37]; and strong wire guards on all windows of the house.[38]

These were all security measures put in place by the society for the detention room. Such physical aspects of a building, which were clearly designed as restraints, defined the despotic aspects of the relationship between the staff of the Toronto Children's Aid Society and juvenile delinquents. Custody at the detention room was in practice punitive confinement, without having the name. Before the establishment of the Juvenile Court in 1911, the detention room was actually used explicitly as a place to serve sentences. One common punishment given by the magistrates who acted as judges of the Children's Court in juvenile cases was the option of a fine or time. In one case in 1903, Donald Hough, age fourteen, was charged in the Police Court with theft for taking leather goods from a store. He was remanded twice and in the end 'committed to Shelter for 15 days.' Fifteen days later, another note in his entry read 'discharged, term having expired.'[39]

Using the prison practice of giving materiality to an identity, in 1907 the shelter committee of the Toronto Children's Aid Society suggested that uniforms be arranged for juvenile delinquents. The board accepted the suggestion and decided to leave the matter in the hands of the ladies. Soon after that, Mrs Lillie and Mrs Sheppard visited different clothiers looking for suits for boys coming from the Police Court. A month later, Sheppard reported to the board that she, along with Mrs Lillie, had arranged for the purchase of 'some cheap suits and pants' at Mr P. Jamieson for the delinquents coming from the Police Court.[40]

The disciplinary and pastoral-care aspects, which were fundamental to the original vision of the detention room, however, were sorely missing. Apparently children in the detention room were merely locked up, fed, and left idle. Not a single person was employed to attend to them. In

1911, an article titled 'The Shelter a Jail' appeared in the Toronto *Telegram.* Although it named the shelter, in fact, the criticism was aimed at the detention room. Within the Toronto Children's Aid Society, attention was first brought to the newspaper article at the meeting of the shelter committee on 9 November 1911. According to the minutes, members of the shelter committee felt that the article cast 'a slur, and [was] misleading as to our Shelter work in connection with Juvenile Offenders.' The matter was referred up to the board.[41] At the board meeting, less than a week later, discussion arose about the article. Some members of the board, if not all, felt that the criticism was not too far off the mark. Dr Smith suggested at the board meeting that the shelter committee secure a man specially to oversee those boys sent to the detention room from the Children's Court, so that their time might be 'profitably employed' while they were in the detention room.[42] In December 1911 the shelter committee formally recommended to the board to secure a man whose duty would be to oversee the delinquents during the day, give them exercise, and improve their tone while they were detained by the order of the magistrate.[43] However, a month later in January 1912, the shelter committee reported that the matter of appointing an additional man to oversee the juvenile delinquents during the daytime had been postponed for the present, owing to the probability that very few delinquents would be sent to the detention room by the new commissioner of the Juvenile Court, the Reverend J.E. Starr.[44] Indeed, Starr rarely remanded juvenile delinquents to the detention room. The number of children in the detention room, however, actually went up slightly in this period because of an increase in the stream of children arrested by the police.

At the end of this incident, even though the Toronto Children's Aid Society had opted not to hire a man to attend to the juvenile delinquents, it did make some minor attempts to improve the detention room. The boys in the detention room were supplied with a crokinole game and a set of dominoes, thanks to a suggestion from the shelter committee. As well, the society approached the YMCA and asked if they would interest themselves so far as to have some of their young men call for an hour in the evenings and speak to or entertain the boys,[45] which they agreed to. Later on the Big Sister and Big Brother associations joined in doing the same kind of work.[46]

For the Toronto Children's Aid Society, resorting to voluntary workers was probably a good way to give its detention work a 'human touch'[47] without increased expenses. However, the introduction of new personnel whose main function was to provide pastoral care meant that the configuration of power relations in the detention room changed. First, the society's relative autonomy was undermined as it put itself under the gaze of outsiders, who not only owed their loyalty to parties other than the society but were a new breed of personnel in social service. Second, even though the Big Sisters and Big Brothers were also authorities so far as the children were concerned, they were nevertheless different from the Children's Aid staff, such as the 'night-watchman.' The presence of Big Sisters and Big Brothers could work as a mechanism for children to exercise their agency, for example, by simply telling a Big Sister that she had been badly treated in the detention room. This was attested to by papers left by a Big Sister, Dorothy Eddis (later Dorothy Glen). The following is based on an examination of Eddis's notes.[48]

Eddis left some notes of her conversation with a couple of children, a conversation with a co-worker of the Big Brothers, and her observations of the operation of the detention room in general. Her notes were brief, but they provided a window for glimpsing how juvenile delinquents experienced their custody at the detention room, as seen through her eyes, and the eyes of children.

On a Friday, 14 July, Eddis wrote:

> [Florence D.] – when leaving the shelter said it was good to be out again – while she was in there she was not out-of-door [*sic*] in the yard once. She was there from the 6th – to the 14th – she also said the room they were in seemed dark & gloomy, and they were given no light in the evening.
>
> Said they were given no potatoes only Beans [*sic*] – very little meat – She is the first child in the shelter who has told me they had anything but bread & jam. She had butter while she was there & toast.
>
> In June [Albert S.] wept because he had to be sent back the shelter & when asked why said they didn't get enough to eat there. Mr. Maughan of the B.B. *told me of this.* [emphasis in original]
>
> [Florence D.]. also had to get up at 6.30 a.m. & wax floors before breakfast said she felt faint.[49]

Her criticisms of the detention home were summarized in another note titled 'Points I think objectionable,' from which we can learn something about the routines in the detention room:

> Boys left alone to play games & read!
> Boys of all ages sleeping in the same room.

Bed at 8 p.m.

Night-watchman an old prison guard.

Sits in the kitchen & if the boys make a noise goes in to see what they are doing – almost every 15 minutes.

Goes upstairs with them when they go to bed stay about 5 min. & then leaves them.

Boys minds allowed to stagnate, no external activities while there.

Food for tea[:] bread & jam ... [illegible] (for tea – bread & jam, thin milk, – prunes -)

Mrs M. thought a little girl of 13 yrs could easily do the work in there ... [illegible]

'She is a smart girl, but was a bit young to be with the boys'

'has been out from Eng. & working here as a slavery [*sic*]

placed by Mrs M. ...

No physical examination – Boys mix indiscriminately.

No provisions at present against vermin.[50]

It was not clear whether Eddis raised her criticisms with the board of the Toronto Children's Aid Society. There is evidence that some communication took place between Kelso and women involved in the detention room's work, probably including Eddis, and that some consensus was reached as to the urgent need to pressure the Toronto Children's Aid Society to improve the situation in the detention room. Evidence for this speculation mainly appeared in the publicized row in 1916 between the Toronto Children's Aid Society and Kelso, along with his ally the Local Council of Women, of which Eddis's Big Sister Association was a member at the time.

The conflict that exploded in March 1916 can actually be traced back to June 1915. At that time, Kelso wrote a letter to Macdonald to raise his concerns about the detention room, particularly, in his opinion, the undue length of time children were detained there. The secretary of the Toronto Children's Aid Society was instructed by the board to prepare a report 'bearing on cases of juvenile delinquents kept on remand at the Shelter from the juvenile court,' and also on the cases of neglected children cared for an inordinate length of time, to answer Kelso's letter. The report gave a detailed statement regarding every child in the shelter, the length of time spent in the shelter, and the causes of the society's inability to place neglected children elsewhere (by now mental defect was frequently cited as a cause). The society formed an ad hoc committee, which had a meeting with Kelso about this matter. Macdonald reported to the board in September that 'the meeting of the committee with Mr Kelso was one that would have good results, inasmuch that [sic] a better understanding of the difficulties of our work in sheltering mental defective children, and children who were physically unfit was shown to and evidently appreciated by Mr Kelso.'[51]

Meanwhile, within the Toronto Children's Aid Society, the board also felt the urgent need to improve the housing situation of the juvenile delinquents in the detention room, as was evident from the preceding discussion. In February 1916, the Toronto Children's Aid Society, together with the city, rented a house for detaining juvenile delinquents. The society was in the process of turning it into a detention home when Kelso made a scandal of the detention work undertaken by the society. Kelso submitted his complaints to the mayor of Toronto, asked for an investigation, and had them published in newspapers such as the *Star*. These caught the society by surprise, since they thought they had defused the tense situation with Kelso by tabling their difficulties in the work the previous year. From Kelso's perspective, nothing had been defused at all. Instead, he felt that he failed to persuade the society to improve their work. Frustrated that he did not have the necessary authority to bring about improvement, he chose the mayor and the board of control to receive his complaints, even though he was fully aware that he was taking an extreme approach. He later recollected that it was 'one of the hardest things I ever had to do, but Presdt. [sic] J.K. [Macdonald] stubborn – refused to improve the work – compelling me to go to extremes. Was denounced and ostracized but three yrs later drastic changes made. Robt. Mills appted [sic] Director and a large staff engaged. No credit ever given to J.J.K.[Kelso]'[52] The regulatory power that the current provincial government has over the operation of children's aid societies is something that Kelso could only have dreamt of having.

In Kelso's letter to the mayor, he confused the detention room with the shelter. He used the term 'shelter,' but it was clear that most of the time he was referring to the detention room for the juvenile delinquents. For example, he wrote that scandalous conditions prevailed in the children's shelter, providing details such as 'lads are locked in a basement room for a week or longer without ... being permitted to enjoy open air.'[53] There was clear evidence that the basement referred to was the detention room, and two possible explanations for this confusion. The first reason lay with the fact that Kelso wrote the letter mainly on the basis of second-hand information. It was apparent in Kelso's careful phrasing that he was referring to 'complaints [which were] frequently made by social workers' and matters of 'common report' in the city. The second and more important reason was that the word 'shelter' was indeed used to refer to the detention room by people ranging from the magistrates of the Children's Court, judges of the Juvenile Court, the Big Sisters and Big Brothers, and sometimes even within the Toronto Children's Aid Society itself. This lack of distinction had reflected the conceptual ambiguity of neglected children and juvenile delinquents and that they were kept in the same building. However, it should also be noted that around this time the Toronto Children's Aid Society began to refine the boundary of its work territory in relation to juvenile delinquents, particularly in its numerous appeals to the city. Thus, it was not a surprise that William Duncan, the then superintendent of the shelter at the Children's Aid Society, contended that 'the detention work and the work of the Children's Aid Society are quite distinct. Mr Kelso is mixing the two activities in his own mind.'[54]

Taken together there were three categories of charges laid by Kelso and his ally the Local Council of Women. The first category concerned the living conditions of the juvenile delinquents, for example the overcrowding in the detention room, the fact that the juvenile delinquents were not given any mattresses, and malnutrition among the children. Second, the management of the detention room was criticized for keeping juvenile delinquents for too long a period. It was asserted that this was a result of the Toronto Children's Aid Society's lack of efficiency in finding homes for children. The third category of complaints were aimed at the lack of proper care for the children, namely, that they had no occupation all day, no supervision, and no association of any 'elevating character,' and that the children were mixed indiscriminately.[55]

Upon hearing these charges, members of the staff, like Duncan, the superintendent, admitted that some of the charges were true, but added that the remedy did not lie in his hands. However, when the board of the Toronto Children's Aid Society, represented by Macdonald, presented its defence before the mayor and the board of control, it rebutted almost every charge that was made. Responding in relation to the undeniable fact that children did not have mattresses to sleep on, Macdonald rationalized it by arguing that 'no one with experience or common sense would dream of mattresses for boys brought in with clothing and heads often filled with vermin.'[56]

It was doubtful whether the society's rebuttals to charges related to the lack of proper care for children were completely truthful. For example, it asserted that 'the boys are taken out every day for fresh air and exercise, and have books and games, and a man detailed to be with them all day, to supervise, and help them.'[57] This, however, was not the experience that Florence D. shared with Eddis. The society's assertion was also contradicted by its 1912 board decision not to hire a man for exactly the same work with delinquent boys. The same applied to its denial of the charge of malnutrition. Eddis's notes cited earlier bear evidence of a lack in both quantity and quality of food in the detention room. As well, the fact that in 1918, two years after this incident, the shelter committee recommended that children in both the shelter and the detention home be given butter at least once a day 'as it was felt that fat of some kind was essential to their health,'[58] indirectly supports the validity of the charge laid in 1916. It would, however, be only fair to point out that the Toronto Children's Aid Society was not guilty of every charge. Some issues, like the inefficiency in placing children, were indeed largely beyond the control of the society. As Macdonald argued, it was simply impossible to place some shelter children; as for juvenile delinquents, the power to place them lay with the Juvenile Court Judge, not the society.[59]

During the confrontations between the Toronto Children's Aid Society and its critics, both sides threatened each other by calling for a judicial investigation. There is no evidence suggesting that this ever happened. In the end, the incident probably reinforced the determination of the Toronto Children's Aid Society to be rid of the detention room. Other than that, a few changes were noticeable in the operation of the detention room, as revealed in existing records. A couple of months after the incident, Dr Millman suggested that more games be supplied to the boys in the detention room.[60] A year later, lady members of the board, who did their routine visit to the shelter and detention home, suggested that a few pictures be obtained for the detention room, since it was so gloomy in comparison with the brightness of the shelter.[61] Lastly, in May 1917, Mr Willie was hired first as an assistant and then as the superintendent of the detention home. According to the minutes of the board, he was a young man of experience with boys and was hired to teach boys 'simple rules of Arithmetic, Reading, Writing and Geography, Manual exercise, etc.'[62]

While defending its work, the Toronto Children's Aid Society also raised questions about financial responsibility. For example, while Kelso used the narrative of superior modern ideas to denounce the society for keeping sixty children in close confinement in the heart of the city, the society retorted by asking 'where are the requisite facilities to be found?

Besides who is to bear the sacrifice of the existing investments in buildings and land? Who is to supply the funds for the acquisition of new buildings and land?'[63] Similarly, it insisted that the society was not designated to undertake the work of operating a detention room for juvenile delinquents. The society then made public its repeated appeals to the city council to take responsibility for juvenile delinquent cases.[64]

The very existence of the detention room at the Toronto Children's Aid Society's building illustrates the interweaving between child saving and juvenile correction during the early period. Its history over the three decades examined here, however, also testifies that the Toronto Children's Aid Society held strong prejudices against juvenile delinquents, who were perceived as rather damaged morally. Its compassion was relative to the perceived degrees of innocence of different children. The closing of the detention room by the society in 1920 was the start of gradually decreasing involvement in juvenile justice system on the part of the society. Today, children's aid societies' involvement in juvenile justice is quite insignificant in comparison with its major operation, the protection of young and innocent children from personal harm.

Chapter 7

Foster Care: Technology for Applying Proper Parental Power

In English Canada, the United States, and Britain, foster care is now generally accepted as the backbone of the child protection system and the best method to care for children who for various reasons are no longer connected to their parents. It has thus received considerable emphasis by many scholars from different stances.[1] Little has been said, though, about the ironic fact that foster care descended from the indenture system, which was often a menace to children's well-being.[2] Indenture usually took the form of apprenticeship to a trade. In early modern Europe and colonial North America, many parents entered agreements with masters of various trades so that their children would stay with a master's family, learn skills, and provide their services in return. By the eighteenth century, the apprenticeship system diminished as industry began to develop. Another form of indenture was what Charlotte Neff calls 'pauper apprenticeship,' apprenticeship indentures used by organizations such as those arranging for the immigration of poor British children and children's homes, to provide for dependent children.[3] Pauper apprenticeship originated in England as part of the English Poor Law.[4] In Ontario despite the province's rejection of the English Poor Law, the indenture of these children, or 'pauper apprentices,' was regulated successively by the Orphans Act of 1799, sections of the Guardian Act of 1827, and the Apprentices and Minors Act of 1851.[5] In the late nineteenth century, institutions such as orphanages continued placing children out with families as domestic servants in the case of girls, or farm helpers in the case of boys.[6]

Justifying Foster Care

It may seem counterintuitive that indenture should be a prototype technology for the child savers. For one thing, it was known that children were vulnerable to exploitation and maltreatment in indenture situations. Ralph Houlbrooke noted in his study of English families during the period from 1450 to 1700 that 'scattered through the archives of various courts are the records of suits undertaken by parents against masters who had maltreated their children, wasted their time, made them do unsuitably menial work or failed to provide them with adequate food and clothing according to their covenant.'[7] In North America, records show that as late as in the second half of the nineteenth century, indenture featured as a prominent setting for violence against children.[8] The question is, then, why did leading child savers choose a technology that had been hazardous to children for their child-saving work and adamantly defended it as a superior method for providing care for the conventional stream of orphans and deserted children and, more importantly, a new stream of children who were protected by the child savers from their own families?

To answer this question, we first need to understand that the superiority of foster care was mostly established in contrast to institutional care.[9] Kelso had played a pivotal role in promoting foster care as an alternative to institutions. An examination of writings by him and some others reveals several rationales for foster care developed in the late nineteenth century. First of all, because of the lack of effective medicine residential facilities for children at the time were frequently afflicted with contagious diseases. The society's shelter did not escape infectious diseases such as scarlet fever and diphtheria, similar to other residential care facilities for children discussed in Rooke and Schnell's study.[10] In contrast, foster care appeared to be a convenient solution to this problem, because clinical medical knowledge prescribed that diseases could be easily contained in individualized and closed-in spaces.

Second, foster homes were considered superior in that children's basic needs for food, clothes, and personal hygiene and so on could be better met in a home setting. A piece of Kelso's writing titled 'Not Enough to Eat' demonstrates how the preferred status of foster care was established.[11] He started with the observation that on the one hand 'it is not uncommon to meet with children from public institutions who complain that they did not get enough to eat'; however, on the other hand, the management of institutions insisted that they never denied children their full supply of food. Kelso provided an analysis of why this was so without accusing either side of lying. Instead, he reasoned that children went hungry because some 'had peculiar tastes and appetites' that could not be satisfied in a group; as well, some children were 'particularly sensitive to the refinement of the table' and thus could 'turn away in disgust and practically lose their appetite because of the oil tablecloth, the battered tin mug or the chipped crockery, together with the coarse manner in which the food is served and the vulgar habits of their companions.' Those issues, however, as Kelso argued, could be easily dealt with in foster homes, where there would be a good variety of food, and a willingness to alter the manner of cooking, or to increase the quantity of butter or sugar. The great lengths to which Kelso went in speculating about why children were hungry in institutions and why foster homes were better is difficult to understand; the simple reason could very well have been a lack of food. In fact, lack of food, both in quantity and quality, was a problem at the society's own shelter and detention room as well, but it was not a problem inherent in institutional care per se.

Another argument for the superiority of foster care, which was stronger than food because it went directly to the fundamental objective of child saving, was concerned with the moral-regulation dimension of care. In this regard, the value of foster care derived from the idea that the home setting was the most appropriate space for individually shaping children into proper adults. Many child savers believed that children in institutions tended to learn 'idle, evil habits from one another.' In contrast, foster homes were considered as being far more suitable for character-building. If women, or foster mothers, could improve children's appetite and diet, their role in properly socializing children was of even greater importance. One of Kelso's stories was about a boy in an orphan's home who found life there monotonous and who was convinced that the 'good ladies of the institution regarded him as an utter failure who would end up in prison.' He wandered away from the orphanage and, fortunately, when he stopped at a farm and asked for something to eat he met a good woman who became his foster mother for the subsequent three years. Years later, the former foster boy had succeeded in business and was 'in good circumstances.' As Kelso suggested, what rescued the boy was the woman's confidence in him, her kindness, and her words of counsel. The inference was that these could not be properly practiced by the 'good ladies of the institution.'[12]

Furthermore, the preference for foster care was justified by the fact that foster homes, most of which were privileged in many ways, were usually located in 'good' communities. As Kelso put it, 'the reason for placing children out is based on the belief that they will in this way become more rapidly and satisfactorily absorbed into the community.'[13]

The ideal outcome would be for a foster child to grow into an adult who 'showed no trace of inferior origin,'[14] as was represented in the after-rescue pictures of children (see Illustration 7). Thus, even though a foster home was not a natural home, it was a 'real home.' To the child savers, not only was it more real than institutions, it was even more real than some natural homes. Kelso made this point in his usual eloquent way when he declared:

> Four walls, a roof, three meals a day and some clothing do not constitute a home – otherwise a prison would be. The home wanted by boys and girls, whose parents are dissolute or incapable, or whose parents have been taken away by death, is a place where their dispositions may be studied and their capabilities gauged; where their natures, if warped, may be straightened; where the wounds and the bruises received in jostling with a cruel or thoughtless world, may be healed; where the cowardice of homelessness, and perhaps disgrace, may be supplanted with the courage born of new hopes, good prospects and worthy aims; where ambition may be quickened, pride aroused, and the honorableness of self-help be shown and made intelligible. That done, the boys and girls are ready for the world of work.[15]

In this sense, foster homes were seen as the ideal setting for shaping children's character, where a variety of 'gardening strategies' – dispersion, separation, classification, diagnosis, and guidance – could be implemented.

Last, but not least in importance, there was the ideological economic argument for foster care as an approach that cost less public money. The economic argument was certainly important, given the reluctance of the provincial government and particularly the city in providing financial support. Comparatively, the cost of foster care was 'a mere fraction of the cost of orphanage maintenance.'[16] Kelso reasoned in the following manner: 'Foster-parents may be inferior to ideal natural parents in affection, interest and training qualities, and yet in results far exceed the possibilities of institutional life. Measured by their fruits in character-building the home-finding plan is far superior to the orphanage. Measured by the financial cost the advantage is equally in favor of the former.'[17]

In some ways, foster care was thought of as a way to prevent the 'abuse' of institutions by parents. Thus, Kelso concluded in later years that 'experience shows that the substitution of the foster home for the large industrial school has had the effect of checking immensely the throwing by parents on the state the maintenance of their children.'[18] The salience of the ideological economic logic also applied to other, smaller rural communities. For example, as Kelso recalled, a deputation from a rural district complained to the provincial government about the expense of having two girls placed in a public institution. Kelso then took charge of the two girls and found them 'free homes.'[19] 'Free homes,' of course, were only possible because of foster children's cheap labour and foster mothers' free labour.[20]

That these rationales were developed shows that foster care was not 'naturally' the best method. Indeed, as the Local Council of Women in Toronto pointed out in a paper in 1933, it was a '"mistaken conception" that a [foster] home was necessarily better than an institution.'[21] The vulnerability of a child in a foster home was one concern. Furthermore, as the Local Council of Women argued, 'there was something to be said for the argument that a natural mother, instead of being forced to give up her child, might have it kept in an institution where she could have access to it and have hope of later reclaiming it.'[22]

Nevertheless, foster care was gradually accepted as the best method in caring for children by the Toronto Children's Aid Society and other child-welfare agencies.[23] Kelso's diaries provided evidence of the techniques used in promoting foster care. For example, in May 1894 he wrote to the president of the Woman's Christian Temperance Union and tried to convince her to cooperate in 'advocating family homes for orphan children.'[24]

Foster care, of course, was not exactly the same as indenture. One difference was that in foster care more emphasis was put on caring for children, particularly their character. The majority of children who were sent to foster homes during the period under examination still laboured in their foster homes, but the expectation of children's economic contribution was decentred, at least on the part of the child savers.[25] This transformation was evidenced by the change of wording in the customary indenture contract, which stated that the child should be received as a domestic servant or helper. An incident which happened to Annie from the Girls' Home, however, shows the resistance to the decentring of economic expectations of children. In this case, the president of the home simply declined to make any alteration in the indenture papers when Kelso found a foster home for Annie and requested dropping the words domestic servant.[26]

Power Relations in Foster Care

Foster care can be seen as a system in which the regulation of children's conduct was delegated by the state through the Children's Aid Society to foster parents. The system consisted of these main procedures: advertising for potential foster parents, selection of foster parents by the society, placing-out of children, and regular inspection by provincial officials. Foster parents were expected to provide for children so as to meet their needs for food, clothes, and shelter. But perhaps more importantly they were also required to send children to school, take them to churches, and see to children's character development. The significance of foster parents' role in moral regulation was made apparent by the criteria of selecting good Christians, and the contents of visitors' reports, which always made note of whether a child received religious education, whether he was honest, and so on. The crucial importance of moral regulation was also revealed by what counted as a success story. In one such story, Kelso reported that a foster mother wrote him about her foster girl: 'It is seldom one can find so dutiful and devoted a daughter as she has proven to be. Has all along been the same, sweet, loving, companionable, trustworthy and truthful girl, now assuming more womanly ways and developing a beautiful Christian character.'[27]

The foster care system constituted power relations among several main parties: foster parents, people in the neighbourhood or relatives, foster children, and the child savers. First, children's real or coerced dependence[28] rendered them objects of their foster parents' authority. The society's case records contain little direct information about mistreatment of children in foster homes in general. However, notes of children being returned by foster parents for being 'unsatisfactory,' children running away,[29] or writing to say that they were not properly treated suggest children's susceptibility to abuse and exploitation, as well as their agency for resistance in some cases.

In her research on pauper apprenticeship in Ontario, Neff argues that pauper apprentices were seen as reliable and cheap sources of labour.[30] It is probably sound to say that foster parents accepted children (most of them were above seven or eight years of age) from the Toronto Children's Aid Society for largely the same reason as people who applied for pauper apprentices throughout most of the nineteenth century. Evidence for this is found in documentation of children's wages as well as discussions of concerns that children might be overworked. Of course, this is not to say that every foster parent was intent on taking advantage of foster children; some truly believed in helping needy children, particularly the quite small proportion of young ones. Whatever their motivations, as soon as they made applications for foster children, foster parents willingly subjected themselves to various sources of power: the society, provincial officials, and the community at large. The screening process gave expression to such authority when the society, and sometimes the provincial Office of Superintendent of Neglected and Dependent Children, gathered information on applicants' 'home surroundings' and reputation. Foster parents then were regulated by a hierarchical surveillance system, similar to that applied to parents in general. The surveillance system targeting foster parents was coordinated by the provincial government even though the guardianship of children was held by the societies. The arrangement was shaped by two factors. One was the geographical dispersion of children and the consequent expense and time involved in supervision, which was almost impossible for a small society to afford. The other factor was the 'continuity and permanency' that state supervision could provide when a local society might not exist or might cease to exist.[31]

All children who were placed in foster homes were reported to the provincial Office of Superintendent of Neglected and Dependent Children. Their names were then recorded both in a central 'supervision book' and on card indexes. Card indexes were divided into towns, cities and counties so as to organize visiting work according to locations. Recording was thus essential to the exercise of power. As Kelso argued: 'The great importance of having all placed out children promptly reported and recorded has been demonstrated over and over again. The smaller Societies pass out of existence, there are frequent changes of secretaries or managers, and if the children were not on record they would in many cases be completely forgotten and lost sight of.'[32]

The supervision system consisted of several components: regular visits of government officials (usually once or twice a year), correspondence with both children and sometimes foster parents, local supervision directed by 'volunteer benevolent committees,' and general oversight by the public – most likely neighbours and family relatives – as established by the technology of reporting. Furthermore, the moral authorities in local communities were also encouraged to communicate regularly with government officials or societies about the state of foster homes. For example, the Toronto society contacted ministers in the local communities where foster children were placed and invited them to report twice a year regarding the welfare of the children.[33]

The supervision of foster parents was expected to serve three purposes: to supervise foster parents, to supervise children, and sometimes to provide encouragement to foster parents to retain children.[34] Given these purposes, little supervision was felt necessary in cases where children were 'adopted' in infancy.[35] Cases involving older children (i.e., children above seven or eight years old), however, required 'special attention,' since usually there was the factor of labour. Kelso observed that 'great care [was] needed to see that they [foster children] receive a fair amount of schooling and are not overworked.'[36] Some foster parents recognized the reason for state supervision and accepted visitors' calls; some even welcomed visitors as an additional resource for keeping foster children under control. However, many were 'apt to resent the call of a visitor as an intrusion' and thus 'raise a fuss over the visit.'[37]

Supervision of foster parents resembled supervision of natural parents in some aspects. For example, foster parents were subjected to regular visits for fear of abuse and neglect of children. There was, however, also a clear double standard in the regulation of foster parents and that of natural parents. The child-savers' power over foster parents was much more compromised by their very reliance on foster parents for the operation of the child-protection system. This reliance could not be more clearly expressed than Kelso's description of the home-finding work as 'begging people to open their homes to ... children.'[38] 'Begging' was hardly an exaggeration given the chronic shortage of foster homes. For example, in 1910, because of the dearth of available foster homes, particularly for boys, the Toronto society wrote to various societies throughout Ontario, asking for homes for boys between the ages of five and ten. When the replies came, however, there was not a single home offered. As these societies explained, they all had the same difficulty in placing children of that age in foster homes.[39] For children with disabilities or diseases, and for non-white children,[40] it was nearly impossible to find homes. Even with healthy white children, one should dress them tastefully[41] and plead for a foster home vigorously: 'advertize your need of homes just as a good salesman advertizes his merchandise. Present it as a privilege and duty to mother the needy child, and point out the joy and reward of such noble service.'[42]

As a solution to the problem of shortage of foster homes, payment of an allowance for foster children's board was started in Boston in 1900. The Toronto Children's Aid Society followed this development about a decade later. It should be noted, however, that such a payment was not conceptualized as a compensation for the labour of foster mothers.

Instead, it was primarily an incentive for people to open their homes, and to some extent a substitute for children's payment for their board through work.[43]

In Toronto, the problem of the lack of foster homes continued into the 1920s (and exists today) even though the Toronto Children's Aid Society tried to attract them by offering payment for board, much to Kelso's criticism. The obvious question is then, if the child savers were beggars, could they be choosers? The power wielded by foster parents on the child savers was reflected in that foster parents could return children as they pleased. For example, a little foster girl was returned because her foster mother 'could not stand the worry of looking after [her].' Similarly, Lydia was sent back because in her foster parents' view 'she did not suit their rough life.'[44] Foster parents' power was also reflected in the instruction to visitors that they should not be too zealous in their supervision work, that 'great care and judgment has to be shown in [the] work of visitation' so as not to 'over-regulate' foster parents.[45] The child-savers' class and race biases in assuming that many foster parents were good people was another factor in the double standard of regulation of foster parents and natural parents.

The genealogy of foster-care technology attests to the central concern of child saving, that is, installing proper parental power to ensure that children would grow up to be perceived good citizens. The superiority of foster homes over institutions was not natural, but had to be buttressed by arguments of disease control, meeting children's individual needs for food, clothes, and personal hygiene, effective moral regulation, and economics. The isolation and vulnerability of a child in a foster home that could only be supervised gently and the interruption, if not severance, of the relation between a child and his mother as raised by the Toronto Local Council of Women suggested that while foster care worked in the eyes of the child savers, it often did not work for children and their families.

In what precedes I have examined the emergence of child protection around the turn of the last century at the threshold of the 'social' era. The historical analyses gave particular attention to the ways that experiences in parent-child relations, knowledge, and power were connected. I have argued that the child-saving movement in the late nineteenth and early twentieth century was primarily a citizenship-building project initiated by the voluntary sector. Its principal objective was to ensure that children as 'citizens in the making' would be properly shaped into 'useful and Christian' adults. It assumed that how children were parented would determine what kind of adults they would be, an idea that had emerged in Western society in the context of sixteenth-century human- ism. In this sense, child saving was a bio-political project that connected the conduct of individual children and parents in the private sphere with issues of societal and national importance.

Specifically, the problematization of cruelty and neglect corresponded to two aspects of the concerns about citizenship. Anti-cruelty activities criticized the immoral use of force on harmless, weak, and lowly subjects, that is, animals and innocent children. These acts of individuals were problems because individual morality was seen as making up the general moral tone of the collective. In other words, cruelty to children emerged as a public problem because it was opposite to civility. Cruelty was thought to be a problem of the heart, usually the heart of a working-class man. The concept of the heart was also central to the question of who could identify cruelty (i.e., those with civilized hearts) as well as how the problem should be addressed (i.e., mainly through education and moral persuasion). Neglectful parenting, from which children were to be pro- tected, was mainly defined as lack of discipline, lack of supervision of children, conduct considered immoral, such as drinking and cohabita- tion, and lack of proper family surroundings, which parents were held responsible to provide. Neglectful parenting, most often mothering, was considered a problem because it failed in building children's character. Neglected children were seen as problematic 'future citizens' in that they were potentially criminals, beggars, prostitutes, or generally immoral. Although problems of cruelty and neglect concerned different aspects of citizenship, they were united in that both, in contrasting directions, devi- ated from emerging middle-class and Anglo-Celtic norms of parent-child relations as conveyed in widely used gardening metaphors.

These norms prescribed a mode of parental power over children that was intimate, gentle, intelligent, and incessant. Thus, cruelty erred on the side of using too much force; neglect erred on the side of too little parenting. The child savers believed that their activities to condemn erring forms of parenting, that is, cruelty and neglect, and, more impor- tantly, activities to cultivate proper parenting conduct were crucial for building the nation's citizenship. At the same time they also believed that their action was a 'noble' way to fulfil their own duties as citizens. Different kinds of knowledge – such as the concept that childhood was important because it determined the character of adults, concepts of character building, moral judgment by the 'civilized heart,' administra- tive and quasi-professional information about the correlation between neglect and crime – were utilized and at the same time generated in child-saving activities. The effect was the constitution of children as 'future citizens,' and parents and/or the child savers as 'gardeners of citizenship.' They were guided by hortisocial strategies that were principally positive, individualized, knowledge-based, and local. The most representative of these strategies included guidance, supervision, investigation, classification, separation, and dispersion. Child-saving technologies of reports, visits, case records, the shelter, the detention room, and foster care embodied these strategies of power. They connected authorities with children and parents in often-complex relations of power and knowledge. These historical analyses can serve as reference points for considering our post-social present, which is the focus of the next chapter.

Chapter 8

Child Protection at the Turn of the Twenty-first Century: 'Keeping Kids Safe'

At the end of twentieth century, sparked by several cases of well-reported child deaths, Ontario's Child Welfare Reform from 1996 to 1999 resulted in a restructuring of the child-protection system. The focus of the Ontario reform on individual cases of child deaths followed a trend across Britain, the United States, Europe, and Australia since the mid-1980s, in which child deaths have emerged as the entry point for public scrutiny of and political deliberation about the child-protection system.[1] In Canada, the province of British Columbia's well-publicized Gove Inquiry into Child Protection (1995) was the first example of initiating restructuring of policy and services through a massive inquiry into the dreadful death of a child involved with the child-protection system.[2] While concern with deaths is no stranger in public policy-making, the 1990s discourse on child deaths is characterized by the format of a personal life story, complete with individual names and faces. Indeed, impersonal and aggregated statistics such as incidence and mortality provided little if any justification for Ontario's Child Welfare Reform. As a social worker commented, 'it is not a quantitative issue. It's the qualitative nature, the tragic nature, that matters.'[3] This perception characterized the focus of the reform, the misnamed Ontario Child Mortality Task Force[4] and a series of coroner's inquests into deaths of children who died while receiving services from a children's aid society. The Child Mortality Task Force and the coroner's inquests were described in the *Toronto Star* on 18 September 1996 as 'a sweeping probe into child deaths ... with a view to saving lives in the future.' They generated a large number of recommendations with three broad themes. First, the courts, professionals in addition to social workers, for example, medical doctors, school teachers, and lawyers, and the general public needed to be more alert to the harmful effects of child abuse and neglect. Second, the principles of 'family preservation' and the 'least restrictive intervention,' which had underlain child-protection law since the 1980s, should be secondary to the protection of children. Third, the child-protection system needed more and stronger legal tools and system supports. The specific recommendations included adding neglect as a ground for child protection, standardized risk assessment tools, interlinked data systems, increased funding and staff for children's aid societies in the province of Ontario, and even creation of new child-specific criminal offences in the Criminal Code at the federal level.[5] During the reform the Ontario Ministry of Community and Social Services adopted an impressive number of those recommendations.

A key component of the reform was the introduction of the Child and Family Services Amendment Act (Child Welfare Reform) in 1998 and then 1999, which became law on 31 March 2000. Major changes brought about by the act include the shift of emphasis from considering the interests of families as a whole to privileging 'children's best interests,' recognizing 'patterns of neglect' as a ground for mandatory protection services, stricter regulation of the duty of professionals to report their suspicions of child abuse and neglect, a shorter timeframe for planning permanent arrangements, and more difficult access by relatives or friends to children who have been made wards of the Crown. Predictably, since the reform there has been a significant increase in the number of reports of child abuse and neglect, interventions, children in care, and children who will not return to their families because of faster planning of permanent arrangements.[6]

As some commentators pointed out, child-protection services are focusing more and more on investigation, assessment, analysis, and documentation of parental inadequacies, than on meeting the needs of families in providing up-to-standard care for children through direct support or helping them to gain access to supplementary resources.[7] Critics of the reform could raise questions such as why the reform took its particular course, what motivations or interests of key players shaped the outcome, and what ideologies were hidden beneath the surface. While these are valuable questions, here I take a different approach in developing critical analysis by following Michel Foucault's use of history to criticize the present.

Using the history to critically understand the present does not imply that I personally endorse the historical ideas and practices of child saving, or that in my opinion a time in the past was superior to the present. Rather, the usefulness of historical analysis is that it has stimulated new insights into the recent Child Welfare Reform in Ontario, illuminated present limitations and possibilities, and suggested possible directions of challenge. What follows turns to the task of confronting influential child-protection ideas and practices that have become canonical at the turn of the twenty-first century. Some of these, for example, the paramount concern with children's personal safety, with few exceptions[8] have been taken for granted and remained unproblematized, even among critics of the child-protection system. The discussion below mainly draws on official child-protection documents in Ontario including speeches, proceedings of the legislature, the report of the Child Mortality Task Force, and recommendations by juries in coroner's inquests. As well, it draws on related documents produced by the federal government, specifically the 1999 consultation paper on Child Victims and the Criminal Justice System.[9]

The analysis presented here is developed in contrast to the history of child saving in the following directions. First, instead of being citizens in the making, or bad citizens in the making in the case of neglected children, today children are very much constituted as ideal citizens, with more legitimate ethical and political claims than adults. Specifically, current child-protection discourse accentuates children's rights to personal safety. If a century ago parents were condemned because they corrupted children and made them potential criminals who would prey on the whole society, today they are condemned as perpetrators of crimes against innocent citizen-children.[10] Second, the primary purpose of current child protection is claimed to be 'keeping kids safe.'[11] The naming and criticizing of this rationality, which is fundamental to today's child protection, was made possible by the preceding historical analysis. In the earlier period, the primary rationality of child saving, as reflected in the Toronto Children's Aid Society's motto, was that 'it is wiser and less expensive to save children than to punish criminals' (see Illustration 8). It assumed that child abuse or neglect is more than a matter of personal danger and harm to children. The current understanding of child abuse and neglect as personal safety issues severely limits the kinds of collective actions to be considered. Third, in the early period 'gardening strategies' were utilized in child-saving work to normalize the conduct of parents, who were supposed to in turn tend to the gardens of their children's character. Child-protection technologies in the late 1990s, however, feature risk management on the one hand and criminal punishment on the other. In contrast to the humanist subject represented in gardening metaphors, risk management and criminal punishment assumes a new conception of the subject, that is, individuals defined through risk factors but who are at the same time held morally culpable for their actions, as Rose observes.[12] The chapter concludes with comments linking child protection to the transformation of citizenship, conceptions of the human subject, and prevalent governing technologies in the general social and political landscape at the turn of the twenty-first century.

The Child as the Ideal Citizen

During the early period examined in preceding chapters, children were considered by the child savers mainly as 'future citizens.' The identity of 'future citizens' was constructed in light of proper citizens, who were at the time white, male, and most important of all in this case, adults. The objective of child saving was to ensure that these 'future citizens' grew up to be good adults. Thus, it can be argued that the governance of wayward children and bad parents was undertaken from the standpoint of adulthood.

This standpoint of adult citizenship had two implications. First, one major difference between children and adult citizens was their perceived property of plasticity. Children's quality of being 'in the making' was precisely the basis for making claims about collective actions, because it promised greater effectiveness in shaping the humanist subject. Second, the identity of 'future citizens' also meant that children in the early period were not thought of as having independent status, either politically, economically, or morally. This was evident in how the rights of children were constituted at the time. The rights of children were certainly part of the child-saving discourse, but, in contrast to today's rights to personal safety, those were rights to a proper environment and careful moral training. They were constituted for the sake of society, not for children as individuals. Thus, although children were sometimes described as victims of cruelty or neglect, their individual victimization was not really the point and was not the justification for intervention. As Kelso put in unambiguous terms, the objective of child protection was 'not so much to rescue the victims ... but rather to reach the children before they have become altogether corrupt'[13] and damage society. Such society-oriented objectives were characteristic of the social era. They were forceful rationalities for child saving and broader social and moral reform in the late nineteenth century. In the name of society,

interventions with mixed purposes and effects of normalizing and providing support for parents (e.g., the Mother's Allowance program) were
also gradually introduced in the twentieth century, since in most cases
parents were conceived of as indispensable gardeners tending to the
development of their children's characters.

In contrast to children's rights as future citizens in the early period,
today children's rights are constructed as those of citizens. A host of
empirical developments around the turn of this century suggest that
children are increasingly constituted as citizens in their own right and as
independent bearers of rights. These include the following: (1) A model
of active citizenship for children has been advanced by movements (of
adults) on behalf of children, child-activist movements, and the United
Nations Convention on the Rights of the Child.[14] (2) Children are
taking a central position in people's awareness and imagination of the
nation and of citizenship. Today children provide images of national
vulnerability, victimization, hope, or degeneracy as in the case of shootings
in schools committed by teenagers.[15] (3) In public policy processes,
rhetoric about children usually attempts to justify claims on collective
resources. One example is the child-poverty campaign. Justification is
usually constructed on the basis of these defining features of children
and childhood: innocence, helplessness, and developmental unique-
ness, especially early neural development.[16]

In the Child Welfare Reform in Ontario at the turn of the twenty-first
century there operated an increasingly influential discourse of innocent
and young children as proper citizens. This discourse of the child-citizen
features a construction of citizenship rights and obligations primarily in
terms of personal safety. Children are considered the most, if not the
only, legitimate citizens with rights to safety and to collective actions to
guarantee their safety. Instead of being seen as potential dangers to
society, as when child protection emerged in the 1890s, children targeted by child protection today are seen as citizen-victims of crime
against them – abuse and neglect committed by their parents. If a
century ago abused and neglected children were often represented by
the image of a dirty-looking, ill-clothed and wayward boy (see Illustration
9), today in the minds of Canadians the typical image of children
protected by children's aid societies is a baby threatened with harm or
even death. Canadians experience thinking of children as citizen-victims
through accounts of how children are victimized by their own parents
and then failed by the system of child protection. Popular and official
narratives of children leading to Ontario's Child Welfare Reform were

preoccupied with child deaths, parent-criminals, and the breakdown of the child-protection system. Although the death of children is the ultimate form of victimization, it certainly is not the only one. Sexually abused children and missing children are two additional, earlier, but also enduring images of child-victims.[17]

The rationality of victimization, of course, is not limited to children. The rights of victims, particularly the victims of personal acts such as drunk driving, have become an effective argument in generating ethical and political claims in recent years. Among various groups of victims, however, children seem to have become the icon or the model. There may be several factors to explain this trend of child-citizen thinking. Innocence is probably one of the most important ideas in the making of the child icon. As Marilyn Ivy observes, 'the child can take on the full weight of victimhood in total purity.'[18] Lauren Berlant also points to the paradox that the child who is made the icon of citizen-victims happens to be incapable of acting as a citizen yet. In this sense, the child icon legitimates having adults articulate the interests of children and wage struggles on their behalf.[19] In addition to these observations, an extension of bio-political thinking from the social era may also be a factor in the iconicity of current model citizen-victim. That is, the value of children to the continuation of the society is also recognized. For example, Janet Ecker, the Ontario Minister of Community and Social Services who presided over the recent Child Welfare Reform, pleaded with her fellow members of the legislature: 'I know that all members will agree with me that children are Ontario's most precious asset. They deserve the best our society can provide – a loving, nurturing environment, and above all, safety and security.'[20] Similarly, in the Department of Justice's Child Victims Consultation, references have been made to societal interests. It was stated that 'the victimization of children and young people has significant costs both for the victims and their families and for the future of our society as a whole.'[21] Although these statements are relatively scant in the official documents examined, they nevertheless indicate some extension of the bio-political thinking that links children's lives to the interests of the society.

Whatever the reasons for manufacturing the icon of child-victim, as a symbol it is very effective in polarizing the dichotomy of innocence and guilt, conveying tragic feelings of loss, and demanding action. Thus, as Joel Best observes, child victims have become important symbols in many movements. The most familiar examples include movements against drunk driving that are organized by describing killer drunks and their child victims, and pro-life attacks on abortion in terms of millions of murdered babies.[22] The central image of children menaced by deviant parents in Ontario's Child Welfare Reform is another example of the discourse of citizenship and child victims. Thinking of problems such as child abuse and neglect as issues of violating the rights of child victims has certain consequences. The most serious one is that it individualizes the analysis of problems, taking it to the level of the personal criminal acts of parents. Thus, the individual rights of children as victims have been invoked (by parties other than children themselves) to position parents as perpetrators 'getting away with murder of children'[23] and to justify harsher regulation and punishment.

Children's citizenship rights are also constructed through their identity as consumers. This fits with the observation that the new citizen at the turn of the twenty-first century is constituted as the consumer of goods and services.[24] Children are represented as the exclusive consumers of the child-protection system, which is supposed to deliver safety. Parents are no longer recognized as consumers of social services, but as perpetrators. This conception of children as the exclusive consumers of child-protection services has shaped the critique of the objective and competence of suppliers of these 'goods or services' – in this case the child-protection system and its staff. Since the late 1960s and 1970s, the rights of individual consumers have proved to be a useful conceptual and political tool in criticizing systems and programs established for the sake of society, particularly their arbitrary, repressive, and intrusive aspects. In earlier times, parents and family units considered themselves consumers and demanded rights on their own. The 'due process' and 'least restrictive or disruptive' principles adopted in Ontario's Child and Family Services Act introduced in 1984 and proclaimed in 1985 resulted from such criticisms. However, these same principles were done away with in the 1990s in the name of protecting the rights of child-consumers.

Children are now seen as the only consumers of the child-protection system and the only ones who can be failed by the system. This is best illustrated by the headline of the *Toronto Star* report referred to earlier: 'How did the system fail these kids.'[25] A staff person at the Toronto Children's Aid Society wrote in 1999: 'A child protection worker's worst fear [was] the death of a child.'[26] That is despite the fact that deaths of children associated with the child-protection system hardly represent the reality of most situations in the system. The vast majority of cases that child-protection workers deal with everyday do not have dramatic endings. For example, in 1995 Ontario children's aid societies provided services to 87,000 families and 150,000 children and youth. Among these children, only fifty-seven died while receiving services from a children's aid society.[27] That is a percentage of 0.038, lower than the death rate for children in Ontario (0.055 per cent). In contrast to the 0.038 per cent of cases ending with child deaths, more than 70 per cent of children involved with the child-protection system live in poverty because their families are poor[28]; 40 per cent of the children involved with the system come from households headed by single mothers; 34 per cent of these children have 'caregivers' who suffer mental health problems.[29] Some scholars have pointed out that child-protection cases are primarily the results of poverty and the effects of associated disadvantages, such as single motherhood, lack of education, substance use, mental health problems, sub-standard housing, or no housing.[30] Instead of being driven by isolated cases of child deaths and treating parents, especially poor single mothers, as potential killers, it would only be sensible to make efforts to improve the child-protection system to focus on far more widespread and chronic issues among its clients, such as poverty and other marginalizations.

To assess the child-protection system exclusively or even primarily by the criterion of whether deaths of children occur is something unique to our time. Certainly in the past some children involved with the child-protection system died. These deaths were undoubtedly considered tragic, but not the result of the system's or individual worker's failure. Instead, in the early period what was most likely to be considered failure on the part of the system and individual workers would be a child's 'criminal career' despite intervention. That shows that the child-protection system had not subscribed to or been judged against the objective of delivering individual safety to children. Indeed, given the correlation between individuals' history with the child-protection system, especially as foster children, and persistent marginalizations in the forms of poverty, homelessness, law-breaking, substance use, and so on, one wonders whether those marginalizations should not be held out as the criteria for assessing the success or failure of the child-protection system and the worst fears for child protection workers.

When children were thought of as 'future citizens,' children's rights were connected with the interests of society. In contrast, today when children are constructed as citizens in the field of child protection, their rights are constituted in personal and private terms and are specifically restricted to safety. Society-oriented rationalities for child protection can be criticized, and rightly so, as not really about children. Nevertheless, such social rationalities also allowed the gradual introduction of social services and benefits beyond child protection. Today's view of children as citizens seems progressive in that it appears to be really about children. However, the theoretical construction of children as independent individuals does not *actually* make it possible for children to define their own interests, and it is doubtful that will ever happen. Certain adults still act on behalf of children, but at present they do so in the name of children's personal human rights. Worse, the conception of children as proper citizens severely limits the scope of their claims when it is articulated with the objective of guaranteeing personal safety.

Rights to Personal Safety

When Minister Ecker introduced the Child and Family Services Amendment Act in Ontario in April 1999, she justified the need for reform by pointing to the rights of children to safety and security. This resonates with how reality is understood in several other sites where the state's authority has been asserted in recent post-deficit years. In Ontario, from the Safe Streets Act, to Child Welfare Reform, to the levy of international adoption fees, the right of individuals to safety and security has proved to be a common and successfully deployed political rationality. The formula is that X (legislation, fee, action) is needed or reasonable because Y's (children, passersby) safety is at stake.

Authority in the name of safety and security needs to be understood in the context of the 'risk society.'[31] It is compatible with and complementary to emphasis on personal fulfillment as free individuals. Rose argues that 'as the twentieth century draws to a close, political reason from all quarters no longer phrases itself in the language of obligation, duty and social citizenship. It now justifies itself by arguing over the political forms that are adequate to the existence of persons as essentially, naturally, creatures striving to actualize themselves in their everyday, secular lives.'[32]

With such a mentality, it is conceivable that safety and security – the very basic conditions for personal fulfillment – have become obvious and reasonable objectives of governing, when the strategy of achieving betterment of society through governing the collective obligations of social citizens is no longer politically viable. Safety, is defined by negation. It is not possible to prove the presence of safety; instead safety exists by means of the absence of risk. Security, meaning being safe from possible harm, also denotes the absence of risk of harm. Thus, the presence of risk of personal harm to children has, to a significant extent, become a tool for processing and making sense of society. The assessment of various aspects of reality and the differentiation of those deemed worthy of political consideration from the unworthy are also organized in terms of the presence or absence of risk of harm and loss.

Among various forms of harm, death is the most dramatic, concrete, and ultimate opposite to individual safety. Thus, death, as the antithesis of the rationality of individual safety, has become one of the most powerful forms of problematization, and the one most likely to lead to political action. From child protection to health care, drug control, and electricity policy, the most compelling stories told by critics of varied political stripes have been those of death.

This discourse of death is overpowering, to the point that it does not take statistically significant patterns of death to initiate policy changes. Indeed, the Child Mortality Task Force and the Coroner's Office did not produce any evidence showing that the death rate for children was on the rise, either in general or in the child-protection system. The whole Child Welfare Reform was sparked by a few high-profile child deaths that did not represent the vast majority of child-protection cases. In the 'social' age, statistics about patterns of death constituted a key knowledge format. In the current climate death as a reality is no longer seen as a regular occurrence with certain statistical probabilities. Instead it is thought of in individualized terms. Death is perceived to be the result of an unacceptable failure to ensure individual safety, the fault of individuals and/or systems. In the domain of child protection, death is blamed on child abuse and neglect, and consequently on parental conduct, even and particularly in the case of accidental deaths.[33] Hence, the attempt to bring child abuse and neglect into the criminal justice system and subject it to the juridical logic of responsibility.[34]

Although the language of safety and security appears neutral and universal, the distribution of entitlement to safety and security is quite uneven. For instance, although some deaths of homeless people have been reported in the media as well, these have never been a cause for panic and/or for an outpouring of compassion. Furthermore, one person's lack of safety, for example, living on the street or being beaten by one's husband, can be construed as danger to another person's safety, for example, a passerby or a child. Hence, 'street people' and an abused mother become (potential) perpetrators who (may) bring harm by their actions, inactions, or mere presence; passersby and children become (potential) victims. The rights of worthy (potential) victims are invoked to position others as perpetrators who deprive victims of their rights.

Thus, the safety of passersby justifies the introduction of the Safe Street Act, which is nothing but anti-'street-people'; the safety of children justified the punishment of parents for being abused themselves, for being poor and living in sub-standard housing, and so on. It is therefore clear that not everyone has rights to safety. The distribution of citizenship, as indicated by the entitlement or disentitlement to personal safety, seems to be shaped by an exclusion of those deemed to be morally unworthy. Children, by reason of their perceived innocence, passiveness, and inherent value to society, enjoy unquestioned rights to safety, which I have discussed in the previous section.

Whereas the rights and obligations of citizens were charted in relation to the collective interests of society at the turn of the last century, personal and private acts and values have become the major criteria for measuring rights and obligations at the turn of the twenty-first century, as Berlant argues perceptively.[35] The case of the Child Welfare Reform supports this observation, and as I have demonstrated here, personal safety is one of the major dimensions of what Berlant calls 'privatized citizenship.' While it is almost impossible to argue against rights to safety, it should be noted that using personal safety as the framework to understand issues does have practical implications. Doing so tends to direct attention to a search for guilty individuals, and it restricts thinking by suggesting that such safety is all we care about. These implications are played out in the restructuring of the child-protection system, which is transforming the system into one that emphasizes risk management on the one hand and punishment on the other.[36]

Risk Management and Child-Specific Criminal Offences

In the early history of child protection, children's rights were defined as rights to a proper environment and proper moral training, in other words, rights to normalization. The assumption was that individuals were products of conditions, and, thus, all deserved a chance of such conditioning. Whether these individuals wished this or not was another matter. This conception of the humanist subject gave rise to social and moral reforms modeled after gardening efforts. The major kinds of work that the Toronto Children's Aid Society undertook, such as inviting and receiving complaints, visits, keeping case records, operating the shelter and the detention room, and foster care, were intended to normalize the conduct of both parents and children.

Today's child-protection approach, which combines risk management with punishment, draws on polarized conceptions of individuals as victims and perpetrators in judicial terms. Such conceptions are radically different from the relatively coherent humanist subject during the 'social' era. First, in people whose rights have been brought to public discussion, such as abused and neglected children and passersby on 'unsafe' streets, we have an image of individuals who are victims.[37] Then, we have an image of individuals who are (potential) perpetrators. Through this image, certain individuals are seen as predisposed to risk. For example, poor single mothers are risky for reasons ranging from being single, to being poor, living in sub-standard housing, being prone to substance abuse, and having experienced abuse and neglect as children. As Rose points out, however, such dispositions, bodily or otherwise, do not serve to excuse individuals from responsibility for their conduct. Quite the contrary, despite these dispositions, individuals are to be held morally and judicially responsible, reflecting a renewal of a moralism that emphasizes moral and political order.[38] These conceptions of new human subjects prescribe governing technologies that feature monitoring, assessment, and management of risk on the one hand, and punishment on the other.

In the summer of 1997, a new standardized risk-assessment model was adopted by Ontario's Ministry of Community and Social Services for all children's aid societies across Ontario. This model had been strongly recommended by the Child Mortality Task Force and coroner's inquests.[39] Prior to the reform, the 1984 Child and Family Services Act adopted the risk-orientation and risk-assessment tools that were then in use in some children's aid societies, including the Toronto society. The 1997 standardized risk-assessment model drew largely on the tools that the Children's Aid Society of Toronto used, which in turn borrowed from the model developed by the New York State Department of Social Services.[40]

The risk assessment model is far more than a tool for assessing risk factors. It is a machinery of child-protection work, which is designed to identify, document, classify, rate, and analyse risk factors related to child safety in the context of abuse and neglect. It has six key components:

1 Eleven risk decision points that describe eleven decisions to be
   made (e.g., risk decision 3: Is child safe now?) and that structure
   the decision-making flow by defining the sequence of decisions
2 Criteria to guide each decision point
3 Eligibility assessment

4 Safety assessment
5 Risk assessment
6 Plan of service connected to the risk assessment.[41]

Among the above six components, eligibility assessment, safety assessment, and risk assessment are considered by the ministry as 'three important phases' incorporated in the risk assessment model.[42] Eligibility assessment is conducted mainly through using the eligibility spectrum tool at the time of referral. According to the ministry, eligibility assessment accomplishes the following three things: (1) It helps ensure that all children and families who are eligible for child welfare services will actually receive those services. (2) It classifies 'reasons for service' requests to enable better planning on the part of children's aid societies. (3) It records all intake activity so that society workloads can be better evaluated. The primary objective of conducting eligibility assessment is to make 'consistent and accurate decisions about eligibility for service.'[43] The outcome in practice is the classification of 'protection investigation cases' and 'non-protection investigation cases.' Classification will likely lean towards more 'protection investigation cases,' partly because it would be better to err on the safe side and partly because the funding formula favours 'protection investigation cases.'

Several observations can be made about the risk assessment model. First, the model structures practice in such a way that the reality of children's existence becomes intelligible only in terms of their individual safety. One senior staff member of a children's aid society explained that the model 'is helpful for making work easier because it organizes your thought and zeroes in on relevant information.'[44] It structures not only the thinking but also action. Following the model, child-protection practices are only concerned with children's needs and define those needs in terms of safety. The result is that for children to receive any professional help, they will have to be deemed to be in an unsafe situation, and parents will have to be perceived, assessed, documented, and acted upon as potential perpetrators posing danger to their children. History has provided ample examples of how a particular definition of need affects practice and the experiences of clients. In the late nineteenth century, when services were devised for meeting the needs of delinquent children, some were sent to industrial schools by parents who wanted them to learn a trade but had to claim that they were incorrigible. Later, when services were devised for children with emotional problems, they would have to be categorized as suffering from emotional problems in order to have access to child-welfare institutions, as illustrated by Carol Baines's study of the Earlscourt Children's Home.[45] Children were given IQ tests in the past; today's children and parents are subject to safety tests and risk-of-harm assessment. The thread running through this is the failure to recognize and address the needs of children and parents from their own perspective.

Second, as critics such as Nigel Parton, Carol Baines, and Karen Swift point out, the technology of risk assessment excludes considerations of the socioeconomic and cultural-ethnic context in which the needs of children and families occur.[46] The risk assessment model embodies the paradigm shift from considering certain aspects of reality to be social problems to considering them to be risk factors. These include poverty, mental illness, single-motherhood, substance use, poor housing, and domestic abuse. These issues are documented in case records not because they are recognized to be problems to be addressed by the society, but because they constitute unsafe situations for children. They have been re-fashioned from social problems into things that are distant, apolitical factors; things that can be taken for granted and dealt with indifferently without relating to collective responsibility; things that can be quantified and rated for their inherent danger to children.

Third, the reduction of risk seems to be the responsibility of the bearer of such risk factors – in this case, parents. Financial and human resources are not spent so much on solving problems, but on rating and analysing and documenting them according to definite formulae, and taking children away if their parents have failed to reduce the magnitude of the danger posed by their conduct to their children's safety. Ironically, despite the reliance on service language, such as 'service eligibility' (for a 'service' for which most do not want to be eligible), services in the sense of providing support to families have apparently been pushed to the very margins of social work.

If at the provincial and local levels parents are primarily risk-managed in the increasingly bureaucratized and 'child-focused' child-protection work, at the federal level they are the central objects of the discussion of toughening criminal punishment. As the Department of Justice explained: 'providing services to children in need of protection is the responsibility of the provinces and territories; ensuring that appropriate offences and penalties are available is the responsibility of the Government of Canada.'[47] The following discussion on the criminal-punishment side of current Child Welfare Reform draws on the Child Victims and the Criminal Justice System consultation started by the Department

of Justice in November 1999. Specifically, I discuss the proposed creation
of child-specific criminal offences, which, I argue, is a technology for
regulating individualized obligations owed by adults, particularly parents, to children.

The consultation paper focused on the deaths of children. It made
substantial reference to recommendations from Ontario, particularly in
relation to the creation of child-specific offences. Among the six coroner's
inquests in Ontario, three recommended that the federal government
amend the Criminal Code. All three recommended the inclusion of an
offence of death by child abuse or neglect in the Criminal Code. One
inquest recommended at the same time the removal from the Criminal
Code of infanticide, which, as a woman-specific offence and separate
from murder and manslaughter, has historically embodied a theme of
tragedy and sympathy, and hence drawn lenient punishment.[48] Another
inquest proposed that the offence of death by child abuse or neglect not
'require the specific intent to kill[,] with a minimum term of imprisonment[,] without eligibility for parole [and] to be classed as second
degree murder,'[49] not recognizing that the very definition of murder
rests on the proof of intent to kill. The objective of creating such a new
offence, as the Department of Justice duly noted, is that it result in more
convictions and lengthier sentences and 'focus attention on society's
condemnation' of such conduct.[50]

It seems clear from the structure of the consultation paper that the
Department of Justice considered the contemplated reform as an extension of legal reforms set in motion by the 1984 report of the Committee
on Sexual Offences Against Children and Youth (the Badgley committee).[51] The principles concerning the special legal status of children laid
down in the context of sexual offences by the Badgley committee are
now being expanded to all other forms of abuse. Then the consultation
paper identified three areas of possible reform of the Criminal Code:

- Creating more child-specific offences, that is, criminal physical abuse
  of a child, criminal neglect of a child, criminal emotional abuse of a
  child, child homicide (a child-specific form of manslaughter), and
  failing to report crimes involving child abuse or neglect
- Sentencing changes to improve protection of children from those
  who might re-offend, in other words, more severe sentences and
  longer terms of supervision and/or treatment
- Facilitating the testimony of child victims and providing for assistance to child witnesses[52]

If reforms are implemented following this direction, what will emerge is a child-specific territory on the map of criminal offences, subject to harsher criminal punishment. The creation of distinct governing spaces is a crucial device for articulating and hence allowing unequal treatment in liberal governance.[53] The basis for creating more child-specific offences, separated from other cases of assault, failure to perform the duty to provide necessities, and homicide, is the adult-child relationship in general, and the parent-child relationship in particular.[54]

The parental obligations of duty and trust are a central theme in child-specific offences and consequent 'appropriately serious penalties.'[55] At the very beginning of the consultation paper, the Department of Justice laid out the terms of parental duties: 'The law has long recognized that parents have the primary role in supporting, protecting and educating their children, and has defined parental duties to take into account the needs of children, as well as the fact that as children grow older, they become less dependent on their parents.'[56]

According to the Department of Justice, one objective of the criminal law is punishment and deterrence of violations of familial and trust relationships; thus, violations of such relationships of trust should be specified as aggravating factors in sentencing.[57] Some ideas tabled in the consultation paper found their way into Bill C-20: An Act to Amend the Criminal Code (Protection of Children and Other Vulnerable Persons) and the Canada Evidence Act, which was introduced in the House of Commons in 2003. The part of the bill relevant to the discussion here was amendments (clauses 11 and 12) to increase the maximum available penalty for child neglect, abandonment, or exposure from the existing maximum of two years' imprisonment to five years. Another proposed amendment (clause 24) deemed an aggravating factor 'evidence that the offender, in committing the offence, abused a child.' Existing provision refers specifically to abuse of the offender's child. Bill C-20 died on the order paper when Parliament was prorogued in November 2003. In February 2004, 2003's Bill C-20 was reintroduced as Bill C-12, which also died on the order paper while waiting second reading in the Senate when the election was called in May 2004.[58] If the widespread criticism of Judge Donald Halikowski's sentencing of a couple near Blackstock, Ontario, who abused their adoptive sons for more than thirteen years might serve as an indicator of public pressure,[59] it seemed likely that the amendments will be reintroduced. Indeed, soon after the opening of the House of Commons in October 2004, Bill C-2, a revised version of Bill C-20 and Bill C-12, was introduced by the minority Liberal government. Revisions were made to clauses concerning child pornography; the content of clauses that are relevant to this discussion remain the same.[60]

The current child-protection approach, which couples preventive risk management with reactive punishment of 'parent perpetrators,' contrasts drastically with the knowledge-based social 'gardening' strategies, which were developed in the nineteenth century for governing the humanist subject mainly through discipline and pastoral techniques. In the early period, child saving was focused on diagnosing the causes of child abuse and neglect and normalizing the conduct of parents accordingly. In contrast, current child protection aims at guaranteeing one minimum condition of life – personal safety. Conceptually, it transforms the causes of child abuse and neglect to personal risk factors. Practically, it shifts the emphasis from treatment to information management, to provide safety and the punishment of perpetrators on an individual basis.

Citizenship, Safety, and Governing Technology

Overall, the lesson from the early history of child protection is that the categories of children, child abuse, and neglect are not self-evident ones, and there are no necessary or neutral ways of organizing child-protection work. The current conception of children as citizens whose rights to safety are violated by parental abuse and neglect is a product of the societal and political obsession with victimization, consumerism, individual safety, blame, and punishment. As much as historical ideas and practices of child protection reflect contemporary concerns with the citizenship of the nation, current ideas and practices exemplify the privatization of citizenship and individualization of responsibility in the larger context.

Ontario's Child Welfare Reform manifests a process of privatizing citizenship at the turn of the twenty-first century, wherein public discussions about rights, power, ethics, and actions by the state or communities are organized by questions of personal significance. Berlant argues that questions of intimacy, sexuality, reproduction and the family 'overorganize' these public discussions, at the expense of excluding questions of capitalism, poverty, environmental degradation, racism, and so on.[61] I have shown that in the area of child protection the question of personal safety has become another dimension of deliberation on the rights and obligations of citizenship. Personal safety is defined as the primary entitlement to which child-victim citizens have rights. Specifically, victimization at the personal level (in contrast to victimization at the structural level such as through poverty resulting from capitalism, racism, and/or patriarchal gender relations) and consumerhood are two of the few things that generate ethical and political claims. This rationality of rights to safety is not monopolized by the political right; in fact, it has also been quite absorbed by those on the left. Safety is a bottom-line condition for personal existence; hence, its paradoxical implications. On the one hand, safety makes a strong, almost irrefutable argument for justifying public spending in the aftermath of privatization and drastic cuts to the welfare state. On the other hand, building claims on safety has serious political consequences.

One effect of the preoccupation with personal safety is that well-being is constituted as if it were primarily a matter of personal safety. This produces the illusion that safety is the only issue important enough to legitimate public actions. No one can argue against the right to safety, because it is so basic to our existence. And yet, the preoccupation with the entitlement to safety severely restricts the scope of other claims. In the early period, the well-being of children was thought of more in terms of the interest of the morality of society rather than as a personal matter. This legitimated child saving and, more importantly, allowed the extension of actions from child saving to more supportive measures, such as playground facilities and Mother's Allowances. Today's preoccupation with personal safety, however, confines actions to those which manage risks of harm and punish perpetrators. It shapes the thinking in such a way that it seems political consensus on collective responsibility is only imaginable in situations where personal safety is violated. In this sense, it is probably sound to say that the long-term effect of the safety discourse will be a drastic lowering of commitments to collective responsibility. One should therefore be wary about deploying the argument of personal safety and building criticisms of the system by referring to individual deaths or other manifestations of a lack of safety.

Another effect of the discourse of safety is that through safety thinking, a logic of crime and justice is introduced that reframes social problems which emerged as public issues during the social era in the twentieth century. Such a logic inevitably seeks to produce individual perpetrators. With such a logic, individuals in the society are positioned within a dichotomy of victims and perpetrators: children versus parent perpetrators, and passersby versus homeless people on the street. These raise serious questions about new conceptions of human subjects. It seems that the population is now divided into two groups: victims with rights and (potential) perpetrators. As a conceptualization device, the division between victims and perpetrators produces innocent young children as the icons of victims with rights, and hence the model citizen. Furthermore, it fragments and weakens familiar categories such as 'youth' and 'mothers' that emerged in the social era and have served as conceptual foundations for various social-engineering programs in the twentieth century. This fragmentation comes from the possibility that individuals can be considered as victims with citizenship rights in one situation and perpetrators in another. For example, a young teenager can be a victim at home but a criminal on the street. Similarly, a woman can be both a victim of domestic abuse and an accomplice to or even perpetrator of child abuse or neglect by exposing her children to domestic violence at the same time. In contrast to the discipline and pastoral power applied to the humanist subject during most of the twentieth century, the new perpetrator subjects are governed through a combination of risk technology and punishment. This new mode of power is manifested not only in child protection, but also in other areas, such as criminal justice, where the rehabilitation model has been challenged. Parental power over children also seems to have started taking on features of this new mode of power. Risk management of children, as opposed to 'gardening,' is beginning to be considered appropriate, at least in some situations such as periodical drug-testing at home.[62] At the same time, corporal punishment of children is defended with increasing vigour.

The analysis of the history and current state of child protection suggests possible challenges to the way in which parents, and especially poor single mothers, are being governed through the spectre of child death by abuse and particularly neglect. First, the argument of 'personal safety' needs to be problematized. We need to document when, where, and how 'personal safety' is posed as a justification for public policy. In the field of child protection the focus on children's personal safety draws on an extremely narrow understanding of needs, from the perspective of people other than parents and children themselves. It does not allow for a good look at resources, because the implied message is that as long as poor kids are safe we do not care about much else, and almost certainly not their quality of life. Furthermore, it pits parents and children against each other as perpetrators and victims, and in effect subsumes the question of child welfare under that of criminality. The preoccupation with safety and the larger trend of discussing citizenship entitlements and responsibilities only in terms of personal criminal acts must be criticized and resisted. Structural questions regarding, for example, capitalism, poverty, patriarchy, and racism need to be brought to the fore in discussions of what ought to constitute entitlements and obligations in child-protection policy, as well as other areas of public policy. It should also be noted that although the safety rationality is different from the rationality of society's interests, they do have one commonality: They both fail to recognize and address the needs of children and parents from their own perspectives. Thus, I argue that the needs of children and parents defined from their own stances must be considered in the making of child-protection policy. The orientation of child protection should be redefined to be supportive not just of children but also supportive of parents rather than hostile.

Second, more empirical studies in diverse areas are needed to grasp the ascendancy of the mode of power coupling risk management technology and punishment. This should in turn provide material with which to think about governance in the broader context, that is, what are the prevailing assumptions about human subjects and how are we governed at the turn of the twenty-first century? Current child-protection technologies, which mainly consist of risk management at the provincial level and criminal punishment at the federal level, should also be questioned. Risk-management and criminal-punishment policies are directed at detecting risk factors for abuse and neglect and punishing offences, without actually addressing problems of poverty, inadequate housing, isolation, and substance use. They also render invisible the fact that resources for meeting the needs of poor parents, particularly poor single mothers, and their children have been drastically diminished in recent years. Larger budgets to do more and better of the same, which Ontario's children's aid societies have received since the Child Welfare Reform, are not the answer to resource deprivation problems confronting parents and children. Instead, public resources should be diverted to establish a support infrastructure. A national child care system would be an immense help to many poor single mothers, whose families constitute the largest category of clients of children's aid societies. Child care would defuse the need for many intrusive child-protection interventions. We need only turn to the history of the shelter of the Toronto Children's Aid Society to see that from the perspective of families who were not able to care for their children because of life exigencies, supportive measures such as residential care or day care were much-needed help and they did not stigmatize or threaten the integrity of families. We also see from the history of the shelter and other child care facilities that society at large as well as much of the social work profession have tended to be hesitant or resistant about such collective community support measures.[63] In a time when the institution of citizenship has been shrunk and privatized and collective actions have become increasingly unthinkable in the public imagination, building community support is harder but also even more vital.

At the theoretical level, this book raises serious questions about citizenship, conceptions of human identity, and modes of power designed for governing human subjects at the turn of the twenty-first century. Those who are interested in debates about the transformation of citizenship should pay attention to both the history and current practices of child protection. Given the ways in which conceptions of children have changed and the ways in which children (particularly those who are victims of personal violence) have become crucial to citizenship today, child protection is an important empirical area for studies of citizenship. In addition, the ways in which child-citizens are constituted in a variety of sites should also be examined. For example, in the area of immigration, children who are adopted from other countries are represented as the perfect immigrants, who are entitled to compassion and preferential treatment. Case studies of the conceptions of children in child protection, immigration, the regulation of drunk drinking, domestic violence, and so on can shed light on the construction of citizenship today – who counts as 'the people,' and how social memberships are measured and valued, and with what consequences.

Notes

Introduction

1 Foucault, 'Politics and Reason,' p. 83.
2 Jones and Rutman, *In the Children's Aid.*
3 See McCullagh, *A Legacy of Caring.*
4 Foucault, 'Nietzsche, Genealogy, History.'
5 Ibid., p. 159.
6 Ibid., p. 149.
7 Ibid.
8 Foucault, 'Governmentality.'
9 Dean, *Governmentality,* p. 11.
10 Rose and Miller, 'Political Power beyond the State,' p. 175; O'Malley, Weir, and Shearing, 'Governmentality, Criticism, Politics,' p. 501.
11 Dean, *Governmentality,* p. 11.
12 O'Malley et al., 'Governmentality, Criticism, Politics,' p. 501.
13 Dean, *Critical and Effective Histories,* p. 182.
14 See Dean's discussion of Foucault's genealogy of governmentality in ibid.
15 Foucault, 'Politics and Reason.'
16 Donzelot, *The Policing of Families.*
17 Valverde, *The Age of Light, Soap, and Water,* pp. 20–2.
18 Foucault, *The History of Sexuality,* vol. 1. Colin Gordon, 'Governmental Rationality.'
19 Gordon, 'Governmental Rationality,' p. 5.
20 For a feminist discussion of social reproduction and social policy, see Pascall, *Social Policy.*
21 O'Malley et al., 'Governmentality, Criticism, Politics.'
22 Rose and Miller, 'Political Power beyond the State,' p. 175.

23 Rose, 'Government, Authority and Expertise in Advanced Liberalism,' p. 293.
24 This part of the discussion draws largely on Hindess, *Discourses of Power.*
25 Ibid., p. 113
26 Ibid., p. 115.
27 Ibid., p. 123.
28 Foucault, 'The Subject and Power,' p. 223.
29 For similar observations of men in administrative positions in Canadian social services see Burke, *Seeking the Highest Good*; Baines, 'From Women's Benevolence to Professional Social Work'; Swift, 'Missing Persons'; and Wills, *A Marriage of Convenience.*
30 Valverde, *The Age of Light, Soap, and Water*, p. 30.
31 Kelso diary, March–April, 1894, Vol. 3, File 'Daily Journals 1894,' Kelso Fonds, National Archives of Canada (NAC).
32 Gordon, *Heroes of Their Own Lives.*
33 Children's Aid Society of Toronto, Annual Report Jan. 1998–March 1999.
34 Rose, 'The Biology of Culpability.'
35 Berlant, *The Queen of America Goes to Washington City.*

1 The Emergence of Child Saving

1 For a discussion of legislation and institutions concerning the welfare of children in the ninetenth century, see for example, Splane, *Social Welfare in Ontario, 1791–1893*, chapter 6. For an overview of provisions for children in England and the United States, see, respectively, Pinchbeck and Hewitt, *Children in English Society*, and Thomas, 'Child Abuse and Neglect, Part I.'
2 Reitsma-Street provides a useful discussion of the history of the doctrine in 'More Control than Care.' See also Labaree, '*Parens Patriae*,' and Custer, 'The Origin of the Doctrine of *Parens Patriae.*'
3 Parallel to measures to protect children from their parents, during the 1880s the province also began to take actions to protect children in industrial plants, which were increasing rapidly in number and size. Splane, *Social Welfare in Ontario*, p. 255.
4 At the time it was common practice for parents to indenture children with skilled craftsmen or tradesmen (i.e., masters) on a one-to-one basis to receive vocational training as apprentices and provide services in return. Neff includes a discussion of such trade apprenticeship in her 'Pauper Apprenticeship in Early Nineteenth-Century Ontario.'
5 Houlbrooke, *The English Family.*
6 Philippe Ariès's *L'enfant et la vie familiale sous l'ancien régime*, which was

translated as *Centuries of Childhood* in 1962, was one of the best-known volumes on childhood. It has influenced many works on the subject since the 1960s. In his review article on recent works on the history of childhood, Hugh Cunningham commented that it was an achievement for Ariès to have convinced nearly all readers that childhood had a history. One of the most famous and controversial arguments in the English version of Ariès's book is that 'in medieval society the idea of childhood did not exist' (p. 125). According to Cunningham, this was a misunderstanding resulting from problematic translation of the French word *sentiment* into the English word 'idea.' The concept of childhood certainly existed in the Middle Ages, as several writers have shown in their rebuttals of this statement in the English translation of Ariès's book. The recent breakthrough in scholarship on the history of childhood, however, as Cunningham argues, is a break away from the 'obsession with defending the Middle Ages against an imagined slur by Ariès' (p. 197). This breakthrough is represented by James Schultz's *The Knowledge of Childhood in the German Middle Ages, 1100–1350.* In his work, Schultz documented the existence of the concept of childhood in the middle ages and showed its fundamental difference from the modern concept of childhood (Cunningham, 'Histories of Childhood').

7 Schultz, *The Knowledge of Childhood in the German Middle Ages.*

8 In *The Knowledge of Childhood,* Schultz identified the eighteenth-century Enlightenment as the turning point for modern concepts of childhood. Steven Ozment, however, suggested that changes in concepts of childhood took place even earlier, probably in the context of the sixteenth-century humanism. See *When Fathers Ruled.*

9 This emphasis is illustrated in Ozment's examination of two widely circulated tracts: *On Disciplining and Instructing Children,* by the Strasbourg humanist and physician Otto Brunfel, and *Behaviour Befitting Well-Bred Youth,* by the Dutch scholar and leading humanist Desiderius Erasmus. See Ozment, *When Fathers Ruled,* p. 136.

10 Gordon, 'Child Abuse, Gender, and the Myth of Family Independence,' p. 523.

11 Ozment, *When Fathers Ruled,* p. 147.

12 Ibid.

13 Ibid.

14 Ibid., p. 134.

15 Ibid., p. 133.

16 Mason, 'Neglected Children Apprenticed by Selectman in Watertown, Mass.,' pp. 212–13.

17 For a history of moral reform in English Canada, see Valverde, *The Age of*

Light, Soap, and Water. For a discussion of theological and intellectual ideas that shaped the urban reform in general, see Cook, *The Regenerators.* A major work on the 'social gospel' aspect of urban reform is Allen, *The Social Passion.* Morrison explores women's roles in the reform in '"Their Proper Sphere" Feminism.'

18 The following works contain influential discussions of the history of child saving in English Canada: Ramsay, 'The Development of Child Welfare Legislation in Ontario'; Jolliffe, 'The History of the Children's Aid Society of Toronto'; Jones and Rutman, *In the Children's Aid*; Sutherland, *Children in English-Canadian Society*; Splane, *Social Welfare in Ontario*; Rooke and Schnell, *Discarding the Asylum*; Bullen, 'J.J. Kelso and the 'New' Child-Savers'; Swift, 'An Outrage to Common Decency'; Comacchio, *Nations Are Built of Babies.*

19 Jones and Rutman, *In the Children's Aid*, pp. 16, 120.

20 Sutherland, *Children in English-Canadian Society.*

21 Swift, 'Contradictions in Child Welfare.'

22 Rooke and Schnell, *Discarding the Asylum.*

23 The following discussion of the Christian mission movement draws largely on Hutchinson, *Errand to the World*; Neill, A *History of Christian Missions*; and Brouwer, *New Women for God.*

24 Brouwer, *New Women for God*, chapter 1; Austin, *Saving China.*

25 For a discussion of the historical relationship between evangelizing and civilizing, see Hutchinson, *Errand to the World.*

26 Kaison, 'The Anti-Cruelty Work in China.' *National Humane Review* regularly carried reports on 'anti-cruelty work in other lands.'

27 Kelso, 'Boarding or Free Homes for Children,' manuscript, n.d., File 'Boarding Homes, n.d.,' Vol. 4, Kelso Fonds, National Archives of Canada (NAC).

28 Brouwer, *New Women for God*, chapter 4. Magic lantern slides were glass lantern slides, often hand-tinted, made for projection on a large screen. Predecessors of the slide projector, they became very popular for entertainment and education around the turn of the twentieth century.

29 Jones and Rutman, *In the Children's Aid.*

30 Platt, *The Child Savers.*

31 Maurutto, *Governing Charities.*

32 Carrigan, *Juvenile Delinquency in Canada.*

33 Ibid., p. 40.

34 Influential discussions of the history of child protection in the United States can be found in Antler and Antler, 'From Child Rescue to Family Protection'; Hiner, 'Children's Rights, Corporal Punishment, and Child Abuse'; Tiffin, *In Whose Best Interest?*; Ashby, *Saving the Waifs*; Thomas, 'Child Abuse and Neglect'; Katz, 'Child-Saving'; Kasinsky, 'Child Neglect and "Unfit"

Mothers'; and several works by Gordon: 'Child Abuse, Gender, and the Myth of Family Independence'; 'Single Mothers and Child Neglect'; 'Family Violence, Feminism, and Social Control'; *Heroes of Their Own Lives.*

35 Influential discussion of the history of child protection in Britain can be found in Pinchbeck and Hewitt, *Children in English Society*; Behlmer, *Child Abuse and Moral Reform in England, 1870–1908*; Parton, *The Politics of Child Abuse*; Holman, 'Prevention'; Cooter, *In the Name of the Child*; Ferguson, 'Cleveland in History'; Violence Against Children Study Group, *Taking Child Abuse Seriously*; and Hendrick, *Child Welfare* and *Children, Childhood and English Society, 1880–1990.*

36 In the 1870s an Ontario Association for the Prevention of Cruelty to Animals was established, modelled after the societies for the prevention of cruelty to animals (SPCAs) in Britain and the United States. Owing to lack of public support, however, the association was active only for a brief period. See Jones and Rutman, *In the Children's Aid*, p. 22.

37 See Jones and Rutman, *In the Children's Aid.*

38 Splane, *Social Welfare in Ontario*, chapter 6. These acts were the first of their kind in English-speaking Canada. Later, other provinces, with the exception of Quebec, the Northwest Territories, and the Yukon, developed similar legislation. Ontario's child protection act of 1893 was amended many times in the twentieth century, and was eventually replaced by the Child and Family Services Act in 1984. Swift, *Manufacturing 'Bad Mothers,'* chapter 3. The Child Welfare Reform (1996–9) included significant amendments to the Child and Family Service Act, as is detailed in chapter 8.

39 *Report of the Commission Appointed to Enquire into the Prison and Reformatory System of Ontario*, 1891, p. 40, Archives of Ontario (AO).

40 Splane, *Social Welfare in Ontario*, chapter 6, p. 270.

41 Jones and Rutman, *In the Children's Aid*, p. 59.

42 Mulvany, *Toronto.*

43 Board of Management Minutes, February 1892. Children's Aid Society of Toronto (CAST) Fonds, City of Toronto Archives (CTA).

44 Jones and Rutman, *In the Children's Aid*, p. 64.

45 According to Jones and Rutman, there was persistent conflict within the Humane Society between those who wished to focus on cruelty to animals and those who believed that children should be the priority. This, together with the lack of legislation concerning child protection, resulted in very limited child-saving work when it was undertaken under the auspices of the Humane Society. Ibid., pp. 48–53.

46 In fact, throughout the history of the Toronto Children's Aid Society in the twentieth century, the largest category of child maltreatment has been

neglect. See Swift, *Manufacturing 'Bad Mothers,'* p. 4, citing Trocmé and Tam, 'Correlates of Substantiation of Maltreatment in Child Welfare Investigations.' It should be noted, however, that neglect cases during the period that I examined differ from today's neglect cases in that most children were older (roughly between the age of 7 and 12) and they were seen more as potential dangers to the society than as innocent victims.

2 The Twin Evils of Cruelty and Neglect

1 This observation is prompted by Mariana Valverde's work on administrative knowledge, contrasted with social scientific knowledge. See Valverde, *Diseases of the Will* and Levi and Valverde, 'Knowledge on Tap.'
2 For a useful discussion in the English context of the movement against cruelty to animals and its class and religious biases see Harrison, 'Animals and the State in Nineteenth-Century England.'
3 Untitled printed material on the organization of the Toronto Humane Society (probably proceedings of the Canadian Institute), 1887, Vol. 1, Kelso Fonds, National Archives of Canada (NAC).
4 Kelso's letter to the editor of the *World*, c. March 1887, Vol. 2, Kelso Fonds, NAC.
5 Breines and Gordon, 'The New Scholarship on Family Violence.'
6 See, for example, Kempe and Kempe, *Child Abuse*; Justice and Justice, *The Abusing Family*; Steele and Pollack, 'A Psychiatric Study of Parents Who Abuse Infants and Small Children.' For critical analysis of these and other concepts, see Breines and Gordon, 'The New Scholarship on Family Violence' and Swift, *Manufacturing 'Bad Mothers.'*
7 See, for example, Spinetta and Rigler, 'The Child-Abusing Parent' and Steele and Pollack, 'A Psychiatric Study of Parents Who Abuse Infants and Small Children.'
8 See, for example, Klaus and Kennell, 'Mothers Separated from Their Newborn Infants'; Money and Needleman, 'Impaired Mother-Infant Pair Bonding in the Syndrome of Abuse Dwarfism'; Schwarzbeck, 'Identification of Infants at Risk for Child Abuse'; Bowlby, *Attachment and Loss.*
9 See, for example, Gil, 'Unraveling Child Abuse.'
10 The Toronto Humane Society's statement of objectives, quoted in Splane, *Social Welfare in Ontario*, p. 266.
11 #9328, Complaint Book, 1903, Children's Aid Society of Toronto (CAST) Fonds, City of Toronto Archives (CTA). In this book, names of clients and case numbers are fictional to protect clients' anonymity.
12 #8, Complaint Book, 1892, ibid.

13 #10, Complaint Book, 1892, ibid.

14 Kelso, untitled manuscript on cruelty charges against institutions, n.d., File 'Reform and Reformatories n.d. 1923,' Vol. 6, Kelso Fonds, (NAC).

15 #9457, Complaint Books, 1903, CAST Fonds, CTA.

16 Newspaper clipping, 'Cruelty to Animals,' c. Feb. 1887, n.s., Vol. 1, Kelso Fonds, NAC.

17 Newsclipping of a report on Kelso's speech in Sarnia on the Children's Aid Society's work, c. June 1906, n.s., File 'General Scrapbook 1905 ...,' Vol. 11, Kelso Fonds, NAC.

18 Foucault, *Ethics*, p. 6.

19 Carrigan, *Juvenile Delinquency in Canada*, pp. 49–50.

20 Kelso, untitled manuscript on mental defects as a major cause of crime, File 'Reform & Reformatories n.d.,' vol. 6, Kelso Fonds, NAC.

21 Newspaper clipping, 'Charities' Conference Begins,' Oct. 5, 1904, n.s., Vol. 13, Kelso Fonds, NAC.

22 Kelso, manuscript titled 'Disappointing Foster Parents,' n.d., File 'Adoption n.d., 1925,' Vol. 3, Kelso Fonds, NAC.

23 See, for example, Sutherland, *Children in English-Canadian Society*, chapter 5. The concept of heredity in the late nineteenth century should not be equated with the panic over 'feeblemindedness.' The latter was a notion specific to the first few decades of the twentieth century.

24 Newspaper clipping, 'Causes of Crime,' 1909, Vol. 14, Kelso Fonds, NAC.

25 Kelso, handwritten notes on the margin of a newspaper clipping of Kelso's letter to the editor of the *Mail and Empire* titled 'A Great Social Problem,' 26 April 1922, File 'Child Welfare 1920–1927,' Vol. 12, Kelso Fonds, NAC.

26 Newspaper clipping, 'Drunkards Are Feeble Minded, Alienist Says,' 15 Oct. 1912, File 'Child Welfare 1920–1927,' Vol. 12, Kelso Fonds, NAC.

27 Newspaper clipping of Kelso's letter titled 'A Great Social Problem,' ibid.

28 For example, Kelso, manuscript titled 'Boys Who Fail' c. 1920s–1930s, File 'Reform and Reformatory,' Vol. 6, Kelso Fonds, NAC.

29 In 1924, Judge Emerson Coatsworth still identified lack of segregation in jails as a factor related to juvenile delinquency. Proceedings of the Canadian Association of Child Protection Officers at the Fourth Annual Meeting, Toronto, 1924, Vol. 24, Kelso Fonds, NAC.

30 Kelso, manuscript titled 'Working Boys' Home,' n.d., Vol. 4, Kelso Papers, NAC.

31 Charlotte Whitton, lecture notes titled 'III. Juvenile Delinquency,' p. 4, File 'MS. – Juvenile Delinquency – 1919–20,' Vol. 19, Whitton Fonds, NAC.

32 Cartoon titled 'The Flaming Youth Problem,' File 4, Vol. 13, Kelso Fonds, NAC.

33 For more on Charlotte Whitton's thinking and her career, see Rooke and Schnell, *No Bleeding Heart*. See also Moffatt, *A Poetics of Social Work*, chapter 6, for a detailed examination of Whitton's philosophy.

34 Whitton, Lecture notes titled 'III. Juvenile Delinquency.'

35 Kelso, manuscript titled 'Newsboys Lodging,' n.d., File 'Kelso, John Joseph. Autobiographical Files. Early Work. n.d.; 1864–1935,' Vol. 1, Kelso Fonds, NAC.

36 Whitton, lecture notes titled 'III. Juvenile Delinquency,' pp. 2–3.

37 Coatsworth, 'The Prevention of Crime,' in 'Proceedings of the Canadian Association of Child Protection Officers, June 24–25, 1924,' p. 17, File 'Canadian Association of Child Protection Officers Annual Meetings,' Vol. 24, Kelso Fonds, NAC.

38 Kelso, notes, n.d., File '230 Diary 1893,' Vol. 34, Kelso Fonds, NAC.

39 Coatesworth, 'The Prevention of Crime,' p. 15.

40 Ibid.

41 Kelso notes, c. 1893, File '230 Diary 1893.'

42 For example, J.K. Macdonald's report on the work of the Toronto Children's Aid Society, 'City Must Care for Delinquents,' newspaper clipping, Nov. 1918, n.s., Vol. 12, Kelso Fonds, NAC.

43 Whitton, lecture notes titled 'III. Juvenile Delinquency,' in which she posed the question 'What contributes to "going wrong" at this age?'

44 Kelso, notes, c. 1893, p. 30, File '230 Diary 1893.'

45 Kelso, notes, n.d., File '229 Diary 1889–93,' Vol. 34, Kelso Fonds, NAC.

46 Whitton, lecture notes titled 'III. Juvenile Delinquency.'

47 For example, the two terms and categories seemed interchangeable in An Act for the Protection and Reformation of Neglected Children, 1888, File 'Kelso, John Joseph 1864–1935 Early Work n.d.,' Vol. 1, Kelso Fonds, NAC. In the 1921 amendments to the Child Protection Act of Ontario, the definition of a neglected child included 'a habitual delinquent or incorrigible.' Newspaper clipping, 'Will Penalize Parents Found Abusing Child,' *Globe*, March 1921, File 'Child Welfare 1920–1927,' Vol. 12, Kelso Fonds, NAC.

48 For example, see Shelter Committee Minutes 11 Oct. 1906, File 3, Vol. 87, CAST Fonds, CTA.

3 'Cultivating Children as You Would Valuable Plants'

1 An earlier version of this chapter appears in Chen, 'Cultivating Children as You Would Valuable Plants.'

2 Kelso, 'A Plea for the City Waif,' pamphlet, 1891, Vol. 1, Kelso Fonds, National Archives of Canada (NAC).

3 I focus on English gardening because this study was located in English-speaking Canada.

4 *Report of the Commission Appointed to Enquire into the Prison and Reformatory System of Ontario*, 1891, p. 40, Archives of Ontario (AO).

5 Bassin, 'The English Landscape Garden in the Eighteenth Century,' p. 26.

6 Davidoff and Hall, '"My Own Fireside."'

7 Gaskell, 'Gardens for the Working Class,' p. 481.

8 Ibid.

9 von Baeyer, *Rhetoric and Roses*. See also von Baeyer, 'Mackenzie King's Gardening and the Horticultural Times.' Martin, 'Reforming the Landscape,' p. 26.

10 Chambers, 'The Translation of Antiquity,' p. 363.

11 Bell, 'Women Create Gardens in Male Landscape,' p. 1.

12 Ibid.

13 von Baeyer, *Rhetoric and Roses*, p. 70.

14 Chambers, 'The Translation of Antiquity,' p. 363.

15 Bell, 'Women Create Gardens in Male Landscapes.' Von Baeyer, *Rhetoric and Roses*, p. 70.

16 Quaintance, 'Walpole's Whig Interpretation of Landscaping History.' In Walpole's prose, the transition from the European formal garden style dominated by 'the line, shears, compass, and square (p. 289)' to the emerging alternative of the English landscape garden recreating nature's picturesque curving lines, irregularity, and asymmetry, was characterized as 'the shift from gross despotic to benign aristocratic design' (p. 292). The former was associated with pompous, inhumane, and arbitrary monarchs, and the latter 'an "English" respect for local vitality' (p. 285) and 'Whig regard for talented initiative, confidence in "improvement," and mistrust of "an arbitrary monarchy"' (p. 285). As a comparison, in his paper on French formal garden design and its parallel to classical theatre, Peter V. Conroy Jr. mentions in passing a comment made by Helen Fox that the gardens of the French garden architect André Le Notre 'express the political and philosophical thoughts of seventeenth-century France' (p. 666) ('French Classical Theatre and Formal Garden Design').

17 Quaintance, 'Walpole's Whig Interpretation of Landscaping History,' p. 297.

18 Valverde, 'The Dialectic of the Familiar and the Unfamiliar.'

19 Ibid., p. 504.

20 Ibid.

21 Kelso, 'Home Wanted,' 1924, Vol. 12, Kelso Fonds, NAC.

22 Hindess, 'Foucault on Power, Domination and Government,' in *Discourses of Power*, p. 115.

23 Kelso diary, 26 Sept., 1894, Vol. 3, Kelso Fonds, NAC.

24　Kelso diary, 28 Nov. 28, 1894, Vol. 3, Kelso Fonds, NAC.

25　Chambers, 'The Translation of Antiquity,' p. 363.

26　Kelso, notes, c. Feb. 1901, Vol. 34, Kelso Fonds, NAC.

27　Unknown author, 'Childhood in the Strategic Period,' Vol. 12, Kelso Fonds, NAC.

28　Kelso, 'Reforming Delinquent Children,' speech delivered at the 13th National Conference of Charities and Correction, Atlanta, GA, 8 May 1903, Vol 1, Kelso Fonds, NAC.

29　Kelso, 'Items of Interest on Social Work,' *Humane Pleader*, 1923, Vol. 7, Kelso Fonds, NAC.

30　Bruce, 'Teach by Example,' *Toronto Star*, Feb. 1916, newspaper clipping, Vol. 14, Kelso Fonds, NAC.

31　Newspaper clipping, 'Childrens' [*sic*] Aid Work,' *The Daily British Whig*, 10 Nov. 1913, Vol. 12, Kelso Fonds, NAC.

32　Kelso diary, n.d., Vol. 34, Kelso Fonds, NAC.

33　The early intervention approach meant a focus on children as opposed to adults. It is different from the current early childhood development approach that emphasizes the first months of life.

34　Kelso, 'Reforming Delinquent Children,' 1903, Vol. 1, Kelso Fonds, NAC.

35　Cowper, cited by Kelso in his diary, 1896, Vol. 34, Kelso Fonds, NAC.

36　Kelso, 'Home Wanted.'

37　Kelso, untitled manuscript, n.d. Vol. 4, Kelso Fonds, NAC.

38　Kelso, manuscript titled 'No Moral Training,' Vol. 6, Kelso Fonds, NAC.

39　Kelso, 'Some Thoughts on Social Problems,' *Canadian Municipal Journal*, Aug. 1917, Vol. 4, Kelso Fonds, NAC.

40　Kelso, 'Home Wanted.'

41　Kelso, 'Can Slums Be Abolished, or Must We Continue to Pay the Penalty?' pamphlet, 1910, p. 8., Vol. 1, Kelso Fonds, NAC.

42　Kelso, printed notes titled 'Suggestions for Dealing with Wayward Boys,' n.d., Vol. 6, Kelso Fonds, NAC.

43　Valverde, *Diseases of the Will*, especially pp. 35–42.

44　Kelso, 'Can Slums be Abolished.'

45　In some other situations, habits can appear as the 'other' of the will, as Valverde points out in *Diseases of the Will*.

46　Kelso, 'Suggestions for Dealing with Wayward Boys.'

47　Unknown author, quoted in Kelso's diary, c. 1884, Vol. 34, Kelso Fonds, NAC.

48　Kelso, manuscript titled 'Civil and Moral Law,' n.d., c. mid-1920s, Vol. 12, Kelso Fonds, NAC.

49　Kelso, 'Items of Interest on Social Work.'

50 Kelso, 'Ontario Child Welfare,' *Humane Pleader*, 1922, Vol. 7, Kelso Fonds, NAC.
51 Kelso, 'Items of Interest on Social Work.'
52 Ibid.
53 Ibid.
54 Kelso, 'Child-Saving: Purpose and Methods of a Boys and Girls Aid Society,' pamphlet, 1890, Vol. 4, Kelso Fonds, NAC.
55 Kelso, 'The Spiritual Hospital,' 1913, Vol. 12, Kelso Fonds, NAC.
56 Kelso, manuscript titled 'Character-building,' n.d., Vol. 4, Kelso Fonds, NAC.
57 Kelso, 'Sparks from the Social Anvil,' pamphlet, n.d., Vol. 7, Kelso Fonds, NAC.
58 Kelso, untitled manuscript, n.d., Vol. 6, Kelso Fonds, NAC.
59 Ibid.
60 Kelso, notes titled 'Moral Virtues Never Flourish When Forced,' 1893, Vol. 34, Kelso Fonds, NAC.
61 Kelso, 'Education of the Heart,' *Humane Review*, Nov. 1930, Vol. 13; the same article was also published in *Canadian Child*, Dec. 1930, Vol. 5, Kelso Fonds, NAC. This piece of writing by Kelso suggests that the heart still featured as a major target of moral reform even in the 1930s, despite the ascendance of social scientific discourse focused on the mind. Because it was a well-written and well-circulated article and it represented the thinking originating in the earlier period, I draw on it despite the fact that it was published in 1930.
62 Kelso, untitled manuscript, n.d., Vol. 6, Kelso Fonds, NAC.
63 Unknown author, 'The Humane Pleader – The Toronto Humane Society or S.P.C.A.' n.d., Vol. 12, Kelso Fonds, NAC.
64 Ibid.
65 Kelso, 'Reforming Delinquent Children.'
66 Kelso, 'Education of the Heart.'
67 Ibid.
68 Kelso, 'Utility of the Curfew,' 1913, p. 8, Vol. 1, Kelso Fonds, NAC.
69 Ibid., p. 3.
70 Ibid.
71 Kelso, 'Home Wanted.'
72 Kelso notes, n.d. Vol. 14, Kelso Fonds, NAC.
73 Unknown author, 'The Weeds that Bothered Dora,' *Juvenile Court Record*, Chicago, Dec. 1907. Vol. 1, Kelso Fonds, NAC.
74 Valverde, 'The Dialectic of the Familiar and the Unfamiliar.'
75 Kelso, manuscript titled 'Guide Instead of Punish,' n.d. Vol. 7, Kelso Fonds, NAC.
76 Kelso, 'Child-Saving.'

77 'Prevention of Cruelty,' newspaper clipping, no source, c. 1887, Vol. 2, Kelso Fonds, NAC.
78 Kelso, manuscript titled 'Causes of Neglect,' n.d., Vol. 4, Kelso Fonds, NAC.
79 Ibid.
80 Quoted by Kelso, Kelso's notebook, Vol. 34, Kelso Fonds, NAC.
81 Kelso, 'Friendly Visiting,' n.d., c. 1910s, Vol. 6, Kelso Papers, NAC.
82 Ibid.
83 See Burke's *Seeking the Highest Good*, a historical study of Toronto's University Settlement as an application of idealism to problems generated by poverty.
84 Kelso, manuscript titled 'Social Settlements,' n.d., Vol. 6, Kelso Fonds, NAC.
85 Kelso, untitled manuscript on neglect and crime, n.d., Vol. 6, Kelso Fonds, NAC.
86 Kelso, 'Utility of the Curfew,' p. 8.
87 Splane, *Social Welfare in Ontario*, p. 270.
88 Unknown author, 'The "Kids" Judge,' *Canadian Epworth Era*, p. 9, June, 1906, Vol. 4, Kelso Fonds, NAC.
89 Mott, 'Social Consciousness in Our Relationships Today,' *The Eighteenth Annual Conference of Association of Children's Aid Societies of the Province of Ontario*, 1930, p. 9. Vol. 4, Kelso Fonds, NAC.
90 Complaint Books, Toronto Children's Aid Society, Children's Aid Society of Toronto (CAST) Fonds, City of Toronto Archives (CTA).
91 Kelso, 'A Plea for the City Waif,' 1891, Vol. 1, Kelso Fonds, NAC.
92 In Toronto, the detention room for the Juvenile Court was in the shelter of the Children's Aid Society from 1894 to 1920. For more details, see chapter 6.
93 Kelso, 'The Ideal Reform School,' Vol. 6, Kelso Fonds, NAC.
94 Kelso, untitled manuscript on reform schools, n.d., c. 1920s, Vol. 6, Kelso Fonds, NAC.
95 For example, Kelso, untitled manuscript on foster homes, n.d., c. 1920s, Vol. 3, Kelso Fonds, NAC.
96 Kelso, 'Utility of the Curfew,' p. 8.
97 Ibid.
98 Ibid.
99 Ibid.
100 Ibid, p. 4.
101 Kelso, untitled manuscript, n.d., File 'Reform and Reformatories, n.d.' Vol. 6, Kelso Fonds, NAC.
102 'Merit of Strap Is Debatable,' newspaper clipping, Vol. 13, Kelso Fonds,

NAC; 'Favor Spanking for Juvenile Offenders,' newspaper clipping, c. 1933, Vol. 13, Kelso Fonds, NAC.
103 See, for example, posters produced by Invest in Kids Foundation, Toronto, 2000. I thank Dawn Moore for drawing my attention to this.

4 Reports, Visits, and Case Records

1 Foucault, 'The Subject and Power,' p. 224.
2 Board of Management Minutes, 23 Feb. 1901, Children's Aid Society of Toronto (CAST) Fonds, City of Toronto Archives (CTA).
3 In one case, a father laid a complaint against his mother-in-law, who held his child because he didn't pay a bill. Complaint Books, CAST Fonds, CTA.
4 Callahan, 'Feminist Approaches.'
5 Constitution and By-Laws of the Children's Aid Society of Toronto, CAST Fonds, CTA. For discussions of the history of Juvenile Court and juvenile justice, see Dorothy Chunn, *From Punishment to Doing Good*; P. Havemann, 'From Child Saving to Child Blaming'; Bryan Hogeveen, '"Winning Deviant Youth Over by Friendly Helpfulness"'; Hogeveen, 'Political Discourse and the Perceived Crisis in Youth Crime in the 1990s'; Franca Iacovetta, 'Parents, Daughters, and Family Court Intrusions into Working-Class Life'; J.E. Laycock, 'Juvenile Courts in Canada'; J.S. Leon, 'The Development of Canadian Juvenile Justice'; J. Trépanier, 'The Origin of the Juvenile Delinquent Act of 1908'; Larry C. Wilson, *Juvenile Courts in Canada*.
6 Board of Management Minutes, 23 Nov. 1905, CAST Fonds, CTA.
7 Ibid.
8 Ibid., 21 May 1896.
9 Ibid., 15 Dec. 1892.
10 Ibid., 19 and 31 May 1895.
11 Ibid., 16 March 1900, 26 March 1903.
12 Ibid., 13 Sept. 1906.
13 Ibid., 15 Jan. 1903.
14 Ibid., 20 June 1907.
15 Ibid., 1 April 1908.
16 Ibid., 30 March 1911.
17 Ibid., 19 Sept. 1907, 16 Jan. 1908.
18 'Half Our Insane Foreigners Ontario Has to Pay,' newspaper clipping, *Evening Telegram*, 25 Nov. 1908, Toronto, Vol. 13, Kelso Fonds, NAC.
19 Kelso, manuscript titled 'The Dominion Juvenile Act,' n.d. Vol. 1, Kelso Fonds, National Archives of Canada (NAC).
20 Chen, 'The Juvenile Court.'

21 Board of Management Minutes, 18 May and 19 Oct. 1911, CAST Fonds, CTA.
22 Newspaper Clipping, 'How "Big Sisters" Help Lonely Girls,' n.d., *Toronto Star*, Glen Papers, CAST Fonds, CTA. See also Robinson, *Decades of Caring.*
23 For example, Kelso diary, 30 July 1893, 13 Sept. 1893, 17 Jan. 1894, 27 Jan. 1894, 9 April 1894, 12 April 1894, 23 April 1894, 23 July 1894, 8 Sept. 1894, 1 Sept. 1894, Vol. 3, Kelso Fonds, NAC. Board of Management Minutes, 15 Dec. 1892, 16 Feb. 1893, CAST Fonds, CTA.
24 Kelso notes, n.d., File '234 Diary 1922–33,' Vol. 34, Kelso Fonds, NAC.
25 Kelso, untitled notes on the work of various organizations concerning children, n.d. Vol. 4, Kelso Fonds, NAC.
26 Iacovetta and Mitchinson, *On the Case.*
27 Valverde, 'Review of *On the Case,*' unpublished ms, July 1999.
28 Board of Management Minutes, 15 June 1905, CAST Fonds, CTA.
29 Maynard, 'On the Case of the Case,' p. 66 n. 3.

5 The Shelter

1 Dean, *Critical and Effective Histories*, p. 20.
2 Kelso, manuscript, 'Children's Shelter,' n.d., File 'Children's Aid Society, Ontario, Notes, Activities n.d., 1906, 1929,' Vol. 4, Kelso Fonds, National Archives of Canada (NAC).
3 Kelso's letter to the Editor of the *World*, c. March 1887. Vol. 2, Kelso Fonds, NAC.
4 Newspaper clipping, c. 12 Dec. 1889, *Globe*, Vol. 2, Kelso Fonds, NAC.
5 As several historians of Canadian social services have observed, these institutions for children, which had child care characteristics, first emerged in the 1830s and flourished during the late nineteenth and the early twentieth centuries. They provided a significant resource for poor families. However, by the 1920s the domination of ideas about the superiority of home-based child care led to the closure of some children's institutions and the transformation of some others to residences for children with special needs. See Rooke and Schnell, *Discarding the Asylum*, and Strong-Boag, 'Intruders in the Nursery.' See also Baines, 'The Children of Earlscourt, 1915–1948,' for a discussion of the history of the Earlscourt Children's Home as an exceptional institution that adhered to its original mission.
6 Board of Management Minutes, 30 March 1892, Children's Aid Society of Toronto (CAST) Fonds, City of Toronto Archives (CTA).
7 Ibid.
8 Ibid., 25 May 1892.
9 Complaint Books, 1913, case 19714, CAST Fonds, CTA.

10 Ibid.
11 Iacovetta, 'Parents, Daughters, and Family Court Intrusions into Working-Class Life.'
12 Complaint Books, 1893, case 73, CAST Fonds, CTA.
13 Ibid., 1892, case 34.
14 Ibid., 1893, case 88.
15 Kelso, untitled manuscript on Emily's fight with her husband, n.d., Vol. 4, Kelso Fonds, NAC.
16 Complaint Books, 1913, case 19868, CAST Fonds, CTA.
17 Ibid., 1903, case 9429. A month later the society apparently persuaded the father to sign papers to give his boy up to the society, because it thought it was in the best interest of the boy that it take charge of him. Later he was placed in a foster home. The last entry in his case record shows that he joined the army.
18 Ibid., 1903, case 9390.
19 See, for example, ibid., 1903, case 9715.
20 Board of Management Minutes, 26 March 1894, CAST Fonds, CTA.
21 Shelter Committee Minutes, 4 Feb. 1904, 10 March 1904, 12 May 1904, 8 Sept. 1904, CAST Fonds, CTA.
22 Samuel Wotton's statement, included in Board of Management Minutes, 16 Dec. 1898, CAST Fonds, CTA.
23 Board of Management Minutes, 30 Nov. 1898, CAST Fonds, CTA.
24 Ibid., 16 Dec. 1898.
25 Ibid., 25 Sept. 1902, 17 Oct. 1902.
26 City of Toronto Board of Control Minutes, 19 April and 9 May 1901, City Executive Committee Fonds, CTA. Board of Management Minutes, 17 May 1901, CAST Fonds, CTA.
27 Board of Management Minutes, 17 May 1901, CAST Fonds, CTA.
28 Children's Aid Society of Toronto 19th Annual Report, 1801, CAST Fonds, CTA.
29 Board of Management Minutes, 21 Feb. 1895. CAST Fonds, CTA.
30 Ibid., 15 Feb. 1894.
31 Ibid., 20 Dec. 1894.
32 Ibid., 21 May 1896.
33 Ibid., 21 March 1912.
34 Ibid., 15 Feb. 1906.
35 Ibid., 21 March 1912.
36 'Complains of the Shelter,' Mail and Empire, 25 March 1916.
37 See Rooke and Schnell's description of Protestant Orphans Home, in Discarding the Asylum.

38 Constitution, Children's Aid Society of Toronto, File 'Printed Material 1891–1970,' Box 87, CAST Fonds, CTA.

39 Kelso diary, 5 July 1893, File 1, 'Daily Journal 1893,' Vol. 3, Kelso Fonds, NAC.

40 Board of Management Minutes, 3 July 1906, CAST Fonds, CTA.

41 Ibid., 17 June 1902, 27 May 1915.

42 See Rooke and Schnell, *Discarding the Asylum*, for references to the Ladies Committee in a House of Industry. At the Toronto CAS, the other committee with female members was the Fresh Air Committee.

43 See Board of Management Minutes, 23 March 1893, CAST Fonds, CTA.

44 Ibid., 6 June 1898.

45 Ibid., 19 May 1904.

46 See ibid., 1 Nov. 1894.

47 Shelter Committee Minutes, 14 May 1903, CAST Fonds, CTA.

48 Kealey, *A Not Unreasonable Claim*, Prentice et al., *Canadian Women*, chapter 7.

49 See, for example, Board of Management Minutes, 17 March 1904, 19 Oct. 1900, CAST Fonds, CTA.

50 Ibid., 18 April 1912, CAST Fonds, CTA.

51 Ibid., 21 March 1907, CAST Fonds, CTA.

52 Kealey, *A Not Unreasonable Claim*; Morrison, '"Their Proper Sphere" Feminism.'

53 Board of Management Minutes, 27 April 1905, CAST Fonds, CTA.

54 Ibid., 31 Oct. 1895.

55 Ibid., 15 March 1917.

56 Ibid., 19 April 1917.

57 Ibid., 17 May 1917.

58 Ibid., 28 June 1917.

59 Ibid., 15 Nov. 1917, 20 Dec. 1917.

60 Ibid., Jan. 1918.

61 Ibid., Jan. 1918.

62 Ibid., 20 June 1918.

63 Ibid., 17 Sept. 1918.

64 Ibid., 20 Feb. 1919.

65 Ibid., 17 Oct. 1919.

66 Ibid., 30 March 1911.

67 Ibid., 17 Oct. 1919.

68 Ibid., 18 Oct. 1919.

69 Ibid., 18 Dec. 1919.

70 Ibid., 15 Jan. 1920.

71 Ibid., 19 Feb. 1920.

72 Ibid., 19 Feb. 1920.

73 Community homes refer to families that are not licensed as foster homes but are considered qualified to provide temporary care.
74 Personal communication with staff of the Children's Aid Society of Toronto, 13 Oct. 2000.
75 Ontario government news release, 'New Funding Framework for Children's Aid Societies,' 3 Dec. 1998, www.gov.on.ca:80/css/page/news (accessed 31 Jan. 2000).

6 The Detention Room

1 The name detention room changed to detention home in 1916, when it was moved to a building separate from the shelter.
2 Authority Record for Division 1, Metropolitan Toronto Police Service Fonds, City of Toronto Archives (CTA).
3 Board of Management Minutes, 24 Feb. 1892, Children's Aid Society of Toronto (CAST) Fonds, CTA.
4 Complaint Books, 1892, CAST Fonds, CTA.
5 Board of Management Minutes, 6 Oct. 1892, CAST Fonds, CTA.
6 Ibid., 20 Oct. 1892.
7 Complaint Books, 1893, CAST Fonds, CTA.
8 'New Ideas Needed by Magistrates,' *Mail and Empire*, 20 Oct. 1909, newspaper clipping, Vol. 13, Kelso Fonds, National Archives of Canada (NAC).
9 Board of Management Minutes, 21 Oct., 11 Nov., 16 Dec. 1915, CAST Fonds, CTA.
10 Kelso, untitled notes, n.d., Vol. 4, Kelso Fonds, NAC.
11 Board of Management Minutes, 1 Nov. 1894, CAST Fonds, CTA.
12 Shelter Committee Minutes, 1903, CAST Fonds, CTA.
13 Board of Management Minutes, 25 Oct. 1906, CAST Fonds, CTA.
14 Shelter Committee Minutes, 14 Oct. 1907, CAST Fonds, CTA.
15 Board of Management Minutes, 17 Oct., 5 Nov., 21 Nov. 1907, CAST Fonds, CTA.
16 Ibid., 21 May 1908.
17 Shelter Committee minutes, 10 Nov. 1914, CAST Fonds, CTA.
18 Board of Management Minutes, 27 Nov. 1914, CAST Fonds, CTA.
19 Ibid., 18 Feb. 1915.
20 Ibid., 21 Oct. 1915.
21 Ibid., 11 Nov. 1915.
22 Ibid., 11 Nov., 16 Dec. 1915.
23 Ibid., Feb. 1916. 'Court's Fullest Inquiry – Children's Aid Society – President J.K. Macdonald Defends the Work of Shelter – Never Meant to Provide for

Delinquent Boys,' newspaper clipping, 5 Dec. 1916, Vol. 12, Kelso Fonds, NAC.

24 'Court's Fullest Inquiry.'
25 Board of Management Minutes, 18 Oct., 15 Nov. 1917, Jan. 1918, CAST Fonds, CTA.
26 Ibid., 17 Sept. 1918.
27 Ibid., 21 Nov. 1918.
28 'City Must Care for Delinquents,' Nov. 1918, newspaper clipping, Vol. 12, Kelso Fonds, NAC.
29 Board of Management Minutes, Dec. 1918, CAST Fonds, CTA.
30 Ibid., 20 Feb. 1919.
31 Ibid., 17 April 1919.
32 Ibid., 19 Feb. 1920.
33 For example, Carrigan, *Juvenile Delinquency in Canada.*
34 Board of Management Minutes, 17 Oct. 1907, CAST Toronto, CTA.
35 Ibid., 8 Dec. 1908.
36 Ibid.
37 Ibid.
38 Ibid., 16 March 1916.
39 Complaint Books, 1903, CAST Fonds, CTA.
40 Board of Management Minutes, 21 Feb., 18 April, 16 May 1907, CAST Fonds, CTA.
41 Shelter Committee Minutes, 9 Nov. 1911, CAST Fonds, CTA.
42 Board of Management Minutes, 16 Nov. 1911, CAST Fonds, CTA.
43 Shelter Committee Minutes, 14 Dec. 1911; Board of Management Minutes, 21 Dec. 1911, CAST Fonds, CTA.
44 Shelter Committee Minutes, 11 Jan. 1912, CAST Fonds, CTA.
45 Ibid., 14 March 1912.
46 Robinson's historical account of the Big Sister Association is a useful source of information. See *Decades of Caring.*
47 'Working among the Young Boys Who Need a Brother's Care,' *Toronto Sunday World,* n.d., newspaper clipping, Dorothy Glen Papers, CAST Fonds, CTA.
48 Glen Papers, 1916–1920, CAST Fonds, CTA. Apparently, Dorothy Glen was never on the staff of the Toronto Children's Aid Society; however, she came to associate with the society in her capacity as a Big Sister. Her papers were donated by her husband, Andrew Glen, to the Metro Toronto Children's Aid Society in 1975. There is evidence that the donation was a response to coverage of the Metro Toronto CAS and its anniversary celebration in 1975 in CBC's *Voice of a Pioneer* program.
49 Glen, notes, n.d. [post-1911], Glen Papers, CAST Fonds, CTA.

50 Glen, notes, n.d. [post-1916], ibid.
51 Board of Management Minutes, 17 June and 16 Sept. 1915, CAST Fonds, CTA.
52 Kelso notes, Vol. 12, Kelso Fonds, NAC.
53 'Complaints of the Shelter,' 25 March 1916, *Mail and Empire*, Vol. 12, newspaper clipping, Kelso Fonds, NAC.
54 Ibid.
55 Ibid.; 'Children's Shelter Under Criticism – Local Council of Women Ask City Council to Hold Investigation,' n.d., n.s., Vol. 12, newspaper clipping, Kelso Fonds, NAC.
56 Macdonald's letter to Mayor T.L. Church, 8 April 1916. Board of Management Minutes, 17 April 1916, CAST Fonds, CTA.
57 Ibid.
58 Shelter Committee Minutes, 20 June 1918, CAST Fonds, CTA.
59 Macdonald's letter to Mayor T.L. Church, 8 April 1916.
60 Board of Management Minutes, 21 Sept. 1916, CAST Fonds, CTA.
61 Ibid., 17 May 1917.
62 Ibid.
63 Macdonald's letter to Mayor T.L. Church, 8 April 1916.
64 Ibid.

7 Foster Care

1 See, for example, Kendrick, *Nobody's Children*; Meyer, 'A Feminist Perspective on Foster Family Care'; Mnookin, 'Foster Care.'
2 Neff, 'Pauper Apprenticeship in Early Nineteenth-Century Ontario.'
3 Ibid.
4 Ibid. Abbott, *The Child and the State.*
5 Splane, *Social Welfare in Ontario*, pp. 266–7. Neff, 'Pauper Apprenticeship in Early Nineteenth-Century Ontario.'
6 For example, the Protestant Orphans Home placed children out and, as Kelso noted in 1893, a Mrs Leigh kept a list of them. Kelso diary, File 1, 'Daily Journal 1893,' Vol. 3, Kelso Fonds, National Archives of Canada, (NAC). See also Neff's discussion of apprenticeship by children's homes during the nineteenth century, in 'Pauper Apprenticeship in Early Nineteenth-Century Ontario,' and Rooke and Schnell, *Discarding the Asylum.*
7 Houlbrooke, *The English Family*, p. 175.
8 Abbott, *The Child and the State.*
9 Rooke and Schnell, *Discarding the Asylum*; Katz, 'Child-Saving' and 'Saving Children.'
10 Rooke and Schnell, *Discarding the Asylum.*

11 Kelso, manuscript, 'Not Enough to Eat,' n.d., File 'Charity & Charity Organization n.d. 1917,' Vol. 4, Kelso Fonds, NAC.
12 Kelso, untitled manuscript on a successful foster care story, n.d., File 'Adoption n.d. 1925,' Vol. 3, Kelso Fonds, NAC.
13 Circular, 'Appointment of Children's Visiting Committee,' 1894, File 'Conference, Ontario – Child-saving Work 1894,' Vol. 4, Kelso Fonds, NAC.
14 Kelso, 'Believed Husband to be Highly Connected,' File 'Adoptions, n.d. 1925, 1930,' Vol. 3, Kelso Fonds, NAC.
15 Circular, 'Child Saving,' 1890, Vol. 4, Kelso Fonds, NAC.
16 Kelso, manuscript, 'Dependent Children,' File 'Adoption n.d. 1925,' Vol. 3, Kelso Fonds, NAC.
17 Ibid.
18 Kelso, notes, n.d., File '234 Diary 1922–33,' Vol. 34, Kelso Fonds, NAC.
19 Kelso, untitled manuscript of anecdotes, Vol. 1, Kelso Fonds, NAC.
20 Smith and Smith, 'For Love and Money'; Meyer, 'A Feminist Perspective on Foster Family Care.'
21 Newspaper clipping, 'Child Welfare Social Duty,' *Globe*, c. March 1933, File 1, Vol. 13, Kelso Fonds, NAC.
22 Ibid.
23 For example, Latimer's study of the Toronto Infants' Homes shows that by 1920 the agency abandoned institutional care as a primary method of caring and began a new era in foster-home care. Latimer, 'Methods of Child Care as Reflected in the Infants' Homes of Toronto.'
24 Kelso diary, 14 May 1894, File 2, 'Daily Journal 1894,' Vol. 3, Kelso Fonds, NAC.
25 Zelizer's *Pricing the Priceless Child* documents the shift in emphasis from the economic value of children to their sentimental value in middle-class families. In the case of child protection, which dealt mostly with working-class children, a parallel and related shift in emphasis was from the economic value of children to the importance of their morals to society.
26 Kelso diary, 4 Aug. 1893, Vol. 3, Kelso Fonds, NAC.
27 Kelso, 'Ontario Child Welfare,' *Humane Pleader*, May 1922, Vol. 6, Kelso Fonds, NAC.
28 Dependence can be seen as coerced in the case of older children who otherwise might have supported themselves by their own labour.
29 For example see Board of Management Minutes, 15 June 1905, Children's Aid Society of Toronto (CAST) Fonds, City of Toronto Archives (CTA).
30 Neff, 'Pauper Apprenticeship in Early Nineteenth-Century Ontario.'
31 Kelso, 'Desirability of State Supervision of Children Placed in Foster Homes,' Juvenile Court Record, Dec. 1907, Chicago, File 'Speeches,' Vol. 1, Kelso Fonds, NAC.

32 Ibid.
33 Board of Management Minutes, 18 March 1897, CAST Fonds, CTA.
34 Ibid.
35 Although the placing-out of infants may have been recorded as adoption even before the passage of the Adoption Act in 1921, legally infants were placed in foster homes, not adopted.
36 Kelso, 'Desirability of State Supervision of Children Placed in Foster Homes.'
37 Ibid.
38 Kelso, manuscript, 'Boarding or Free Homes for Children,' File 'Boarding Homes n.d.,' Vol. 4, Kelso Fonds, NAC.
39 Board of Management Minutes, 17 March 1910, CAST Fonds, CTA.
40 See, for example, Kelso's story about finding a Chinese foster home for a baby born to a white girl and a 'Chinaman,' n.d. File 'Unmarried Parents Act 1906–07, 1917, 1922, 1926, 1930,' Vol. 5, Kelso Fonds, NAC.
41 Kelso, untitled manuscript on how to present a child to potential foster parents, n.d., File 'Child Placement n.d. 1908, 1917,' Vol. 4, Kelso Fonds, NAC.
42 Kelso, untitled manuscript on how to seek out foster homes, File 'Children's Aid Society, Notes, historical,' Vol. 4, Kelso Fonds, NAC.
43 Kelso, 'Boarding or Free Homes for Children,' n.d., File 'Boarding Homes n.d.,' Vol. 4, Kelso Fonds, NAC.
44 Kelso diary, 19 April, 12 Sept. 1894, Vol. 3, Kelso Fonds, NAC.
45 Kelso, 'Desirability of State Supervision of Children Placed in Foster Homes.'

8 Child Protection at the Turn of the Twenty-first Century

1 Ontario Child Mortality Task Force, p. 2. See Parton, 'Reconfiguring Child Welfare Practices,' for a discussion of the emergence of child abuse inquiries into the deaths of children in Britain in the 1970s and the mid-1980s.
2 Gove Inquiry into Child Protection, *Report of the Gove Inquiry into Child Protection in British Columbia.*
3 Personal communication, 13 Oct. 2000.
4 The name of Ontario's Child Mortality Task Force may suggest that it was not consistent with the 1990s norm of individualized discourse about deaths, as it considers statistics. However, its blatantly problematic assembling and interpretation of data actually illustrate the current policy-making trend, which strives for some kind of qualitative measure of reality, such as the tragic nature of child deaths or single-mother households, rather than being attuned to issues of quantitative magnitude, such as the lower rate of child

deaths among children involved with the child protection system. For a detailed critique, see Chen, 'Constituting 'Dangerous Parents' through the Spectre of Child Death.'

5 See Ontario Child Mortality Task Force, *Ontario Child Mortality Task Force Final Report*; Ontario Association of Children's Aid Societies, *Inquest Recommendations by Topic*; Ontario Association of Children's Aid Societies, *Ontario Child Mortality Task Force Recommendations*; Department of Justice, 'Child Victims and the Criminal Justice System: A Consultation Paper'; Karstulovich, 'New Legislation Paves the Way to Protecting Children Better.'

6 Ontario Association of Children's Aid Societies Web site, www.oacas.org (accessed 23 April 2001), cited in Chen, 'Constituting "Dangerous Parents."'

7 Baines, 'Restructuring Services for Children'; Parton, 'Risk, Advanced Liberalism and Child Welfare.'

8 See Anglin, 'Meaning and Implication of the Move to Paramountcy of the Safety and Well-Being of the Child.'

9 Department of Justice, 'Child Victims and the Criminal Justice System: A Consultation Paper' and 'Child Victims and the Criminal Justice System: Technical Background Paper.'

10 See Chen, 'The Birth of the Child-Victim Citizen.'

11 Children's Aid Society of Toronto, Annual Report Jan. 1998–March 1999.

12 Rose, 'The Biology of Culpability.'

13 Newspaper clipping of a report on Kelso's speech in Sarnia on the Children's Aid Society's work, c. June 1906, n.s., File 'General Scrapbook 1905 ...,' Vol. 11, Kelso Fonds, National Archives of Canada (NAC).

14 Minow, 'Rights for the Next Generation'; O'Neill, 'Children's Rights and Children's Lives'; Stasiulis, 'The Active Child Citizenship.'

15 Best, *Threatened Children*; Ivy, 'Have You Seen Me?'; Berlant, *The Queen of America Goes to Washington City*; Scobey, 'The Specter of Citizenship'; Chen, 'The Birth of the Child-Victim Citizen.'

16 Chen, 'Tending the Gardens of Citizenship'; Jenson, 'Canada's Shifting Citizenship Regime'; Wiegers, *The Framing of Poverty as 'Child Poverty' and Its Implications for Women*; Nadesan, 'Engineering the Entrepreneurial Infant'; Currie, 'Child Citizenship in the Infancy of the Synaptic Self.'

17 Best has provided a useful analysis of the rise of the child-victim in America, especially the panic about missing children in the 1980s. Best, *Threatened Children*. See also Marilyn Ivy for a discussion of the centrality of child victimization discourse (particularly around missing children) in American culture and politics in 'Have You Seen Me?'

18 Ivy, 'Have You Seen Me?' p. 235.

19 Berlant, *The Queen of America Goes to Washington City*.
20 Ontario Ministry of Community and Social Services news release, 26 April 1999.
21 Department of Justice, 'Child Victims and the Criminal Justice System: A Consultation Paper,' p. 26.
22 Best, *Threatened Children*.
23 'Getting Away with Murder of Children,' *Toronto Star*, 18 May 1997.
24 Lister, 'Dialectics of Citizenship'; Neysmith, 'Networking across Difference.'
25 'How Did the System Fail These Kids,' *Toronto Star*, 18 Sept. 1996.
26 Karstulovich, 'New Legislation Paves the Way.'
27 Ontario Child Mortality Task Force, *Final Report*. For a critical analysis of the report, see Chen, 'Constituting "Dangerous Parents."'
28 The Children's Aid Society of Toronto (CAST) Web site, www.casmt.on.ca (accessed 23 April 2001).
29 Trocmé et al., *Canadian Incidence Study of Reported Child Abuse and Neglect*.
30 Armitage, 'The Policy and Legislative Context'; Swift, *Manufacturing 'Bad Mothers*,' and 'Failure to Protect.'
31 Beck, *Risk Society*.
32 Rose, *Powers of Freedom*, p. 166.
33 For a detailed examination of the social construction of accidental death as a major problem confronting the child protection system, see Chen, 'Constituting "Dangerous Parents."'
34 Ewald, 'Insurance and Risk.' In her research on the history of infanticide, Kirsten Johnson has found that a pathologist at the Toronto Hospital for Sick Children put down 'child abuse' as cause of death in many cases, including accidental deaths and suicides. This supports the argument that child welfare issue are now being subsumed under criminality. Personal communication, 10 Feb. 2000.
35 Berlant, *The Queen of America Goes to Washington City*.
36 For comments on the British Columbia experience since 1996, see Anglin, 'Meaning and Implication of the Move to Paramountcy of the Safety and Well-Being of the Child.' Current transformation of service to a community-based governance may have quite different implications for policy and practice.
37 In her examination of recent legal moves in Britain, Vikki Bell argues that members of a family have been treated as individuals. However, she observes that simultaneously there is contradictory manoeuvre of 'befriend[ing] "the family" as a unit' (p. 390). This does not seem to apply in Ontario. Bell, 'Governing Childhood.'
38 Rose, 'The Biology of Culpability.' See also Valverde's analysis of alcoholism

in recent law, which shows that alcoholism is no longer a defence, even if one does not know what one is doing. Valverde, *Diseases of the Will.*

39 Ontario Association of Children's Aid Socities, *Child Mortality Task Force Recommendations,* p. 5.

40 Personal communication with staff of CAST, 11 Aug. 1999.

41 Ontario Ministry of Community and Social Services, *Risk Assessment Model for Child Protection in Ontario, Executive Summary,* p. 3.

42 Ibid., p. 1.

43 Ibid.

44 Personal communication with staff at CAST, 21 July 1999.

45 Baines, 'The Children of Earlscourt' and 'From Women's Benevolence to Professional Social Work.'

46 Parton, 'Risk, Advanced Liberalism and Child Welfare.' Baines, 'Restructuring Services for Children'; Swift, 'Failure to Protect.'

47 Department of Justice 'Child Victims and the Criminal Justice System: A Consultation Paper,' p. 2.

48 For historical writings on infanticide, see Backhouse, 'Desperate Women and Compassionate Courts' and *Petticoats and Prejudice.*

49 Ontario Association of Children's Aid Societies, *Inquest Recommendations by Topic,* p. 17.

50 Department of Justice, 'Child Victims and the Criminal Justice System: Technical Background Paper,' p. 19.

51 For critical perspectives on the report of the Badgley committee, see Brock, *Making Work, Making Trouble.*

52 Department of Justice, 'Child Victims and the Criminal Justice System: Technical Background Paper,' p. 19.

53 Valverde, '"Despotism" and Ethical Liberal Governance.'

54 One historical example of relation-specific offences is petit treason in eighteenth-century England. Petit treason was a criminal offence limited to a particular class of murder: murder of a husband by his wife, of a master by a servant, or of a religious superior by a religious inferior. We can draw some inferences from the example of petit treason regarding the creation of child-specific offences. As Shelley Gavigan suggests, petit treason reflected the pre-capitalist social and economic relations in England, which were based on 'obligations of duty, subjection, and allegiance' (p. 347). The murder of one's master was greater than murder because it was 'the conscious and deliberate breach of one's duty' and 'the abuse of a confidence' (p. 347). The murder of one's husband was also greater than murder, as it was the violation of subjection and obedience that was due (only) from the

wife to the husband. Thus, such murders were treachery exceeded only by disloyalty to the king, which was high treason. In her article, Gavigan emphasizes petit treason cases in which wives were accused of murdering their husbands. Women convicted of killing their husbands were burned at the stake as traitors. The exemplary penalties for women were considered necessary on the basis of their violation of the 'most sacred obligation' (p. 358). Thus, the law of petit treason both reflected and reinforced social and economic relations of gender and class, which were anchored in feudal forms of obligations.

55 For example, Department of Justice Canada, 'Child Victims and the Criminal Justice System: Technical Background Paper,' p. 15.

56 Ibid., p. 1. Also, Department of Justice, 'Child Victims and the Criminal Justice System: A Consultation Paper,' p. 2.

57 Department of Justice, 'Child Victims and the Criminal Justice System: Technical Background Paper,' p. 8.

58 See Legislative Summaries, Bill C-12, for more details, www.parl.gc.ca/common/Bills   (accessed 15 June 2004).

59 Globe and Mail, 6 July 2004.

60 Bill C-2, www.parl.gc.ca/common/Bills   (accessed 10 Oct. 2004). Personal communication with Department of Justice personnel, 15 Oct. 2004.

61 Berlant, The Queen of America Goes to Washington City, p. 8.

62 Personal communication with Dawn Moore, 13 Dec. 2000.

63 For discussions on child care services in Canada, see Teghtsoonian, 'Neoconservative Ideology and Opposition to Federal Regulation of Child Care Services in the United States and Canada'; Prentice, ed., Changing Child Care.

References

Archival Sources

City of Toronto Archives (CTA), Toronto:
  Children's Aid Society of Metropolitan Toronto Fonds
  City Executive Committee Fonds
  Metropolitan Toronto Police Service Fonds
Archives of Ontario (AO), Toronto:
  Commission Appointed to Enquire into the Prison and Reformatory
    System of Ontario, 1890
National Archives of Canada (NAC), Ottawa:
  John Joseph Kelso Fonds
  Charlotte Whitton Fonds
  William Louis Scott Fonds

Other Primary Sources

Children's Aid Society of Toronto. 'Annual Report Jan. 1998 to March 1999.'
– *Communication Online, www.casmt.on.ca/co.*
– *Eligibility Spectrum and Family Service Case Management Systems Users' Manual.* July
    1999.
Department of Justice, Canada. 'Child Victims and the Criminal Justice System:
    A Consultation Paper.' Nov. 1999. *www.canada.justice.gc.ca/en/cons/child/*
    toc.html (accessed on 18 Feb. 2000).
– 'Child Victims and the Criminal Justice System: Technical Background Paper.'
    Nov. 1999.
Gove Inquiry into Child Protection (British Columbia, Canada). *Report of the*
    Gove Inquiry into Child Protection in British Columbia: A Commission of Inquiry into

the Adequacy of the Services, Policies and Practices of the Ministry of Social Services as They Relate to the Apparent Neglect, Abuse and Death of Matthew John Vaudreuill. Thomas J. Gove, the Commissioner. Victoria: The Commission, 1995.

Ontario Association of Children's Aid Societies. *Inquest Recommendations by Topic.* Feb. 1998.

– *Ontario Child Mortality Task Force Recommendations: A Progress Report.* April 1998.

Ontario Child Mortality Task Force. *Ontario Child Mortality Task Force: Final Report.* Ontario Association of Children's Aid Societies and the Office of the Chief Coroner of Ontario, July 1997.

Ontario Ministry of Community and Social Services. *Child Welfare Accountability Review: Final Report.* Jan. 1998.

– News releases. *www.gov.on.ca:80/CSS/page/news* (accessed on 31 Jan. 2000).

– *Risk Assessment Model for Child Protection in Ontario.* 2000.

– *Risk Assessment Model for Child Protection in Ontario: Executive Summary.* Oct. 1997.

Ontario Office of the Chief Coroner. *Report on Inquests into the Deaths of Children Receiving Services from a Children's Aid Society,* vols. 1–7. Nov. 1998.

Ontario Panel of Experts on Child Protection. *Protecting Vulnerable Children: Report of the Panel of Experts on Child Protection.* March 1998.

Secondary Sources

Abbey, Sharon, and Andrea O'Reilley, eds. *Redefining Motherhood: Changing Identities and Patterns.* Toronto: Second Story Press, 1998.

Abbott, Grace, compiler. *The Child and the State,* vols. 1 and 2. Chicago: University of Chicago Press, 1938.

Allen, Richard. *The Social Passion: Religion and Social Reform in Canada, 1914–1928.* Toronto: University of Toronto Press, 1971.

Alston, P., S. Parker, and J. Seymour, eds. *Children, Rights, and the Law.* Oxford: Clarendon, 1992.

Anglin, Jim. 'Meaning and Implication of the Move to Paramountcy of the Safety and Well-Being of the Child in Child Welfare Legislation.' A report prepared for the Department of Justice. Ottawa: Department of Justice, 1999.

Antler, Joyce, and Stephen Antler. 'From Child Rescue to Family Protection: The Evolution of the Child Protective Movement in the United States.' *Children and Youth Services Review* 1 (1979), 177–204.

Ariès, Philippe. *Centuries of Childhood: A Social History of Family Life.* Translated by Robert Baldick. New York: Vintage Books, 1962.

Armitage, Andrew. 'The Policy and Legislative Context.' In *Rethinking Child Welfare.* Brian Wharf, ed. Toronto: McClelland and Stewart, 1993, 37–63.

– Marilyn Callahan, and Chris Lewis. 'Social Work Education and Child

Protection: The B.C. Experience.' Paper presented at the Canadian Association of Schools of Social Work Annual Conference, June 1999, Sherbrooke, Quebec.

Ashby, LeRoy. *Saving the Waifs: Reformers and Dependent Children, 1890–1917.* Philadelphia: Temple University Press, 1984.

Austin, Alvyn. *Saving China: Canadian Missionaries in the Middle Kingdom, 1888 – 1959.* Toronto: University of Toronto Press, 1986.

Backhouse, Constance B. 'Desperate Women and Compassionate Courts: Infanticide in Nineteenth-Century Canada.' *University of Toronto Law Journal* 34 (1984), 447–78.

– *Petticoats and Prejudice: Women and Law in Nineteenth-Century Canada.* Toronto: Women's Press, 1991.

Baines, Carol T. 'The Children of Earlscourt, 1915–1948: All in the Same Boat – "Except we were in a better boat."' *Canadian Social Work Review* 11, no. 2 (1994), 184–200.

– 'From Women's Benevolence to Professional Social Work: The Case of the Wimodausis Club and the Earlscourt Children's Home, 1902–1971.' Doctoral dissertation, Faculty of Social Work, University of Toronto, 1990.

– 'Restructuring Services for Children: Lessons from the Past.' In *Restructuring Caring Labour: Discourse, State Practice, and Everyday Life.* Sheila M. Neysmith, ed. Don Mills, Ont.: Oxford University Press, 2000, 164–84.

Baines, Carol T., Patricia Evans, and Sheila Neysmith, eds. *Women's Caring: Feminist Perspectives on Social Welfare.* Toronto: Oxford University Press, 1998.

Bassin, Joan. 'The English Landscape Garden in the Eighteenth Century: The Cultural Importance of an English Institution.' *Albion* 11, no.1 (1979): 15–32.

Beck, Ulrich. *Risk Society: Towards a New Modernity.* London: Sage, 1992.

Behlmer, George K. *Child Abuse and Moral Reform in England, 1870–1908.* Stanford, Calif.: Stanford University Press, 1982.

Bell, S.G. 'Women Create Gardens in Male Landscape: A Revisionist Approach to Eighteenth-Century English Garden History.' *Feminist Studies* 16, no. 3 (1990), 1–9 (electronic journal version).

Bell, Vikki. 'Governing Childhood: Neo-liberalism and the Law.' *Economy and Society* 22, no. 3 (1993), 390–405.

Berlant, Lauren Gail. *The Queen of America Goes to Washington City: Essays on Sex and Citizenship.* Durham and London: Duke University Press, 1997.

Best, Joel. *Threatened Children: Rhetoric and Concern about Child-Victims.* Chicago and London: University of Chicago Press, 1990.

Bowlby, John. *Attachment and Loss,* vols. 1 and 2. New York: Basic Books, 1969.

Bradbury, Bettina. *Working Families: Age, Gender, and Daily Survival in Industrializing Montreal.* Toronto: McClelland and Stewart, 1993.

Brannen, Julia, and Margaret O'Brien. 'Childhood and the Sociological Gaze: Paradigms and Paradoxes.' *Sociology* 29, no. 4 (1995), 729–37.

Breines, Wini, and Linda Gordon. "The New Scholarship on Family Violence." *Signs* 8, no. 3 (1983), 491–531.

Brickey, S., and E. Cormack, eds. *The Social Basis of Law.* Toronto: Garamond, 1986.

Brock, Deborah. *Making Work, Making Trouble: Prostitution as a Social Problem.* Toronto: University of Toronto Press, 1998.

– ed. *Making Normal: Social Regulation in Canada.* Toronto: Thomson Nelson, 2003.

Broder, Sherri. 'Child Care of Child Neglect? Baby Farming in Late-Nineteenth-Century Philadelphia.' *Gender and Society* 2, no. 2 (1988): 128–48.

Brodie, Janine, and Linda Trimble, eds. *Re-inventing Canada: Politics of the 21st Century.* Toronto: Pearson Education Canada, 2003.

Brouwer, Ruth Compton. *New Women for God: Canadian Presbyterian Women and India Missions, 1876–1914.* Toronto: University of Toronto Press, 1990.

Bullen, John. 'J.J. Kelso and the "New" Child-Savers: The Genesis of the Children's Aid Movement in Ontario.' *Ontario History* 82, no. 2 (1990), 107–28.

– 'Orphans, Idiots, Lunatics, and Historians: Recent Approaches to the History of Child Welfare in Canada.' *Histoire Sociale – Social History* 18, no. 35 (1985), 133–45.

Burchell, G., C. Gordon, and P. Miller, eds. *The Foucault Effect: Studies in Governmentality.* Chicago: University of Chicago Press, 1991.

Burke, Sara. *Seeking the Highest Good: Social Service and Gender at the University of Toronto, 1888–1937.* Toronto: University of Toronto Press, 1996.

Callahan, Marilyn. 'Feminist Approaches: Women Recreate Child Welfare.' In *Rethinking Child Welfare in Canada.* Brian Wharf, ed. Toronto: McClelland and Stewart, 1993, 137–56.

– 'Public Apathy and Government Parsimony: A Review of Child Welfare in Canada.' In *The Challenge of Child Welfare.* Kenneth L. Levitt and Brian Wharf, eds. Vancouver: University of British Columbia Press, 1985, 1–27.

Carrigan, D. Owen. *Juvenile Delinquency in Canada: A History.* Concord, Ont.: Irwin, 1998.

Chambers, Douglas. 'The Translation of Antiquity: Virgil, Pliny and the Landscape Garden.' *University of Toronto Quarterly* 60, no. 3 (1991), 354–73.

Chambon, Adrienne, Allan Irving, and Laura Epstein, eds. *Reading Foucault for Social Work.* New York: Columbia University Press, 1999.

Chen, Xiaobei. 'The Birth of the Child-Victim Citizen.' In *Re-inventing Canada: Politics of the 21st Century.* Janine Brodie and Linda Trimble, eds. Toronto: Pearson Education Canada, 2003, 189–203.

- 'Constituting "Dangerous Parents" through the Spectre of Child Death: A Critique of Child Protection Restructuring in Ontario.' In *Making Normal: Social Regulation in Canada.* Deborah Brock, ed. Toronto: Thomson Nelson, 2003, 209–34.
- '"Cultivating Children as You Would Valuable Plants": The Gardening Governmentality of Child Saving, Toronto, Canada, 1880s–1920s.' *Journal of Historical Sociology* 16, no. 4 (2003), 460–86.
- 'The History of Child Protection: Class, Race, Gender: The United States, England, and English Canada, 1870–1920.' Comprehensive paper, Faculty of Social Work, University of Toronto, 1998.
- 'Is It All Neo-Liberal? – Some Reflections on Child Protection Policy and Neo-Conservatism in Ontario.' *Canadian Review of Social Policy* 45 and 46 (2000), 237–46.
- 'The Juvenile Court: Producing Social Scientific Knowledge at A Cost.' Chapter 5, 'Tending the Gardens of Citizenship: Child Protection in Toronto, 1880s–1920s.' Doctoral dissertation, Faculty of Social Work, University of Toronto, 2001.
- 'Personal Safety as a Public Policy Objective? Implications to Social Development.' Paper for the Eleventh Biennial Canadian Social Welfare Policy Conference, University of Ottawa, Ottawa, June 2003.
- 'Tending the Gardens of Citizenship: Child Protection in Toronto, 1880s–1920s.' Doctoral dissertation, Faculty of Social Work, University of Toronto, 2001.
Chunn, Dorothy E. *From Punishment to Doing Good: Family Courts and Socialized Justice in Ontario 1880–1940.* Toronto: University of Toronto Press, 1992.
Comacchio, R. Cynthia. *Nations Are Built of Babies: Saving Ontario's Mothers and Children.* Montreal and Kingston: McGill-Queen's University Press, 1993.
Conroy, Peter V. Jr. 'French Classical Theatre and Formal Garden Design.' *Dalhousie Review* 59, no. 4 (1979–1980), 666–82.
Cook, Ramsay. *The Regenerators: Social Criticism in Late Victorian English Canada.* Toronto: University of Toronto Press, 1985.
Cooter, Roger, ed. *In the Name of the Child: Health and Welfare, 1880–1940.* London and New York: Routledge, 1992.
Corrigan, Philip. 'On Moral Regulation: Some Preliminary Remarks.' *Sociological Review* 29, no. 2 (1981), 313–37.
Cunningham, Hugh. *Children and Childhood in Western Society since 1500.* London and New York: Longman, 1995.
- 'Histories of Childhood.' *American Historical Review* (Oct. 1998), 1195–1208.
Currie, Gail. 'Child Citizenship in the Infancy of the Synaptic Self: The Neuron-Nation Connection in Canada's Social Policy Renewal.' Paper presented at

the Canadian Sociology and Anthropology Association Annual Meeting,
Dalhousie University, Halifax, Nova Scotia, 1–4 June, 2003.

Custer, Lawrence B. 'The Origin of the Doctrine of *Parens Patriae.' Emony Law
Journal* 27, no. 2 (1978), 195–208.

Davin, Anna. 'Imperialism and Motherhood.' *History Workshop*, no. 5 (1978),
9–65.

Davidoff, Leonore, and Catherine Hall. *Family Fortunes: Men and Women of the
English Middle Class, 1780–1850.* London: Hutchinson, 1987.

– '"My Own Fireside": the Creation of the Middle-class Home.' In *Family Fortunes: Men and Women of the English Middle Class, 1780–1850.* London:
Hutchinson, 1987, 257–96.

De Montigny, Gerald A.J. *Social Working: An Ethnography of Front-Line Practice.*
Toronto: University of Toronto Press, 1995.

Dean, Mitchell. *Critical and Effective Histories: Foucault's Methods and Historical
Sociology.* London and New York: Routledge, 1997.

– *Governmentality: Power and Rule in Modern Society.* London and Thousand Oaks,
Calif.: Sage, 1999.

Denison, George Taylor. *Recollections of a Police Magistrate.* Toronto: Musson,
1920.

Donzelot, Jacques. *The Policing of Families.* Robert Hurley, transl. Baltimore and
London: Johns Hopkins University Press, 1997.

– 'The Promotion of the Social.' *Economy and Society* 17, no. 3 (1988), 395–427.

Dreyfus, Hubert L., and Paul Rabinow. *Michel Foucault: Beyond Structuralism and
Hermeneutics.* Chicago: University of Chicago Press, 1983.

Ewald, François. 'Insurance and Risk.' In *The Foucault Effect: Studies in Governmentality.* G. Burchell, C. Gordon, and P. Miller, eds. Chicago: University of
Chicago Press, 1991, 197–210.

Ferguson, Harry. 'Cleveland in History: The Abused Child and Child Protection, 1880–1914.' In *In the Name of the Child: Health and Welfare, 1880–1940.*
Roger Cooter, ed. London and New York: Routledge, 1992, 146–73.

– 'Rethinking Child Protection Practices: A Case for History.' In *Taking Child
Abuse Seriously: Contemporary Issues in Child Protection Theory and Practice.* Violence Against Children Study Group. London, Unwin Hyman, 1990, 121–42.

Foucault, Michel. *Discipline and Punish: The Birth of the Prison.* Transated by Alan
Sheridan. New York: Vintage Books, [1975] 1995.

– *Ethics: Subjectivity and Truth.* Paul Rabinow, ed., and Robert Hurley and others,
transl. (see M. Margin). New York: New Press, 1997.

– 'Governmentality.' In *The Foucault Effect: Studies in Governmentality.* G. Burchell, C. Gordon, and P. Miller, eds. Chicago: University of Chicago Press,
1991, 87–104.

- *The History of Sexuality, vol. 1.* Translated by Robert Hurley. New York: Vintage Books, [1978] 1990.
- *Language, Counter-memory, Practice: Selected Essays and Interviews.* Donald F. Bouchard, ed., and Donald F. Bouchard and Sherry Simon, transl. Ithaca, New York: Cornell University Press, 1977.
- 'Nietzsche, Genealogy, History.' In *Language, Counter-memory, Practice: Selected Essays and Interviews.* Donald F. Bouchard, ed. and Donald F. Bouchard and Sherry Simon, transl. Ithaca, New York: Cornell University Press, 1977, 149–64.
- 'Politics and Reason.' The Tanner Lectures. Reprinted in *Politics, Philosophy, Culture: Interviews and Other Writings, 1977–1984.* Lawrence D. Fritzman, ed. and transl. New York: Routledge, 1988, 57–85.
- *Power/Knowledge: Selected Interviews and Other Writings 1972–1977.* Colin Gordon, ed. and Colin Gordon, Leo Marshall, John Mepham, and Kate Soper, transl. New York: Pantheon Books, 1980.
- 'The Subject and Power.' In *Michel Foucault: Beyond Structuralism and Hermeneutics.* Hubert L. Dreyfus and Paul Rabinow, eds. Chicago: University of Chicago Press, 1983, 208–26.
- Fraser, Nancy, and Linda Gordon. 'A Genealogy of Dependency: Tracing a Keyword of the U.S. Welfare State.' *Signs* 19, no. 2 (1994), 309–36.
- Garland, David. 'The Limits of the Sovereign State.' *British Journal of Criminology* 36, no. 4 (1996), 445–71.
- *Punishment and Welfare: A History of Penal Strategies.* Brookfield, Vt.: Gower Publishing, 1985.
- Gaskell, S. Martin. 'Gardens for the Working Class: Victorian Practical Pleasure.' *Victorian Studies* 23, no. 4 (1980), 479–501.
- Gavigan, Shelley A.M. 'Petit Treason in Eighteenth-Century England: Women's Inequality before the Law.' *Canadian Journal of Women and the Law* 3 (1989–1990), 335–74.
- Gelles, Richard. 'Child Abuse and Psychopathology: A Sociological Critique and Reformulation.' In *Family Violence.* Richard Gelles, ed. Beverly Hills, Calif.: Sage, 1979, 27–41.
- ed. *Family Violence.* Beverly Hills, Calif.: Sage, 1979.
- 'The Social Construction of Child Abuse.' *American Journal of Orthopsychiatry* 45, no. 3 (1975), 363–56.
- Gil, David C. 'Unraveling Child Abuse.' *American Journal of Orthopsychiatry* 45, no. 3 (1975), 346–56.
- *Violence against Children.* Cambridge, Mass.: Harvard University Press, 1970.
- Gordon, Colin. 'Governmental Rationality: An Introduction.' In *The Foucault Effect: Studies in Governmentality.* G. Burchell, C. Gordon, and P. Miller, eds. Chicago: University of Chicago Press, 1991, 1–51.

Gordon, Linda. 'Child Abuse, Gender, and the Myth of Family Independence: Thoughts on the History of Family Violence and Its Social Control, 1880–1920.' *New York University Review of Law and Social Change* 12 (1983–1984), 523–37.

– 'Family Violence, Feminism, and Social Control.' *Feminist Studies* 12, no. 3 (1986), 453–78.

– *Heroes of Their Own Lives: The Politics and History of Family Violence: Boston, 1880–1960.* New York: Penguin, 1988.

– 'The New Feminist Scholarship on the Welfare State.' In *Women, the State and Welfare.* Linda Gordon, ed. Madison: University of Wisconsin Press, 1990, 9–35.

– Preface to *Taking Child Abuse Seriously*, by Violence against Children Study Group. London: Unwin Hyman, 1990, xv–xviii.

– 'Single Mothers and Child Neglect, 1880–1920.' *American Quarterly* 37, no. 2 (1985), 173–92.

– ed. *Women, the State and Welfare.* Madison: University of Wisconsin Press, 1990.

Hacking, Ian. 'The Making and Molding of Child Abuse.' *Critical Inquiry* 17 (1991), 253–88.

Harrison, Brian. 'Animals and the State in Nineteenth-Century England.' *English Historical Review* 88 (1973), 786–820.

Havemann, P. 'From Child Saving to Child Blaming: The Political Economy of the Young Offenders Act 1908–1984.' In *The Social Basis of Law.* S. Brickey and E. Comack, eds. Toronto: Garamond, 1986.

Helfter, Ray, and C. Henry Kempe, eds. *The Battered Child.* Chicago: University of Chicago Press, 1968.

Hendrick, Harry. *Child Welfare: England, 1872–1989.* London and New York: Routledge, 1994.

– *Children, Childhood and English Society, 1880–1990.* Cambridge: Cambridge University Press, 1997.

Hindess, Barry. *Discourses of Power: From Hobbes to Foucault.* Oxford: Blackwell, 1996.

Hiner, N. Ray. 'Children's Rights, Corporal Punishment, and Child Abuse: Changing American Attitudes, 1870–1920.' *Bulletin of Menninger Clinic* 43, no. 3 (1979), 233–48.

Hogeveen, Bryan. 'Political Discourse and the Perceived Crisis in Youth Crime in the 1990s.' In *Youth Justice: History, Legislation, and Reform.* R. Smandych, ed. Toronto: Brace/Harcourt, 2001, 144–68.

– '"Winning Deviant Youth Over by Friendly Helpfulness": Transformations in the Legal Governance of Deviant Children in Canada, 1857–1908.' In *Youth Justice: History, Legislation and Reform.* R. Smandych, ed. Toronto: Brace/Harcourt, 2001, 43–64.

Holman, Bob. 'Prevention: The Victorian Legacy.' *British Journal of Social Work* 16 (1986), 1–23.

Houlbrooke, Ralph. *The English Family, 1450–1700.* London and New York: Longman, 1984.

Houston, Susan. 'The "Waifs and Strays" of a Late Victorian City: Juvenile Delinquents in Toronto.' In *Childhood and Family in Canadian History.* Joy Parr, ed. Toronto: McClelland and Stewart, 1982, 129–42.

Hutchinson, William R. *Errand to the World: American Protestant Thought and Foreign Missions.* Chicago: University of Chicago Press, 1987.

– *The Modernist Impulse in American Protestantism.* Cambridge, Mass.: Harvard University Press, 1976.

Iacovetta, Franca. 'Parents, Daughters, and Family Court Intrusions into Working-Class Life.' In *On the Case, Explorations in Social History.* Franca Iacovetta and Wendy Mitchinson, eds. Toronto: University of Toronto Press, 1998, 312–37.

Iacovetta, Franca, and Wendy Mitchinson. 'Introduction: Social History and Case Files Research.' In *On the Case: Explorations in Social History.* Franca Iacovetta and Wendy Mitchinson, eds. Toronto: University of Toronto Press, 1998, 3–21.

– eds. *On the Case: Explorations in Social History.* Toronto: University of Toronto Press, 1998.

Irving, Allan. 'The Scientific Imperative in Social Welfare Research in Canada, 1897–1945.' *Canadian Social Work Review* 9 (1992), 9–27.

Ivy, Marilyn. 'Have You Seen Me? Recovering the Inner Child in Late Twentieth-Century America.' *Social Text* no. 37 (1993), 227–52.

Jenson, Jane. 'Canada's Shifting Citizenship Regime: Investing in Children.' In *The Dynamics of Decentralization: Canadian Federalism and British Devolution.* Trevor C. Salmon and Michael Keating, eds. Published for the School of Policy Studies, Queen's University. Montreal and Kingston: McGill-Queen's University Press, 2001, 107–24.

Jolliffe, Russell. 'The History of the Children's Aid Society of Toronto, 1891–1947.' Master's dissertation, Faculty of Social Work, University of Toronto, 1952.

Jones, Andrew, and Leonard Rutman. *In the Children's Aid: J.J. Kelso and Child Welfare in Ontario.* Toronto: University of Toronto Press, 1981.

Justice, Blair, and Rita Justice. *The Abusing Family.* New York: Human Sciences Press, 1976.

Kaison, Tong. 'The Anti-Cruelty Work in China.' *National Humane Review* Jan. (1913), 10–11.

Kakar, Suman. *Child Abuse and Delinquency.* Lanham, Md.: University Press of America: 1996.

Karstulovich, Dawn. 'New Legislation Paves the Way to Protecting Children

Better.' *Communication Online*, the electronic newspaper of the Children's Aid Society of Toronto, Fall 1999. www.casmt.on.ca/co/99fall01 (accessed 31 Jan. 2000).

Kasinsky, Renee. 'Child Neglect and "Unfit" Mothers: Child Savers in the Progressive Era and Today.' *Women and Criminal Justice* 6, no. 1 (1994), 97–129.

Katz, Michael. 'Child-Saving.' *History of Education Quarterly* 26, no. 3 (1986), 413–23.

– In the Shadow of the Poorhouse: A Social History of Welfare in America. New York: Basic Books, 1986.

– 'Saving Children.' In *In the Shadow of the Poorhouse: A Social History of Welfare in America*. New York: Basic Books, 1986.

Kealey, Linda, ed. *A Not Unreasonable Claim: Women and Reform in Canada, 1880s–1920s*. Toronto: Women's Press, 1979.

Kelso, J.J. 'Children's Courts.' *Canadian Law Times* 28 (1908), 163–66.

– 'Delinquent Children: Some Improved Methods Whereby They May Be Prevented from Following a Criminal Career.' *Canadian Bar Review* 6 (1907), 106–10.

Kempe, Ruth S., and C. Henry Kempe. *Child Abuse*. Cambridge, Mass.: Harvard University Press, 1978.

Kendrick, Martyn. *Nobody's Children: The Foster Care Crisis in Canada*. Toronto: Macmillan, 1995.

Klaus, Marshall, and John Kennell. 'Mothers Separated from Their Newborn Infants.' In *Traumatic Abuse and the Neglect of Children at Home*. Gertrude Williams and John Money, eds. Baltimore: Johns Hopkins University Press, 1980, 208–27.

Kunzel, Regina. *Fallen Women, Problem Girls: Unmarried Mothers and the Professionalization of Social Work, 1890–1945*. New Haven and London: Yale University Press, 1993.

Labaree, David F. '*Parens Patriae*: The Private Roots of Public Policy toward Children.' *History of Education Quarterly* 26, no. 1 (1986), 111–16.

Latimer, Elspeth. 'Methods of Child Care as Reflected in the Infants' Homes of Toronto 1875–1920.' Master's thesis, Faculty of Social Work, University of Toronto, 1953.

Laycock, J.E. 'Juvenile Courts in Canada.' *Canadian Bar Review* 21 (1943), 1–22.

Leashore, Bogart R., and Jerry R. Cates. 'Use of Historical Methods in Social Work Research.' *Social Work Research and Abstracts* 21, no. 2 (1995), 22–7.

Leiby, James. *A History of Social Welfare and Social Work in the United States*. New York: Columbia University Press, 1978.

Leon, J. S. 'The Development of Canadian Juvenile Justice: A Background for Reform.' *Osgoode Hall Law Review* 15, no. 1 (1997), 71–106.

Levi, Ron, and Mariana Valverde. 'Knowledge on Tap: Police Science and

'Common Knowledge' in the Legal Regulation of Drunkenness.' *Law and Social Inquiry* 26, no. 4 (2001), 201–28.

Levitt, Kenneth L., and Brian Wharf., eds. *The Challenge of Child Welfare.* Vancouver: University of British Columbia Press, 1985.

Lindsey, Duncan. *The Welfare of Children.* New York: Oxford Unversity Press, 1994.

Lister, Ruth. 'Dialectics of Citizenship.' *Hypatia* 12, no. 4 (1997), 6–27.

Little, Margaret J. H. *'No Car, No Radio, No Liquor Permit': The Moral Regulation of Single Mothers in Ontario, 1920–1997.* Toronto, University of Toronto Press, 1998.

Locke, John. *An Essay Concerning Human Understanding.* Oxford: Clarendon Press, [1689] 1957.

Martin, Carol. *A History of Canadian Gardening.* Toronto: McArthur, 2000.

– 'Reforming the Landscape,' in *A History of Canadian Gardening.* Toronto: McArthur, 2000, 77–89.

Mason, Joseph. 'Neglected Children Apprenticed by Selectman in Watertown, Mass.,' 27 March 1726/7, in *The Child and the State.* Grace Abbott, comp. Chicago: University of Chicago Press, 1938. Vol 1, part 3, pp. 212–13.

Maurutto, Paula. *Governing Charities: Church and State in Toronto's Catholic Archidiocese, 1850–1950.* Montreal and Kingston: McGill-Queen's University Press, 2003.

Maynard, Steven. 'On the Case of the Case: The Emergence of the Homosexual as a Case History in Early Twentieth-Century Ontario.' In *On the Case: Explorations in Social History.* Franca Iacovetta and Wendy Mitchinson, eds. Toronto: University of Toronto Press, 1998, 65–87.

McCullagh, John. *A Legacy of Caring: A History of the Children's Aid Society of Toronto.* Toronto: Dundurn Press, 2002.

Meredyth, Denise, and Deborah Tyler. *Child and Citizen: Genealogies of Schooling and Subjectivity.* Queensland: Institute for Cultural Policy Studies, Faculty of Humanities, Griffith University, 1993.

Meyer, C. 'A Feminist Perspective on Foster Family Care: A Redefinition of the Categories.' *Child Welfare* 64 (1985), 249–58.

Miller, Perry. *Errand into the Wilderness.* Cambridge: Harvard University Press, 1956.

Minow, Martha. 'Rights for the Next Generation: A Feminist Approach to Children's Rights.' *Harvard Women's Law Journal* 9, no. 1 (1986), 1–24.

Mnookin, R. 'Foster Care – In Whose Best Interests?' *Harvard Educational Review* 43 (1973), 599–638.

Moffatt, Ken. *A Poetics of Social Work: Personal Agency and Social Transformation in Canada, 1920–1939.* Toronto: University of Toronto Press, 2001.

Money, John, and Andrea Needleman. 'Impaired Mother-Infant Pair Bonding in the Syndrome of Abuse Dwarfism.' In *Traumatic Abuse and the Neglect of*

Children at Home. Gertrude Williams and John Money, eds. Baltimore: Johns Hopkins University Press, 1980, 228–39.

Morrison, T.R. '"Their Proper Sphere" Feminism, the Family, and Child-Centered Social Reform in Ontario, 1875–1900.' *Ontario History* 68, nos. 1 and 2 (1976), 45–74.

Mulvany, C. Pelham. *Toronto: Past and Present. A Handbook of the City.* Toronto: W.E. Caiger, Publisher, 1884.

Murray, Karen. 'Upsetting the Public-Private Divide: The Third Sector and the Governance of Single Mothers in 20th Century.' Doctoral dissertation, Department of Political Science, University of British Columbia, 2001.

Nadesan, Majia Holmer. 'Engineering the Entrepreneurial Infant: Brain Science, Infant Development Toys, and Governmentality.' *Cultural Studies* 16, no. 3 (2002), 401–32.

Neff, Charlotte. 'Pauper Apprenticeship in Early Nineteenth-Century Ontario.' *Journal of Family History* 21, no. 2 (1996), 144–71.

Neill, Stephen. *A History of Christian Missions.* Harmondsworth: Penguin, 1971.

Neysmith, Sheila M. 'Networking across Difference: Connecting Restructuring and Caring Labour.' In *Restructuring Caring Labour: Discourse, State Practice, and Everyday Life.* Sheila M. Neysmith, ed. Don Mills, Ont.: Oxford University Press, 2000, 1–28.

– ed. *Restructuring Caring Labour: Discourse, State Practice, and Everyday Life.* Don Mills, Ont.: Oxford University Press, 2000.

O'Malley, Pat. 'Genealogy, Rationalisation and Resistance in "Advanced Liberalism."' In *Rethinking Law, Society and Governance: Foucault's Bequest.* G. Wickham and G. Pavlich, eds. Oxford: Hart, 2001.

– 'Risk, Crime and Prudentialism Revisited.' In *Crime, Risk and Justice: The Politics of Crime Control in Liberal Democracies.* K. Stenson and R. Sullivan, eds. London: Willan, 2001.

O'Malley, Pat, Lorna Weir, and Clifford Shearing. 'Governmentality, Criticism, Politics.' *Economy and Society* 26, no. 4 (1997), 501–17.

O'Neill, Onora. 'Children's Rights and Children's Lives.' In *Children, Rights, and the Law.* P. Alston, S. Parker, and J. Seymour, eds. Oxford: Clarendon, 1992, 24–42.

Ozment, Steven. *When Father Ruled: Family Life in Reformation Europe.* Cambridge, Mass.: Harvard University Press, 1983.

Parr, Joy, ed. *Childhood and Family in Canadian History.* Toronto: McClelland and Stewart, 1982.

Parton, Nigel. *The Politics of Child Abuse.* London: Macmillan, 1985.

– '"Problematics of Government," (Post)modernity, and Social Work.' *British Journal of Social Work* 24, no. 1 (1994), 9–32.

– 'Reconfiguring Child Welfare Practices: Risk, Advanced Liberalism, and the

Government of Freedom.' In *Reading Foucault for Social Work.* A. Chambon, A. Irving, and L. Epstein, eds. New York: Columbia University Press, 1999, 101–30.

– 'Risk, Advanced Liberalism and Child Welfare: The Need to Rediscover Uncertainty and Ambiguity.' *British Journal of Social Work* 28 (1998), 5–27.

Pascall, Gillian. *Social Policy: A Feminist Analysis.* London and New York: Tavistock, 1986.

Pinchbeck, Ivy, and Margaret Hewitt. *Children in English Society.* London: Routledge and Kegan Paul, 1969.

Platt, Anthony M. *The Child Savers: The Invention of Delinquency.* Chicago: University of Chicago Press, 1977.

Prentice, Alison, Paula Bourne, Gail Cuthbert Brandt, Beth Light, Wendy Mitchinson, and Naomi Black. *Canadian Women: A History.* Toronto: Harcourt Brace Jovanovich, 1988.

Prentice, Susan, ed. *Changing Child Care: Five Decades of Child Care Advocacy and Policy in Canada.* Halifax. Fernwood, 2001.

Quaintance, Richard. 'Walpole's Whig Interpretation of Landscaping History.' *Studies in Eighteenth-Century Culture* 9 (1979), 285–300.

Ramsay, Dean P. 'The Development of Child Welfare Legislation in Ontario.' Master's thesis, Faculty of Social Work, University of Toronto, 1949.

Reitsma-Street, Marge. 'More Control than Care: A Critique of Historical and Contemporary Laws for Delinquency and Neglect of Children in Ontario.' *Canadian Journal of Women and Law* 3 (1989–1990), 510–30.

Robinson, Helen Caister. *Decades of Caring: The Big Sister Story.* Toronto: Dundurn Press, 1979.

Rooke, P.T., and R.L. Schnell. *Discarding the Asylum: From Child Rescue to the Welfare State in English Canada, 1880–1950.* Lanham, Md.: University Press of America, 1983.

– *No Bleeding Heart: Charlotte Whitton, a Feminist on the Right.* Vancouver: University of British Columbia Press, 1987.

Rose, Nikolas. 'Beyond the Public/Private Division: Law, Power and the Family.' *Journal of Law and Society* 14, no. 1 (1987), 61–76.

– 'The Biology of Culpability: Pathological Identities in a Biological Culture.' Paper presented at the Centre of Criminology, University of Toronto, 25 May 1999.

– 'The Death of the Social? Re-figuring the Territory of Government.' *Economy and Society* 25, no. 3 (1996), 327–56.

– 'Government, Authority and Expertise in Advanced Liberalism.' *Economy and Society* 22, no. 3 (1993), 283–99.

– *Powers of Freedom: Reframing Political Thought.* Cambridge: Cambridge University Press, 1999.

Rose, Nikolas, and Peter Miller. 'Political Power beyond the State: Problematics of Government.' *British Journal of Sociology* 43, no.2 (1992), 172–205.

Sager, Eric W. 'Employment Contracts in Merchant Shipping: An Argument for Social Science History.' In *On the Case: Explorations in Social History*. Franca Iacovetta and Wendy Mitchinson. eds. Toronto: University of Toronto Press, 1998, 49–64.

Salmon, Trevor C., and Michael Keating, eds. *The Dynamics of Decentralization: Canadian Federalism and British Devolution*. Published for the School of Policy Studies, Queen's University. Montreal and Kingston: McGill-Queen's University Press, 2001.

Schultz, James A. *The Knowledge of Childhood in the German Middle Ages, 1100– 1350*. Philadelphia: University of Pennsylvania Press, 1995.

Schwarzbeck, Charles III. 'Identification of Infants at Risk for Child Abuse.' In *Traumatic Abuse and the Neglect of Children at Home*. Gertrude Williams and John Money, eds. Baltimore: Johns Hopkins University Press, 1980, 240–46.

Scobey, David. 'The Specter of Citizenship.' *Citizenship Studies* 5, no. 1 (2001), 11–26.

Scott, W.L. *The Juvenile Court in Law and the Juvenile Court in Action*. CCCW Publication no. 34. Ottawa: Canadian Council on Child Welfare, 1927.

Smandych, R., ed. *Governable Places: Readings in Governmentality and Crime Control*. Aldershot, U.K.: Dartmouth Publishing, 1999.

– *Youth Justice: History, Legislation and Reform*. Toronto: Brace/Harcourt, 2001.

Smandych, R., G. Dodds, and A. Esau, eds. *Dimensions of Childhood: Essays on the History of Children and Youth in Canada*. Winnipeg: University of Manitoba Legal Research Institute, 1991.

Smith, B., and T. Smith. 'For Love and Money: Women as Foster Mothers.' *Affilia* 5, no. 1 (1990), 66–80.

Spinetta, John, and David Rigler. 'The Child-Abusing Parent: A Psychological Review.' In *Traumatic Abuse and Neglect of Children at Home*. Gertrude Williams and John Money, eds. Baltimore: Johns Hopkins University Press, 1980, 117–29.

Splane, Richard B. *Social Welfare in Ontario, 1791–1893: A Study of Public Welfare Administration*. Toronto: University of Toronto Press, 1965.

Stasiulis, Daiva. 'The Active Child Citizenship: Lessons from Canadian Policy and the Children's Movement.' *Citizenship Studies* 6, no. 4 (2002), 507–33.

Steele, Brandt, and Carl Pollack. 'A Psychiatric Study of Parents Who Abuse Infants and Small Children.' In *The Battered Child*. Ray Helfter and C. Henry Kempe, eds. Chicago: University of Chicago Press, 1968, 103–47.

Stenson, K., and R. Sullivan, eds. *Crime, Risk and Justice: The Politics of Crime Control in Liberal Democracies*. London: Willan, 2001.

Strong-Boag, Veronica. 'Intruders in the Nursery: Child Care Professionals Reshape the Years One to Five, 1920–1940.' In *Childhood and Family in Canadian History.* Joy Parr, ed. Toronto: McClelland and Stewart, 1982, 160–78.

Sutherland, Neil. *Children in English-Canadian Society: Framing the Twentieth-Century Consensus.* Toronto: University of Toronto Press, 1976.

Swift, Karen. 'Contradictions in Child Welfare: Neglect and Responsibility.' In *Women's Caring: Feminist Perspectives on Social Welfare.* Carol Baines, Patricia Evans, and Sheila Neysmith, eds. Toronto: Oxford University Press, 1998, 160–87.

– 'Failure to Protect.' Presented at the Annual Conference of the Canadian Association of Schools of Social Work, Université de Sherbrooke and Bishop's University, Quebec, June 1999.

– *Manufacturing 'Bad Mothers': A Critical Perspective on Child Neglect.* Toronto: University of Toronto Press, 1995.

– 'Missing Persons: Women in Child Welfare.' *Child Welfare* 74, no. 3 (1995), 486–502.

– 'An Outrage to Common Decency: Historical Perspectives on Child Neglect.' *Child Welfare* 76, no. 1 (1995), 71–91.

Teghtsoonian, Katherine. 'Neo-conservative Ideology and Opposition to Federal Regulation of Child Care Services in the United States and Canada.' *Canadian Journal of Political Science* 26, no. 1 (1993), 97–121.

Thomas, Mason P. 'Child Abuse and Neglect, Part I: Historical Overview, Legal Matrix and Social Perspectives.' *North Carolina Law Review* 50 (1971–1972), 293–4.

Tiffin, Susan. *In Whose Best Interest? Child Welfare Reform in the Progressive Era.* Westport, Conn.: Greenwood, 1982.

Trépanier, J. 'The Origin of the Juvenile Delinquents Act of 1908: Controlling Delinquency through Seeking Its Causes and through Youth Protection.' In *Dimensions of Childhood: Essays on the History of Children and Youth in Canada.* R. Smandych, G. Dodds, and A. Esau, eds. Winnipeg: University of Manitoba Legal Research Institute, 1991, 205–32.

Trocmé, N., and K.K. Tam. 'Correlates of Substantiation of Maltreatment in Child Welfare Investigation.' Paper presented at the National Research and Policy Symposium in Child Welfare, Kananaskis, Alberta, May, 1994.

Trocmé, N., et al. *Canadian Incidence Study of Reported Child Abuse and Neglect: Final Report.* Ottawa: Health Canada, 2001.

Valverde, Mariana. *The Age of Light, Soap, and Water: Moral Reform in English Canada, 1885–1925.* Toronto: McClelland and Stewart, 1991.

– 'As If Subjects Existed: Analysing Social Discourses.' *Canadian Review of Sociology and Anthropology* 28, no. 2 (1991), 173–87.

– '"Despotism" and Ethical Liberal Governance.' *Economy and Society* 25, no. 3 (1996), 357–72.
– 'The Dialect of the Familiar and the Unfamiliar: "The Jungle" in Early Slum Travel Writing.' *Sociology* 30, no. 3 (1996), 493–509.
– *Diseases of the Will: Alcohol and the Dilemmas of Freedom.* Cambridge: Cambridge University Press, 1998.
– ed. *New Forms of Governance: Theory, Practice, Research.* Conference Proceedings. Toronto: Centre of Criminology, University of Toronto, 1997.
– 'Review of *On the Case.*' Unpublished manuscript, July 1999.
– 'Poststructuralist Gender Historians: Are We Those Names?' *Labour / Le Travail* 25 (1990), 227–36.
– compiler. *Radically Rethinking Regulation: Workshop Report.* Toronto: Centre of Criminology, University of Toronto, 1994.
Valverde, Mariana, and Lorna Weir. 'The Struggle of the Immoral: Preliminary Remarks on Moral Regulation.' *Resources for Feminist Research* 17, no. 3 (1988), 31–4.
Violence Against Children Study Group. *Taking Child Abuse Seriously: Comtemporary Issues in Child Protection Theory and Practice.* London: Unwin Hyman, 1990.
Von Baeyer, Edwinna. *Garden of Dreams: Kinsmere and Mackenzie King.* Toronto: and Oxford: Dundrum Press, 1990.
– 'Mackenzie King's Gardening and the Horticultural Times.' Introduction to *Garden of Dreams: Kinsmere and Mackenzie King.* Toronto and Oxford: Dundrum Press, 1990, 11–22.
– *Rhetoric and Roses: A History of Canadian Gardens 1900–1930.* Markam, Ont.: Fitzhenry and Whiteside, 1984.
Wharf, Brian. 'Rethinking Child Welfare.' In *Rethinking Child Welfare in Canada.* Brian Wharf, ed. Toronto: McClelland and Stewart, 1993.
– ed. *Rethinking Child Welfare in Canada.* Toronto: McClelland and Stewart, 1993.
Wickham, G., and G. Pavlich, eds. *Rethinking Law, Society and Governance: Foucault's Bequest.* Oxford: Hart, 2001.
Wiegers, Wanda. *The Framing of Poverty as 'Child Poverty' and Its Implications for Women.* Ottawa: Status of Women Canada, 2002.
Williams, Gertrude, and John Money, eds. *Traumatic Abuse and the Neglect of Children at Home.* Baltimore: Johns Hopkins University Press, 1980.
Wills, Gale. *A Marriage of Convenience: Business and Social Work in Toronto, 1918–1957.* Toronto: University of Toronto Press, 1995.
Wilson, Larry C. *Juvenile Courts in Canada.* Toronto: Carswell, 1982.
Zelizer, Vivian. *Pricing the Priceless Child: The Changing Value of Children.* New York: Basic Books, 1985.

Index